言葉の橋

アメリカと日本の見方

佐藤 紘彰

A Bridge of Words

Views across America and Japan

Hiroaki Sato

Foreword by Geoffrey O'Brien

Published by
Stone Bridge Press
P. O. Box 8208, Berkeley, CA 94707
TEL 510-524-8732 • sbp@stonebridge.com • www.stonebridge.com

Second and third photos on page 258 by William Irwin, courtesy of the Donald Keene Center. Third photo on page 140, fifth on page 141, and first on page 258 by Seiji Kakizaki. All other photos by the author.

Calligraphy on the half-title is courtesy of Hirata Takako.

Printed in the United States of America.

p-ISBN 978-1-61172-078-5
e-ISBN 978-1-61172-958-0

Dedicated to my parents
Masao (1908–85) and Michiko (1910–80)
and to Nancy and her parents
Lewis (1905–85) and Florence (1909–2009)

CONTENTS

FOREWORD

As poet, scholar, and literary translator, Hiroaki Sato has created a body of writing of such proportions that it might constitute a library in itself, ranging over centuries of poetic and cultural tradition, from his landmark translations of a multitude of poets—including Miyazawa Kenji, Takamura Kōtarō, Hagiwara Sakutarō, and the many contributors to his extraordinary anthology *Japanese Women Poets* (2007)—to such indispensable recent books as *On Haiku* (2018) and *Forty-Seven Samurai* (2019). The present volume reveals another aspect of Sato's work, as an essayist and commentator whose probing curiosity darts freely from personal history and close-up observation to the widest perspectives of history and ecology. Throughout, we are given insights into Sato's life and the history of his family. A group of tributes under the rubric "Teachers and Friends" movingly evoke some crucial figures in his life, such as the poet Lindley Williams Hubbell, who as a naturalized Japanese citizen took the name Hayashi Shūseki, and was Sato's professor of English poetry at Doshisha University in the 1960s.

These pieces, most of which appeared originally as columns in the *Mainichi Daily News* and the *Japan Times*, have a conversational informality that allows for unexpected digressions and interjections. "I am prejudiced against golfing and golf courses," he announces, and explains why. He quotes a scientist's argument for limiting wild geese populations—"When you see geese, they're eating or they're defecating"—and immediately responds: "Isn't that what we human beings do as well, too well?" The back and forth is continual, and continually energizing.

We have the impression of listening in on a long ongoing conversation with interlocutors living and dead, the talk of friends and correspondents blending with the words of a remarkable variety of writers. The talk can be contentious. Sato never hesitates to engage with cruxes and controversies. His judgments are precisely argued but not categorical or final. He prefers to pose questions designed to spur further thought and deeper investigation: "Reassessing history is a constant activity," he writes. It is certainly a constant activity in these pages, particularly in those pieces in which Sato focuses on the causes and consequences of World War II, frequently targeting unexamined assumptions that over time have hardened into historical certainties: "When it comes to Japan and World War II, some Americans are incapable of accommodating different viewpoints."

Of such viewpoints an abundance can be found here, many of them from relatively obscure or previously untranslated writers. The net effect is to convey a sense of complexity that eludes easy slogans. In the process we learn about individuals and situations that for most American readers are likely to be unfamiliar. These tantalizing glimpses provide steady encouragement for additional research, all the more so as Sato describes his own process of delving into the records or consulting with others for further knowledge.

He explores the meaning of terms deployed by the Japanese government during World War II (*ichioku gyokusai* or *hitobashira*), examines the variegated representations of carp in Japanese poetry, and provides an altogether fascinating account of the first Japanese diplomatic mission to the U.S. in 1872. The restless desire to know more—to illuminate large things by attention to the smallest of details—might be the bass note of this collection; and what Sato uncovers, whether it concerns the origins of the 442nd Regimental Combat Team (the famous "Go For Broke" regiment) or the representation of kissing in Japanese erotic art or the significance of spirit possession in *The Tale of Genji*, is full of surprises and odd angles.

A significant part of the book deals with "invasive species"—a term Sato dislikes and whose implications he tracks in a series of pieces on the arrogance of human campaigns against crows, Canada geese, seagulls, kudzu, purple loosestrife, and other insufficiently loved fauna and flora. He finds beauty in the supposedly intolerable cawing of crows—"the *kah-kah* of the thick-billed crow or the *gah-gah* of the thin-billed crow"—and uncovers a rich Japanese literary tradition in praise of kudzu. In a magisterial essay on cicadas, he points out that the sound described by an American journalist as "the threat of shrieking hell to come" has inspired Japanese poetry from the eighth-century *Man'yōshū* ("the cicadas' voices roaring like rock-rushing waterfalls") to the seventeenth-century haiku master Bashō ("Quietness: seeping into the rocks the cicada's voice"). For the poet and sculptor Takamura Kōtarō, "the way their rasps pierce the core of my brain is very pleasant." In a note added in 2021, Sato sums up this section nicely: "The ideal natural equilibrium . . . may well have been a phantom. Nature has been in perpetual motion since time immemorial. Didn't Lao Tzu say that?" The poem "Seagulls" which follows this note, from Sato's collection *That First Time* (1988), provides a supremely appropriate coda.

Geoffrey O'Brien

AUTHOR'S NOTE

Many of these articles originally appeared in my column, "Here and Now—in New York," for the *Mainichi Daily News*, which I wrote once every two weeks, from April 2, 1984 to May 29, 1989, and in my monthly column, "The View from New York," for the *Japan Times*, which I wrote from April 2000 to October 2017. For both dailies I also reviewed books and contributed commentaries.

I have indicated for each piece when and where it appeared, retaining the heading of each as it appeared, as appropriate. However, I have changed the order of Japanese names, surname first.

My poem "Seagulls" first appeared in my book of poems, *That First Time: Six Renga on Love and Other Poems* (St. Andrews Press, 1988).

I thank my sister Hirata Takako for her calligraphy of the book title and my name in kanji.

I

Wars and Consequences

Shattering the Mirror That Distorts Japan

December 25, 1995, *Japan Times*

One book that has recently caused a stir in certain circles in Japan is a new translation of *Mirror for Americans: Japan*. It is not the latest tract—God forbid—that purports to show lessons that the United States ought to learn from Japan. Rather, it is a sober look at the postwar U.S.-Japanese relationship at its incipient stage.

Written by the American writer Helen Mears and published in 1948, *Mirror for Americans* was so bluntly critical of the premises on which the Occupation was based that its translation into Japanese was prohibited. Indeed, its first translation did not see print until after the peace treaty was signed. The recent translation was prepared following "rediscovery" of Mears' original.

Mears' thesis was as simple as her analysis was persuasive. In occupying defeated Japan for the purpose of "punishing the Japanese and re-educating and reforming them," she said, MacArthur and his deputies were basing their policies on "exaggerated" and "distorted" images of Japan created in the heat of war. And Mears made each of her points by dispassionately looking at each claim made.

Take the central issue—the notion that the Japanese are "inherently militaristic and expansionist." It was largely on this charge that the Occupation was instituted, and it was because of it that MacArthur equipped the Constitution he gave Japan with an extraordinary "no-war" clause. This characterization of the Japanese has lost none of its power today, half a century later.

Just a few weeks ago, for example, at a cultural society in New York, when the talk turned to a possible reconsideration of the U.S.-Japan Security Treaty, at least two Americans in the relatively small audience—one young, the other somewhat advanced in age—voiced concerns about a "resurgence of militarism" in Japan. The idea that Japan, given a chance, would quickly turn itself into a nation of warmongers is so ingrained in the American psyche that it pops back at the drop of a hat. The speaker that evening was Frank Gibney, whom I admired.

Mears had no inclination to entertain such a view. Writing only three years after the fury of the war, she argued that a quick look at the history of the world since the sixteenth century would prove that view to be mostly wrong. From 1600 until the U.S. Navy pried its doors open in 1853–54, Japan was a "peace-loving" nation nonpareil. It traded with a few countries but otherwise tightly held to itself and showed no expansionist signs. It was during the same 250-year period, in fact, that expansionism ran rampant elsewhere, with Portugal, Britain, France, The Netherlands, Russia, and "even" the United States busily "conquering the world."

What about the decades preceding Pearl Harbor?

It took Japan forty-five years, until 1899, to shed the last of the "unequal treaties," so we could look at what had happened from the last decade of the nineteenth century onward. Then, we would see, Mears said, that Japan turned "warlike." Still, even during that period of international transformation, Japan became no more warlike or expansionist than any other power.

It is a telling comment, Mears said, that "at the time of Pearl Harbor, the Japanese controlled only two tenths per cent [*sic*] of the islands in the entire Pacific area." Japan's seizure of Manchuria, which began in 1931, is taken today—as it was right after Japan's defeat—to be a turning point in Japan's expansionist policy. Yet, even when the puppet Manchukuo was included, Japan's foreign territories—again at the time of Pearl Harbor—amounted to less than what France had in Asia and the Pacific alone. When it comes to Britain, its holdings in the same regions were thirteen times larger.

Such things do not of course absolve Japan of its effort to emulate Western powers in imperialism and its consequences. Nonetheless, the West's postwar condemnation of Japan *"in toto"* would be "a perfect illustration," Mears said, "of respectable people smashing their own glass houses." After all, until Japan plunged into war with Western powers, it was "generally accepted as a modern progressive nation—the vanguard of Westernization in Asia." For them, Japan was a competitor of some stature but also a convenient ally. None of them voiced a demurrer, for example, when Japan annexed Korea, in 1910.

That Western powers had regarded Japan more or less as one of their own is clear from their failure to take any decisive action against it following "the Manchurian Incident," in 1931, and, again, following "the China Incident," in 1937. They each had their own stake in the region and needed to engage in complex maneuvers to protect them. All that changed with Japan's successful assaults on them and its eventual defeat.

To go with the condemnation of the "inherently militaristic" character of the Japanese people was the characterization of the Japanese soldier as "a diabolical, unpredictable, unconquerable savage . . . who preferred death to surrender." By citing contemporary newspaper accounts (mostly the *New York Times*), Mears demonstrated that this, too, was a willful distortion.

True, the Japanese soldier sometimes chose death over surrender. He was told to do so. Yet, the choice in no time became a non-choice because of several stark realities. The Japanese military became quickly overextended. America's material superiority came to the fore in short order. And the United States zealously engaged in "a war of extermination." As a result, in a great many engagements, the Japanese side "fighting to the last man" was not so much an act of bravado as a necessity.

In a dispatch of March 8, 1944, for example, Frank Kluckhohn described "a slaughter in which the cream of Japanese fighting men died like sheep in a packing-house" because of the staggering U.S. firepower. In another for the *Times,* dated February 5, 1945, George E. Jones reported: "Organized resistance [on Namur] was ended, and even the toughened battle-hardened Marines were disgusted with the task of wiping out Japanese troops who hovered on the borderline of insanity as the result of the Allied bombardment and the ensuing hopeless retreat across the island."

On Okinawa, W. H. Lawrence wrote, in June 1945: "Stated in its simplest terms we were able to announce the victory of Okinawa because the enemy had run out of caves and boulders from which to fight and we were nearly out of Japanese to kill."

Mears cited a number of other examples. Indeed, contrary to the benign images of the U.S. military that were later generated, the U.S. policy in the Pacific War, "on the whole, was not to take prisoners." Mears went a step further: "There was little question but that our policy was, on the whole, to fight it out as a war of extermination."

The upshot of all this was the kill ratio of fourteen Japanese soldiers to one American, according to the Strategic Bombing Survey.

Speaking of benign images, Mears showed that the Occupation was less than benign in certain important respects. At the start of his rule MacArthur declared that "the punishment for [Japan's] sins ... will be long and bitter." Indeed, in large measure the Occupation was not a form of noblesse oblige, as was depicted later. Instead, it was designed to be and was a full burden on a defeated, half-starved country.

"In the first three months," Mears noted, "the Occupation—which is run in an extravagant American style—cost the Japanese more than the entire yearly expense for their armed forces in 1930. . . . By August, 1947, the Japanese Government budget had mounted to ... over 184,500,000,000 yen, of which more than forty-three per cent was allocated to Occupation costs."

Mears detailed in a footnote: "The Japanese have been charged for flowers for officers' billets and homes; telegrams and telephone calls to the United States; the maintenance of rest camps; high salaries for civilian experts and secretaries, and various other niceties of life," as well as for "Japanese individuals who were injured in traffic accidents by members of the Occupation." As Lucy Herndon Crockett, Mears' contemporary but with a totally different outlook and attitude, said of the Occupation in her account, *Popcorn on the Ginza* (William Sloane,

1949), "Americans in Japan are enjoying to the fullest the privileges that constitute the spoils of war." In the midst of a starving people Crockett said this without irony, with full approval.

That *Mirror for Americans: Japan* did not sit well with U.S. authorities at the time is understandable. But it was also subjected to a "historical blackout," according to Richard Minear, a professor of history at the University of Massachusetts at Amherst. Minear, who regards *Mirror* as "the most important book on Japan written by a westerner in the entire decade 1940–50," which far outclassed the writings of influential academics like Edwin O. Reischauer and Ruth Benedict, believes that had Helen Mears' views been taken more seriously, the United States might have avoided some of its blunders in Asia in the decades that followed.

I would like to think if this writer of profound sensitivity and unerring intelligence had not been ostracized, as she was, she might have helped soften the American perception, which persists to this day, that Japan, for some reason, is the odd man out in international transactions.

It was in the frontispiece of Mirror for Americans *that I learned John Quincy Adams' famous speech before the U.S. House of Representatives on July 4, 1821, which included these words for the United States: "Wherever the standard of freedom and independence has been or shall be unfurled, there will her heart, her benedictions and her prayers be. But she goes not abroad, in search of monsters to destroy."*

When this article appeared in the Japan Times, *Donald Richie wrote to tell me that he had reviewed* Mirror for Americans: Japan *for* Stars and Stripes *when the book came out, agreeing with Mears completely.*

In 1998 I gave a speech based on this article at a brownbag lunch at the New York University Stern School of Business. I remember an elderly woman getting upset by my talk. Later, I was told that her deceased husband was the captain of a destroyer who had taken part in some of the operations in the South Seas of the Pacific during the war.

War Perspective of Poets Oceans Apart

October 27, 2003, *Japan Times*

A gentleman named Paul Preusser, describing himself as "a composer and fresh graduate from the New England Conservatory," has recently written to ask if I could help him with poems of Takamura Kōtarō (1883–1956). He has been commissioned to compose "a song cycle using poetry which is influenced by war," and plans to include poems in six languages: English, French, German, Polish, Russian, and Japanese. With Takamura he'd like to use a jingoistic poem as well as one expressing regret over his stance during the war.

Preusser's preliminary research was correct. Takamura wrote both kinds of poems. In his youth a powerful advocate of "Western values," among them the need for an artist to be independent and true to himself, rather than, say, digesting and mastering traditions, he began to accept and uphold his country's nationalist causes during the 1930s as Japan's military meddling in China faced mounting international criticism. Many of the poems he wrote from the end of the decade until Japan's defeat, in 1945, were certainly jingoistic, studded as they were with right-wing slogans and self-serving arguments, such as that Western powers were in East Asia only "for profit," while Japan was "for justice."

When the Japanese regained some footing from the furies of war that ended in their country's utter ruin, a serious charge, albeit literary, was leveled against Takamura. "Among the many poets Takamura Kōtarō not only directly bears the greatest war responsibility to the people," a prominent leftist scholar thundered, "he must take the supreme responsibility for the degradation of poets as a whole."

Such a highhanded indictment could be made because of Takamura's seeming betrayal of the values he had championed when young and because of his service during the war as head of the poetry branch of the Patriotic Literary Association formed under government pressure.

Partly in response to the accusation, Takamura "exiled" himself from Tokyo and in time wrote a sequence of twenty poems titled *A Brief History of Imbecility*. More than anything else a reflection on the spiritual journey of someone who was at once intimidated and exhilarated by the West in his youth—he studied sculpture in New York, London, and Paris, from 1906 to 1909—and then was gradually caught up with his country in danger, the sequence is not an outright expression of about-face remorse. Still, it ends with the poet expressing readiness to "submit to the extreme penalty," if that was what society wanted.

I translated a body of Takamura Kōtarō's poems years ago, but newly translating for Mr. Preusser some of the poems he wrote around the outbreak of the Pacific War, I couldn't help contrasting Takamura and some of the American poets at the time. It's not that at present the United States is at war amid worldwide criticism. It's that I've been reading *Poets of World War II* (Library of America, 2003), which Harvey Shapiro edited.

The first thing that comes to mind is that ordinary American people may have been unaware of the imminence of war in the Pacific in the fall of 1941. I have read so many stories of American men and women who reacted to Japan's "sneak attack" on Pearl Harbor with towering indignation. But Robinson Jeffers (1887–1962), for one, had known for some years that his country was brewing a war with Japan. A resident of Carmel, California, he began "Pearl Harbor" by saying:

Here are the fireworks. The men who conspired and labored
To embroil this republic in the wreck of Europe have got their bargain,—
And a bushel more.

I can't tell exactly when Jeffers wrote the poem, but it clearly was not long after the assault, for he ends the poem telling the reader to enjoy the "great beauty" restored along the "long shore" of California as a result of the attack:

> . . . our prudent officers
> Have cleared the coast-long ocean of ships and fishing-craft, the sky of
>   planes, the windows of light: these clearings
> Make a great beauty.

That was after the fact. About three weeks *before* the fateful day, Takamura wrote a poem whose title may be translated as "A Time of Certain Death" or "A Desperate Time" (the poet uses both Chinese and Japanese senses of the word *hisshi*). It is a hortatory piece telling the reader that the destruction Japan is about to face is likely to be deadly. Not that Takamura was privy to the planned top-secret assault on Pearl Harbor. Earlier in November, Mishima Yukio, then just sixteen years old, had written to a friend of his: "We appear to be going to war with America, but I think it's too late now"—too late because Germany's general offensive against Moscow was thought to fail. It did.

Between Takamura and Jeffers there was an ocean of difference. Whereas Takamura's forebodings of the impending war typified a people who felt impossibly hemmed in, Jeffers' reaction after the initial attack was one of disbelief that, to quote Allen Tate, "the puny Japanese" dared assault the giant America. While fulminating against the warmongers of his country, Jeffers reminded himself:

> (Oh, we'll not lose our war: my money on amazed Gulliver
> And his horse-pistols.)

There was also some similarity between the Japanese and American poets. Despite his sense of doom, Takamura spoke of "Nature's grace in certain death." While deriding "our leaders" for making "orations" about a war they provoked, Jeffers spoke of "the prehuman dignity of night," which came back as a result of the black-out, "as it was before and will be again."

Takamura of course exulted at the news of Pearl Harbor.

Remember December the 8th
that split world history into two

he wrote. (The assault took place on the 7th Hawaiian time, on the 8th Japan time.) There was no way for him to know either that "Remember Pearl Harbor" would become key to a merciless retribution or that it would change America's military strategy forever after the war.

For that matter, Takamura also exulted at the news of the fall of Singapore, on February 15, where the British Empire had maintained its "impregnable" fort. He wrote:

They possessed it, it meant trouble.
We possess it, it means justice.
Those suffocated over the years are about to be liberated.

Little did he know that, even as he wrote, the Japanese military was rounding up and killing large numbers of inhabitants of the Lion City, throwing many in the Strait of Singapore to drown on suspicion of harboring anti-Japanese sentiments. The total of those so killed is put anywhere between 5,000 and 50,000.

Those at the home front seldom imagine what may ensue after such a "victory."

Robinson Jeffers, who called himself an "Inhumanist," wrote, in "Pearl Harbor," of "The war that we have carefully for years provoked," etc., and expressed in it and other poems from 1942 to 1947 such antipathy against Franklin Delano Roosevelt that when the Random House published his poems during that period under the title of The Double Axe, *in 1948, its editors felt compelled to "suppress" eleven poems, with one resurrected from Jeffers' "manuscript worksheets." ("Pearl Harbor" was not omitted.) In 1977,*

Liveright restored those suppressed poem in Robert Jeffers: The Double Axe and Other Poems.

In one of the suppressed poems, "Fantasy," written in June 1941, Jeffers wrote, "On that great day the boys will hang / Hitler and Roosevelt in one tree," and in another, "Wilson in Hell," written in 1942, Woodrow Wilson, who had been accused of having the United States take part in the European War, tells Roosevelt, "But you / Blew on the coal-bed, and when it kindled you deliberately / Sabotaged every fire-wall that even the men who denied / My hope had built." In this, Jeffers was like the great historian Charles A. Beard (1874–1948). Among others, Beard published, in 1948, President Roosevelt and the Coming of the War, 1941: A Study in Appearances and Realities.

It was another Californian poet, Dion O'Donnol (1912–2007), who told me about Jeffers while driving me around to various places, such as La Jolla, San Diego, and Watts—the last of which was where great riots had occurred in the previous year. I spent two summer months of 1966 with Alice Boaz and her family in Redondo Beach, CA, thanks to her sister, poet Edith Shiffert's, kindness. Mrs. Shiffert taught at the English Department of Doshisha University, Kyoto, where I was a graduate student, and she introduced me to Mr. O'Donnol in LA. I didn't know at the time or later, but now I see Mr. O'Donnol created "Dionol" meter, an octave with a rentrement as an added line, the last phrase of L2 is repeated as L9.

Was Pearl Harbor Really a Surprise?

January 29, 2001, *Japan Times*

My young colleague at work, Donald Howard, comes to me, and wryly asks: Why is this Japanese office having a Christmas party on December 7? Impressed by his historical acuity, I only manage: Well, from the Japanese perspective, the Pearl Harbor assault didn't take place on December 7, but on December 8, during the predawn hours. . . .

I remembered this exchange when I received, from a friend of mine in Tokyo, the bulletin of the Foreign Correspondents' Club of Japan carrying a transcript of Herbert Bix's talk, including questions and answers, at FCCJ toward the end of last August. In response to one questioner, Bix, now famous for his *Hirohito and the Making of Modern Japan* (HarperCollins, 2000), says:

> . . . the struggle over historical consciousness is heating up again in Japan today, and there are those who are recycling old FDR notions from the isolationist literature of the '30 and '40s, you know: FDR maneuvered to get the Japanese to fire first, and the Hull note was an effort to get Japan to attack. Some of the worst myths from that era appear all the time in Japanese journals like *Shokun* among others.

I haven't read (sorry!) *Shokun* and other articles pertaining to this particular "myth" that Bix had in mind, but I have the feeling that in this instance Bix is putting the cart before the horse. It is hard to imagine Japanese willingly promoting the idea of their Navy falling into a trap. That would require a twisted sense of nationalism. The Pearl Harbor attack led to Japan's overwhelming defeat, but it was, tactically, a spectacular success, or so most Japanese would like to think, I would imagine.

In point of fact, it is Americans, not Japanese, who are and have been "recycling" the notion of FDR entrapment.

Suppose Bix was thinking of some specific Japanese writers who brought up the "myth" in the early part of the year 2000, the impetus for them was most likely the publication, toward the end of 1999, of Robert Stinnett's *Day of Deceit: The Truth about FDR and Pearl Harbor* (Free Press). Stinnett is described as "a World War II veteran who served with Lt. George H. W. Bush."

On the other hand, if Japanese do that "all the time," as Bix asserts, that may be because Stinnett is only among the most recent American writers to suspect and conclude that FDR knew what was coming but, for political reasons, let it run its course. The suspicion goes right back to the first few days after the attack, if not before, as is familiar to anyone who has scanned the literature on Pearl Harbor.

There were, in the first place, a series of government investigations. Counting Secretary of the Navy Knox's inquiry, December 11 and 12, 1941, and the Congressional hearings shortly after the war, there were a total of nine of them in less than four years. But it was apparently felt that each was politically biased or distorted, so none of them succeeded in allaying the suspicions. When it comes to books and articles, I cannot begin to imagine how many there are.

Such things, of course, are well known. Equally well known is the fact that there are any number of people who, like Herbert Bix, dismiss FDR's alleged maneuver as a "myth," or worse. I have just taken the number of investigations from John Toland's *Infamy: Pearl Harbor and its Aftermath* (Doubleday, 1982), a book representing a famous change of heart. As it happens, Toland is one of the two "distinguished historians," albeit "revisionist," that David Kahn cites by way of condemning *Day of Deceit* as "the most irrational of the revisionist books," in the *New York Review of Books*. The suggestion is that, when it comes to Pearl Harbor, "revisionists" are altogether nuts.

Yet, the other historian Kahn cites is no less than Charles Austin Beard, at one time president of the American Historical Association. Beard published, in 1948, *President Roosevelt and the Coming of the War, 1941,* and it is this book Gore Vidal mentions in the afterword to *The Golden Age* (Doubleday, 2000), the first half of which is written to bring to life Vidal's observation: "It was well known within the whispering gallery [to wit, of those in the know, in Washington, D.C.] of the day that FDR had provoked the Japanese into attacking us."

Yes, Gore Vidal is a novelist, and *The Golden Age* is a "historical novel." But about this category, Vidal has something to say for "those who mistakenly regard history as a true record and the novel as invention." Vidal fans may remember what has happened to his depictions of Jefferson and his slave in *Burr* and of Lincoln and his proposals for blacks in *Lincoln.*

Is FDR's alleged maneuver a myth? I am in no position to do archival research or wade through mountains of diaries, but I do think much of history writing is a matter of interpretation and, let's say, viewpoint.

For a minor example, compare how Toland treats Labor Secretary Frances Perkins' description of FDR after he was informed of the Pearl Harbor disaster and how Doris Kearns Goodwin treats the same thing in *No Ordinary Time: Franklin and Eleanor Roosevelt: The Home Front in World War II* (Simon and Schuster, 1994). Goodwin, a Harvard historian turned TV commentator, apparently approached FDR and Pearl Harbor with the thought that "the charge is absurd that [FDR] somehow connived in the Japanese attack." The quote comes from Arthur Schlesinger.

What was Bix's angle? To use a phrase he employed in his 1980 article for the *Bulletin of Concerned Asian Scholars,* it was that Hirohito spearheaded "emperor-system fascism." The historian George Akita wrote to tell me about the Bix article.

What in the end bothers me about Bix's remark is the reference to "the struggle over historical consciousness." The suggestion is that such a struggle, when it occurs in Japan, is dangerous or else nonsensical. Is it that Bix, having emerged victorious in the battle over Hirohito's culpability as a war criminal, can't brook anything similar over FDR?

Old Prejudices Burn
Bright in a War Account

May 29, 2000, *Japan Times*

A new book on Iwo Jima demystifies the flag, said Richard Bernstein, reviewing it for the *New York Times*.

What James Bradley calls "The Photograph" in *Flags of Our Fathers* (Bantam, 2000) is only too famous: a picture of a small band of soldiers in battle fatigues struggling to raise the U.S. flag on what appears to be a devastated, windswept hilltop. Almost accidentally taken by Joe Rosenthal, the photo instantly captured the American imagination as the very image of valor and patriotism.

The idea for what finally became the 100-ton bronze statue, the Marine Corps War Memorial, was proposed less than twenty days after the flag-raising, before the battle was over. The Congressman who introduced a bill for the idea said, "I do not believe any product of the mind of the artist could equal this photograph in action."

Three of the six "flagraisers" were killed in subsequent battles. The three survivors were summoned home as "heroes" to spearhead a war-bond campaign. The campaign was a glorious success. It raised $26.3 billion—twice the original target. The sum was equal to one half of the U.S. budget for the year.

Yet, already during the fervent national tour, a schism began to appear between the "heroes" and the adulators, Bradley reports. For the "heroes," there was nothing heroic about the flagraising. The first flag raised was small. When the replacement flag was raised, they happened to be around, so they lent a hand. It was as simple as that.

And the flagraising and the adulation affected the three men differently. For Ira Hayes, a Pima Indian from Arizona, it became in the end a sort of stigma—something that would be brought up when he least needed it. For Rene Gagnon, a mill worker from Manchester, it became a phantom on which he could never build an imagined career. And for John Bradley, a future owner of a funeral home in a small town in Wisconsin, it became something to be avoided whenever possible. Most insistent on "no heroism" during the bond tour, he saw the discrepancy between image and reality most clearly.

Indeed, it was his father's lifelong reticence on the subject of Iwo Jima and flagraising, and the posthumous discovery that his father, a medical corpsman, had even been decorated with the Navy Cross, that compelled James Bradley to look into the lives of the six men, piece together the battles they fought, and examine what happened afterward. The result is a son's heartfelt tribute to his beloved father.

Knowing it is a filial tribute, I nonetheless find *Flags of Our Fathers* bumpy in places—yes, where Bradley describes the enemy, the Japanese. In demystifying the flagraisers, I wish he had demystified the defenders. Instead, he resorts to unthinking wartime contrasting.

So, the U.S. Marines are "the cream of American democracy," while the Japanese soldiers are "the elite minions of a thoroughly militarized society." In one passage, he exalts the Marine Corps for breaking the "individualists" (they are American!) into "powerlessness" in order to turn them into cogs of a "human war machine"; in another, he condemns the Japanese military for doing just about the same thing.

The slogan "Death Before Dishonor" is a fine expression for the American fighting man; for the Japanese, it is a "myth-obsessed" absurdity or else a manifestation of a "corrupt" samurai code. Likewise, Bradley at one point speaks of Japanese soldiers as "suicidal"; in the next breath he mentions "brave Marines trained to advance despite any conditions and all losses."

Bradley apparently does this in part out of a filial remorse. He attended college in Tokyo (days of "study or sushi") and once thought he had figured the "real" reason the United States fought Japan: "FDR's severing of their oil lines forced Japan—an industrial beached whale—to attack Pearl Harbor in self-defense." And once, at a Thanksgiving dinner, he expounded this view in his attempt to "enlighten" his father.

Years later, perhaps after he discovered the "secret" of his father's reluctance to talk, he decided this "self-defense" argument was "bogus." What was John Bradley's secret? During the heat of battle, his best friend was captured by the Japanese; when his body was found, it was mangled from torture and had its penis stuffed in its mouth.

Yet, with due respect to James Bradley's filial love and remorse, I wonder if this was reason enough for him to talk, half a century later, like a Marine who's just survived a hellish battle.

In writing about Rear Adm. Ichimaru Rinosuke, one of the two commanders of Iwo Jima, Hirakawa Sukehiro, a former professor of English at the University of Tokyo, has suggested that history may be judged by the units of day, month, year, and century.

We need not use the unit of century to see that the battle of Iwo Jima was a battle in which an overwhelming force set out to annihilate a trapped enemy, and did. The facts and figures that Bradley has marshaled (at times with boyish glee) to write *Flags of Our Fathers* show this: "70,000 assault-troop Marines" lined up against a garrison whose strength was originally put at 14,000 men; "seventy-two consecutive days" of bombing and bombardment, before the first landing, of what is "only about a third the mass of Manhattan Island"; and so forth.

As Gen. Graves Erskine said at the dedication of a cemetery on Iwo Jima on March 14, while the battle was still going on, "Victory [for the United States] was never in doubt." In the circumstances, to speak of enemy savagery makes little sense.

James Bradley is "straightforwardly patriotic," to quote the reviewer Richard Bernstein. But *Flags of Our Fathers*, which has since become a bestseller, has left me wondering if straightforward patriotism was what Bradley's father wanted.

In 2016 James Bradley wondered if his father was one of the six "flagraisers."

Doing One's Duty in a Desperate Situation

May 27, 2002, *Japan Times*

In April, when a young Palestinian woman exploded herself, killing and wounding many, White House spokesman Ari Fleischer said, "The president condemns this morning's homicide bombing."

A flurry followed in the mass media about the term that seemed intended to replace "suicide bomber." But perhaps because it was redundant (a bomber is homicidal) or too one-sidedly condemnatory to be politically sensible, the term did not survive for long. But it led me to one of the more durable books to come out of Japan's war in Asia and the Pacific: *Listen—Voices from the Deep (Kike wadatsumi no koe)*. It contains the musings of some of the members of the special attack forces, commonly known as kamikaze.

As originally compiled in 1947, with the title *In Distant Mountains and Rivers (Harukanaru sanga ni)*, it was a selection of letters and excerpts from diaries left by graduates of the Imperial University of Tokyo killed in the war. In effect a shorthand epic of the horrendous military venture that had just ended, it became a bestseller. When it had sold 200,000 copies, the book was taken out of print to make way for a new edition to include writings of graduates of other colleges and universities. The result, published in 1949 with the present title, has remained in print ever since.

If the first selection emphasized "humanity" (relief that the war was over), one of the editors said later, the second one emphasized "peace" (the Cold War was setting in fast). Both, in any event, were designed to condemn "that extremely asinine war." That editorial policy precluded writings expressing "radical Japanese spiritualism" or those "exalting war." For that matter, the Occupation's censors wouldn't have permitted publication of such things, either.

Still, *Voices from the Deep* isn't entirely "an eloquent cry for peace," as John Dower puts it in *Embracing Defeat* (Norton, 1999), though there certainly is a strong undercurrent of that. Kawashima Tadashi put that yearning most straightforwardly: "I will not make my son a soldier, never a soldier. . . . Peace, the world of peace, is best!" A graduate of the Tokyo University of Agriculture, Kawashima wrote that sentence on January 31, 1943, after witnessing his fellow soldier savaging an innocent Chinese man, his officers coldly looking on. Kawashima, who thought the retribution was deserved when he learned shortly afterward that more than twenty Japanese soldiers were killed by Chinese peasants, was himself killed in China two years later.

For most able-bodied young men of the day, there was little choice but to become soldiers. Japan at the time was, in the leftist scholar Odagiri Hideo's metaphor, "a house of death." During the Pacific phase of the war alone, a cumulative total of ten million men were drafted and sent to the front and two million were killed or became MIAs. In June 1943, student mobilization was instituted. The departing students' pledge, "We naturally do not expect to return alive," though based on the conventional notion of fighting hard, took a dark, sinister turn.

Most were starkly aware of the impossible position into which Japan had led itself, and they knew what the alternative ought to be. Uehara Ryōji, mobilized while studying economics at Keio University, left a will before plunging his plane into a U.S. task force on Kadena Bay, Okinawa, on May 11, 1945. "For Japan to last forever, it needs liberalism," he wrote, not "the totalitarian atmosphere that envelops it. . . . Whether a country will win or lose in a war you can tell in advance by looking at its ideology. Victory for a nation with one that naturally fits man's true nature is as clear as daylight."

In the face of the heightened likelihood of death, many expressed doubts about the standard reasons given for self-sacrifice. Kikuyama

Hiro'o, like Uehara mobilized while studying economics at the Imperial University of Tokyo, asked himself shortly before induction into the
army: "Am I taking up the gun for His Majesty? Or for my homeland (as
an idealistic concept) or for the love of my parents that I cannot possibly
doubt, or even for Japan's Nature which has always been my hometown.
. . ? But for me at present, (the question of) betting my own death on
any of these remains unsolved." Kikuyama was killed in battle on Luzon,
on April 29, 1945.

However, some also had an unmistakable willingness to be part of
history in the making. Sasaki Hachirō, yet another student mobilized
while studying economics at the Imperial University of Tokyo, has left us
detailed reasoning for his decision. In his diary entry on June 11, 1943, he
explained to himself why he was taking an active role in the war. He did
so in response to his friend Ōuchi Tsutomu's letter. Ōuchi, later a distinguished professor of economics, evidently wrote to counsel against such
a move, pointing out that seeking a certain death would not only be to
indulge in "momentary heroism" but "stupid" as well, because if Sasaki
thought it was his duty, that duty was a "reactionary" one.

"As a young man living in Japan at present," Sasaki wrote, "I regard
it as an extreme honor to be able to take part in this opportunity to create world history. We have studied economics furiously as a duty given
us. . . . In addition, being blessed with physical strength and endowed
with more than the average ability to act, I have the happy duty to be
able to dedicate myself to my country. I think (serving my country and
studying economics) are both sublime responsibilities."

Not that Sasaki chose to be blind or ignorant. In February 1943,
when he learned of the German defeat in Stalingrad and the Japanese
defeat at Guadalcanal, he saw that Japan would be in dire straits very
soon. In May he felt compelled to note: "We are already as helpless as
'a carp on a cooking board.' I'm not being pessimistic but we must recognize fact."

And the country for which he decided to sacrifice himself was far
from pretty. "The life of the wealthy I saw in Karuizawa, the conduct
of soldiers you see and hear about these days who behave as if this was

the time of their life, the government officials and capitalists as they are today," he wrote, "make me boiling mad."

Yet he argued, citing Thomas Carlyle, that there would be no progress in world history unless each made every effort to carry out his duties in circumstances that are only accidentally his, even though he also believed that what moves the world are "foreordained, inevitable forces lying beyond individuals' idealistic efforts." Sasaki died as a kamikaze pilot off Okinawa, on April 14, 1945.

Watanabe Kazuo, the scholar of French who wrote the preface to *Listen—Voices from the Deep*, judged that these young men's deaths were "not of course natural deaths, nor suicides, but 'homicidal deaths' (*tasatsu-shi*)." For many, that was undoubtedly true. But for many others, doing one's duty in a desperate situation was also imperative. To assume otherwise would be an insult to them.

Gyokusai or "Shattering Like a Jewel"
Reflection on the Pacific War

February 1, 2008, *The Asia-Pacific Journal: Japan Focus*

This past fall I was thinking once again about the intractability of Japan's part in the Pacific phase of World War II when the news came: Okinawans had staged a huge rally to protest the Japanese government's banning of textbook references to the military's role in "group suicides" among civilians during the Battle of Okinawa. According to some reports, a single examiner at the Japanese Ministry of Education and Science, with dubious outside connections, made the change. To explain it, he pointed to a suit recently filed against Ōe Kenzaburō's 1970 assertions.

The examiner, if he was thinking at all, took an action as improbable as the war itself. Yes, Japan may have been pushed up against the wall by America's compromise-be-damned approach to international complications. But the Japanese leaders who started the war did so in the perfect knowledge that the odds were overwhelmingly against them. After the initial series of victories, Japan had its first big defeat in the Battle of Midway, a mere six months after Pearl Harbor. From then on, it was all downhill, for reasons many had foreseen. And as matters turned bad, then disastrous, the military leadership's reactions became ever more irrational, as if starting the war itself wasn't irrational enough. One of the more infamous examples of that irrationality is the use of the word *gyokusai*, the ancient Chinese word *yusui* pronounced the Japanese way, meaning "to die gallantly as a jewel shatters."

With the annihilation of its 2,500-man force on Attu Island, in the Aleutian Archipelago, a year after Midway, the Japanese military used the term for the first time in a formal document, it is said. The official announcement on May 30, 1943 stated that those unable to take part in the final attack because of wounds or illness committed suicide in advance of it. The annihilations termed *gyokusai* after that saw the number of "shattered" soldiers increase: the Battle of Tarawa (November 21–23, 1943), 4,600 (17 surviving); the Battle of Kwajalein (January 30 to February 5, 1944), 7,900 (105 surviving); the Battle of Biak (May 27 to June 20, 1944), more than 10,000 (520 surviving); the Battle of Saipan (June 15 to July 9, 1944), 29,000 (921 surviving); and so on.

In that light, you might say that the Battle of Iwo Jima (February 19 to mid-March 1945), about which Clint Eastwood recently made twin films, one from the perspective of the defenders, did not create more deaths among Japanese forces than the Battle of Saipan only because the sulfuric island, one third the size of Manhattan, could not sustain more soldiers. The *gyokusai* there claimed 21,000 lives (1,000 surviving).

As a matter of fact, more than a year before the U.S. decided to send its soldiers into Iwo Jima, that is, in February 1944, Prime Minister Tōjō Hideki, in his "emergency declaration," had made the sweeping call: *ichioku gyokusai*, "100 million *gyokusai*." It was a demand that the entire Japanese population be prepared to die. Japan's mainland population at the time was seventy million, so he was also ordering Taiwanese and Koreans to meet the same fate. Japan had gotten Taiwan following the Sino-Japanese War (1894–95) and annexed Korea in 1910.

The Battle of the Philippines, from 1944 to August 1945, is not usually cited as an example of *gyokusai*, but its essence was the same. Lt. Gen. Yamashita Tomoyuki, whom Tōjō had demoted after he made his reputation in Malaysia, suddenly found himself assigned to a place where no fortification efforts had been made and where his troops were woefully equipped and provisioned. What was the mission given him, then? Prolonging the war as long as possible against an enemy materially and numerically vastly superior. Yamashita told his troops, "Carry out resistance in perpetuity to provide assistance to the never-ending Imperial Fortune, by turning yourselves into human pillars, unperturbed, for the Imperial Nation." The "human pillar," *hitobashira,* is an idea dating from mythological times of sacrificing a human being to placate whatever is creating havoc. The result: more than 450,000 Japanese soldiers died.

The so-called kamikaze tactic was put into practice during the Battle of Leyte Gulf (October 23–25, 1944). Less than half a year later, when Vice Adm. Itō Seiichi showed reluctance to lead Japan's last sizable naval sortie, without air cover, to Okinawa on a similar suicidal mission, he was told, "You are requested to die gallantly ahead of the 100 million *gyokusai*." The result: six of the ten warships that made up Itō's fleet were sunk, including the flagship Yamato, with more than 4,000 men lost. Itō was one of them.

Not that the Japanese high command was as callous or as irrational as that from the outset. When they learned of U.S. forces massing toward Attu in the spring of 1943, they tried to send a fleet to rescue the island's defense unit but the distance from the South Sea to the Aleutian Archipelago was too great and the mission was aborted. The Japanese forces were overstretched, as Faubion Bowers learned firsthand earlier that year when he found himself in New Guinea. Bowers, later Gen. MacArthur's aide-de-camp and personal interpreter, read, among captured Japanese documents, booklets on edible plants and animals. The Japanese troops were expected to survive in any area where they were deployed. The Japanese military had lost its logistical ability by then— actually, long before then.

"Kill yourself, don't be captured alive"

In any event, that one notion behind *gyokusai*, the injunction "Die, rather than become a POW," in the *Senjinkun*, The Code of Conduct on the Battlefield—was not exactly what I was thinking when I heard the news of the Okinawan protest rally, but just then I happened to be looking at the injunction and the code, in puzzlement and wonderment.

Issued in January 1941 in the name of Tōjō Hideki, then minister of the army, the *Senjinkun* is known today virtually for that command alone. Because of that, I was doubly surprised when I actually read the code, along with an account of how it came into being.

First, I learned that the Japanese army prepared it in an attempt to counter the widespread collapse of military discipline on the Chinese front: "violence against superior officers, desertions, rape, arson, pillage"—the kind of criminal acts "not seen on the battlefields during the Sino-Japanese and Russo-Japanese Wars," wrote Shirane Takayuki, one of the small group of officers tasked to write it. Shirane was just a cavalry lieutenant in the spring of 1939 when he was pulled from the unit confronting Chiang Kai-shek's army to work on the code, but he had studied philosophy and education at the Imperial University of Kyūshū. By then, evidently, the Imperial Rescript to the Soldiers, issued in 1882, had lost much of its hold. It had told the soldiers to be loyal, courteous, brave, faithful, and frugal.

What came to be known as the Nanjing Massacre, from December 1937 to early next year, was just one heinous manifestation of the loss of military discipline and order. So, most of the *Senjinkun* was devoted to reminding the soldiers, in much greater detail than the rescript, of the importance of upholding the honor of imperial soldiers. Don't get drunk, don't get carried away by lust, do treat non-combatants with kindness, and so on.

What surprised me equally was the command in question, Part II, Article 8. As Shirane put it, after Japan's defeat, the code as a whole won notoriety "from the humanistic viewpoint" because of the injunction, "Die, rather than become a POW." But the wording confused me. A sentence with two parts in apparent parallelism, it did not entirely make sense to me. It said, as I saw it, something like, "Thou shall not suffer the shame of being taken prisoner while alive; thou shall not leave the infamy of crime and penalty when you die." In short, it did not seem to say, "Rather than be taken prisoner, kill yourself." Put another way, it seemed to say, "Do your best not to be taken captive." Minus "shame," the injunction to avoid capture may be universal. It occurs in the Code of the U.S. Fighting Force, for example.

So I asked my erudite friend at Cornell University, Kyoko Selden. After carefully parsing the two-part sentence, she concluded that the original does not seem to say what it has always been taken to mean. The "traditional" interpretation may have been deliberately encouraged, she suggested, or the existing idea led to that reading. I can readily support the latter possibility from Japan's long military tradition.

Commander of the Attu Garrison Col. Yamazaki Yasuyo, in any event, knew exactly what the article meant when he cited it in his wire, on May 29, 1943:

> Under ferocious attack by enemy land, sea, and air, the two battalions to the fore were both almost smashed. We have barely been able to sustain this day. I arranged so the wounded and the ill in the field hospital were disposed of, the mild ones by themselves, the serious ones by the medics. I had the civilian employees who were noncombatants each take up a weapon, form a unit, both army and navy combined, and follow the attack unit. We had them make a resolve [to die], lest we together suffer the shame of being taken prisoner while alive. It is not that there is no other way; I simply did not wish to sully the soldiers' last moments. We will carry out a charge with the heroic spirits [of those killed in battle].

"To go to war is to die"

Other than Japan's military tradition, there were a few factors that may have made the notion of *gyokusai* more or less acceptable, rather than condemnable as an outright military failure. Going to war was long equated with meeting death. Many military songs at the time attest to this. Most important among them perhaps is "Umi Yukaba" (When Seagoing), which Japan Broadcasting Corporation (NHK) in 1937 commissioned Nobutoki Kiyoshi to compose. The lyrics were an ancient military vow that Ōtomo no Yakamochi (716?-785) incorporated in his poem in the *Man'yōshū* (Collection of Ten Thousand Leaves), the oldest extant anthology of Japanese poetry, and went:

> *Umi yukaba mizuku kabane*
> *yama yukaba kusamusu kabane*
> *Ōkimi no he ni koso shinane*
> *kaerimi wa sezu*

When seagoing, we'll be waterlogged corpses,
mountain-going, grass-grown corpses.
We may die with our Great Lord
but will never look back.

This song, which was often sung in gatherings to send soldiers off to the front, went on to be known as a "semi-national anthem."

Another song, which is said to have become the most popular, was also composed in 1937. It started with these words:

Katte kuru zo to isamashiku
chikatte kuni o detakarawa
tegara tatezuni shinaryōka....

I'll win and return, I pledged,
and gallantly left the country.
How can I die without exploits....

and the third stanza has:

yume ni detekita chichiue ni
shinde kaere to hagemasare

my father, appearing in a dream,
urged me, "Come home in death."

"Come home in death" (*shinde kaere*), to paraphrase, means, "Fight with resolve to die on the battlefield and come home only as a soul." These words are from *"Roei no uta"* (Song of the Bivouac). The lyrics were selected from those submitted by ordinary people in a 1937 newspaper contest. Koseki Yūji provided it with rhythmical music that befit a march. It at once became a big hit.

There was another factor. Despite the Geneva Convention, "take no prisoners" was the prevailing practice at the time—not just in the Japanese but in the Chinese military as well. The U.S. military, too, largely followed it in practice, if not as a matter of policy.

"We of course do not expect to return alive" (*Seira motoyori seikan o gosezu*)—so vowed Ebashi Shinshirō, representing all 25,000 university students, on October 21, 1943, at the ceremony in the Meiji Jingu Gaien stadium, in Tokyo, to send them off to the military. Earlier that year, the Tōjō cabinet had raised the eligible draft age to forty-five and then abolished draft exemptions for university students. Ebashi was a student at the Faculty of Literature of the Imperial University of Tokyo. Prime Minister Tōjō himself gave the farewell speech.

Tōjō Hideki was forced out as prime minister following the defeat at Saipan, which included 5,000 civilian suicides; some say there were a far greater number of them. There evidently was military coercion, though coercion in that milieu doesn't carry much meaning. It was a total war; civilians were regarded as part of the war. There was the frenzy and hysteria created by furious bombing, bombardment, strafing, machine-gunning, napalm spewed from flamethrowers—although Helen Mears made a notable observation about the effects of the tremendous firepower that the United States brought to bear in her 1948 book *Mirror for Americans: Japan.*

"The mass suicides, by deliberate drowning or by rushing futilely against an overwhelming force, were, from the evidence, due to hysteria and despair," Mears wrote after cataloguing the myths being created and perpetuated by the *New York Times* editorialists and others even as their own reporters were saying different things. "There is strong reason to believe that the chief motive in many of the mass suicides was fear of what we would do to them should they surrender," she went on. "Japanese propaganda against us (like ours against them) emphasized our savagery and ruthlessness as a foe. It is significant that we responded to such propaganda by killing more Japanese."

This brings us to the Battle of Okinawa, the biggest *gyokusai* as far as the military clashes to which the term is applicable are concerned. On this battle, the *New York Times* reporter W. H. Lawrence filed a report, in June 1945, using blunt language that his successors at the newspaper sixty years later would not imagine deploying in reporting from Iraq, even though a vastly superior power does exactly the same thing:

"Stated in its simplest terms we were able to announce the victory of Okinawa because the enemy had run out of caves and boulders from which to fight and we were nearly out of Japanese to kill."

A later official U.S. account put the number of Japanese soldiers killed in action at 110,070, with 7,401 captured. In addition, an estimated 100,000 civilians, between one quarter and one third of the Okinawa population, were killed. To quash the Japanese forces defending the fragile archipelago, the U.S. amassed 550,000 soldiers with a vast armada of air and sea power.

Island people called the American assault "an iron storm"—a series of "shock and awe," if you will, that lasted for three months. The government structure quickly disintegrated; the military command system rapidly splintered. With the idea of death over retreat or surrender prevailing, it would have been a miracle had no Japanese soldiers forced civilians to kill themselves or killed them outright in that chaos and madness.

This article is fully annotated in the Internet magazine The Asia-Pacific Journal: Japan Focus *where it first appeared; here it is somewhat revised. I should bring up a single piece of information from the endnotes: The U.S. forces had assaulted Okinawa with a large fleet six months before they attempted landing it and destroyed most of the prefectural capital, Naha, with more than 1,000 bombers. That was on October 10, 1944. In Okinawa it is known as the 10/10 Air Raid.*

On August 9, 2021, the New York Times *carried an article, "How a Star Times Reporter Got Paid by Government Agencies He Covered." The reporter in question was W. H. Lawrence, "Atomic Bill." This explains his exultation, even delirium, in reporting the bombing of Hiroshima. You can read it in the* New York Times, *of course, but also in* Reporting World War II: 1944–1946 *(Library of America), which includes it.*

Creator of "Go for Broke"

August 15, 29, and September 19, 1988, *Mainichi Daily News*

Reading Mike Masaoka's autobiography with Bill Hosokawa, *They Call Me Moses Masaoka: An American Saga* (William Morrow, 1987), I remembered an unexpected response to a column I wrote here, nearly four years ago. In it I outlined Henry Mittwer's story of his life, *Caught Between Fatherland and Motherland (Sokoku to bokoku no hazama de,* Sankei Shuppan, 1983)—quite innocuously, I thought. Not long after the column appeared, though, a Raymond Okamura, a lawyer in Berkeley, sent me a clipping of his letter to the editor of *Hokubei Mainichi,* a Californian daily where, evidently, my piece was reprinted. In his letter Okamura chastised both Mittwer and me for failing to "grasp the true significance" of the incarceration in the United States of 115,000 Japanese residents and Japanese Americans during World War II.

Few of the readers are likely to have read Henry Mittwer's autobiography. It is written in Japanese, and it is not the sort of book that comes naturally your way.

To briefly retell his life, Mittwer was born in Yokohama, in 1918, of the marriage between a geisha and an American, a film distribution agent for Hollywood. When he was nine, his father returned to the United States. Mittwer, the youngest of three sons, stayed in Japan with his mother and his oldest brother.

In 1940 with the money provided by a family acquaintance, Mittwer bought a one-way ticket to this country to find out his father's plans for his wife and two sons left in Japan; Mittwer Sr. hadn't sent them much money or many letters. In Los Angeles he found his father a pauper. His middle brother, though doing pretty well, wasn't willing to help. While he was drifting from one temporary job to another, Japan attacked Pearl Harbor.

The roundup of Japanese residents and Japanese Americans on the West Coast began in a matter of months. Mittwer looked more Caucasian than Oriental, and his friends told him he would be overlooked if he lay low. But he decided not to hide his Japanese blood and chose to be "relocated." From the time he was taken out of Los Angeles in 1942 until 1946, he was an inmate of three different camps and two jails. At the first camp he gave up his American citizenship in protest to the "loyalty" questionnaire. He did not regain it until 1952.

After the war he met Nyogen Senzaki, the first Zen monk to open a Zen center in the United States and, by the time Mittwer met him, himself a former camp inmate. The meeting seems to have led to Mittwer's decision, in 1961, to move back to Japan and take Buddhist vows. He is now a monk in one of the largest temples in Kyoto, Tenryū-ji.

So, what prompted Raymond Okamura to write me a letter of chastisement? Well, in his story—and in my retelling of it—Mittwer says he doesn't want to make a big deal of his relocation and jailing experiences in the United States because the Japanese in Japan suffered far more greatly under the American bombings and because the foreign residents in Japan and those Japanese related to foreigners, like his mother, were treated far more harshly by the Japanese authorities. This reasoning Okamura found offensive.

Okamura emphasized that Mittwer, though "a derivative American citizen" by the law of that time, was "definitely Japanese by culture," as he was "mostly raised by his mother in the authoritarian/militaristic atmosphere of the 1930s." Mittwer missed the chance to experience the American educational process, which "stressed individual rights, presumption of innocence, fair trial by jury, equality under the law, and 'liberty and justice for all.' Despite his American citizenship," therefore, he "did not comprehend what it meant to be an American and yet be imprisoned without evidence, without charge, without trial, and without a verdict of personal guilt."

Yes, the lawyer Okamura said, the Japanese perpetrated much greater atrocities, such as "the use of live human beings for bayonet practice and medical experimentation." But such things are "not germane to the issue," he wrote, because the "mass incarceration of Japanese Americans" in the United States "must be evaluated on the basis of American legal principals and moral standards—not those of another nation."

I think Okamura's argument is faulty on two counts.

First, Mittwer's lack of American education and knowledge of the U.S. Constitution does not have to be central to the issue. After all, Earl Warren, the Attorney General of California at the time and later the Chief Justice of the Supreme Court, advocated the incarceration, and Franklin Roosevelt, the then President of the U.S., ordered it. Weren't they the cream of the crop of the U.S. education that Okamura idealizes? Weren't they among the top custodians of the U.S. Constitution?

Second, comparative perspectives *are* "germane." The mass incarceration in question can be argued from the viewpoint of U.S. laws; it can also be looked at from a larger standpoint of human follies and sufferings. Denying the latter approach will be denying much of the meaning of our attempt to understand the human condition.

Yet, in assessing an experience in one country, someone from another must be careful.

Anyone who honors bravery and sacrifice is likely to be moved by Daniel Inouye's account of a retreat parade of the 442nd Regimental Combat Team—a unit formed entirely of Nisei during the Second World War. As *Personal Justice Denied,* the report of the Commission on Wartime Relocation and Internment of Civilians, puts it, "the 442nd took 9,486 causalities—more than 300 per-cent of its original infantry strength, including 600 killed." The total number of Nisei who served the unit was 18,000, so more than half became casualties. Inouye, a Democratic Senator from Hawaii who lost his right arm during the war, has given one view of the aftermath in his autobiography, *Journey to Washington* (Prentice-Hall, 1967):

When General Dahlquist called the regiment out for a retreat parade to commend us personally, he is reported to have said to the CO, 'Colonel, I asked that the entire regiment be present for this occasion. Where are the rest of your men?' And Colonel Pence, as bone-weary as any dogface in the outfit, replied, 'Sir, you are looking at the entire regiment. Except for two men on guard duty at each company, this is all that is left of the 442nd Combat Team.' ... My outfit, E Company, with a normal complement of 197 men, had exactly 40 soldiers able to march to the parade ground.

What makes this inordinate casualty rate ennobling is the purpose for which the military unit was formed: to prove the Japanese Americans' loyalty to the United States. Mike Masaoka was a prime mover in the formation of the 442nd, as he makes clear in his autobiography, *They Call Me Moses Masaoka.* If one recalls how, not long after Japan's Pearl Harbor attack in December 1941, a total of 115,000 West Coast Japanese residents and Japanese Americans were forced by the U.S. government to abandon their homes and properties to be "relocated" in various camps, one may ask why Masaoka, a Nisei, urged "shedding blood" for the government that treated his fellow Japanese Americans so unjustly.

Though not emphasized by Masaoka himself, perhaps because officially recognized now, the determining factor was the amorphous status of Japanese immigrants and their offspring in America at the time. Like most other immigrants, the Nisei strove to forget their ancestral heritage and become pure American, as they were taught to, but they were never fully accepted as such. Masaoka recalls how in 1936, when he, a student at the University of Utah, won the top ratings at a national debate and oratory contest, the *Salt Lake Tribune* chose to print a full-length editorial to praise him, but deliberately or otherwise referred to him as "an alien of Asiatic heritage."

This frustrating situation, coupled with the mounting hostility against Japan for its military conduct in Asia, made many of the Nisei "pathetically eager to show (their) loyalty" to the United States, as reported by Curtis B. Munson, a well-to-do businessman who was hired by the State Department to do some internal snooping. Masaoka, who became the Washington representative of the Japanese American Citizens League (JACL) shortly before the outbreak of war, makes it abundantly clear that he was one such "eager" person.

Yet, as might be expected, the notion of the Nisei asking the government to allow them to rejoin the military as "the most dramatic demonstration" of their loyalty troubled a sizable number of Nisei at the time, as it apparently has some Japanese Americans since. The contemporary opposition was put cogently and concisely in a remark quoted by Masaoka himself as made by a participant in a JACL conference in the fall of 1942: "'We want the government to let us out of the camps, to let us go home as full-fledged citizens, before we offer our lives in defense of our country.'"

From Masaoka's point of view, the primary goal of that particular conference was to win a "ringing, unequivocal resolution demanding" that the government accept Nisei in the military service. He was prepared to resign unless such a resolution was made. But he wasn't prepared, he reports, for "the depth and sincerity," let alone the persuasiveness, of the opposition. The resolution, which was won, prompted rioting in some of the camps. Troops were brought in, shooting, killing, and beatings occurred. Some JACL leaders had to be placed in a special camp for safety.

It must be noted that the formation of an all-Nisei military unit was *not* what Masaoka and other JACL leaders had in mind; all they had wanted at the outset was "restoration of Selective Service responsibilities for the Nisei." To them, the War Department's idea of such a unit, when broached, was "a bombshell." In the scheme of things, however, the special combat team worked far better in achieving the goal of proving loyalty, though the sacrifice might have been a little too "dramatic."

As Masaoka says, the inability to see that one doesn't have to be white to be an American is "a problem that has remained with Japanese Americans to this day." But after the war he used the records of the 442nd Combat Team effectively to help eliminate racially discriminatory laws and statutes. To that extent his advocacy of proof on the battlefield has been vindicated.

The resolve to remain loyal to his country, rather than to his wishes, at some critical junctures of the Second World War was pivotal to the achievements of Mike Masaoka, as we learn from *They Call Me Moses Masaoka.* But it also has raised some questions.

Masaoka, who was born in Fresno, California, in 1915, and brought up in Salt Lake City, has been a strong advocate of "100% Americanism." When the U.S. government decided to remove West Coast Japanese residents—most of them legally unable to become American citizens—and Japanese Americans to special camps for security, he actively cooperated with the authorities in the belief that "it was [American people's] patriotic duty in wartime to obey government orders no matter how repugnant."

Masaoka then worked hard to send his fellow Nisei, himself included, to the battlefields in order to prove, in blood, their loyalty to their country. The direct result was the formation of the 442nd Regimental Combat Team. With the motto, Go for Broke, the regiment became one of the most decorated during World War II. To put it differently, it sustained a disproportionately high rate of causalities.

His moves troubled some of his contemporaries. Since the ending of the war they have also prompted some Japanese Americans to question his motives. Around 1970, for example, he was "savagely pilloried" by some "young activists," he tells us, who charged that he had "sold Japanese Americans down the river in 1942." Reassessing history is a constant activity, so I'm certain that similar charges will continue to be made.

For the most part, though, Masaoka's explanations of his motives from the standpoint of national loyalty are likely to win the day as long as the view remains unassailable that the Second World War was a "good war." The fact that the United States came out of the war victorious should also strengthen Masaoka's argument.

When a country wages a "bad war" and loses it, as Japan did in that war, the question of national loyalty becomes complex. It has provoked tortuous emotions in Japan. This may not be too clear to those who hear about Japanese references to their country's military roles in the 1930's and 1940's only in a highly politicized way.

On one hand, there have been reports on the Japanese government's attempts at textbook revisions that obscure Japanese atrocities in China, Korea, and other Asian nations. Occasional remarks by senior government officers to the effect that Japan needn't be apologetic about what it did decades ago have also made headlines in this country. On the other hand, the American media, the *New York Times* among them, makes the point of noting, whenever an opportunity arises, that the Japanese tend to underplay their roles in the war.

Among those who ponder the question, however, there have been a simmering question: What about those Japanese who were troubled by the aims and deeds of their country but remained loyal, fighting and dying for it?

The most recent article touching on this question that I've read is written by the critic Yamamoto Shichihei, who took it up in the November 1986 issue of the monthly *Bungei Shunjū*. The occasion was the publication of the "complete works" of Yoshida Mitsuru (1923–79) who is best known for his epic description of the sinking of the largest battleship ever built, *Senkan Yamato no saigo*, which Richard Minear translated as *Requiem for Battleship Yamato* (University of Washington Press and Kodansha, 1985).

Yoshida, an ensign on the bridge of the Yamato when it was sunk in April 1945, became an ardent pacifist after the war. But throughout his life he was unable to reconcile himself with the view, successfully propagated by the Occupation Forces, that, as he put it, "the war was a sheer misery, a sheer emptiness, and was unilaterally meaningless to Japan." It was because of such views, he believed, that his book depicting men who, while recognizing the absurdity of the cause, fought to the end, was banned. For him, his fellow men in uniform were honorable men who knew exactly what they were doing.

One memorable character Yoshida recreates in his epic is Lt. Usubuchi. An outspoken critic of Japan and its navy, Usubuchi knew fully well the hopelessness of going out on a naval sortie without air cover into the midst of swarms of enemy aircraft. Still, he declared that if he and his fellow men died, their country might finally wake up; the impending defeat would be vital for Japan's rebirth. Soon afterward he was blasted out of existence by a 1000-pound bomb—killed like nine out of ten men on board the Yamato. Were their hopes understood by the survivors and the postwar generations? That's what Yoshida kept asking.

The central concern for Yamamoto Shichihei, a survivor of the war as Yoshida was, is the seemingly innocuous question often asked of him: "Why didn't you oppose the war?" He says he sometimes tries to explain the why of it by asking the questioner to imagine himself to be an employee at a large company that is in turmoil and facing bankruptcy. Will he jump ship or will he try to execute his daily assignments faithfully? (This corporate analogy is unlikely to work for most Americans, except perhaps Vietnam veterans, and for many young Japanese. Yamamoto says he has never come away feeling he has convinced the questioner.)

I am treading treacherous ground. Mike Masaoka may be right in saying "it is important not to judge long-past decisions by contemporary values." Clearly, however, Yoshida and Yamamoto were on the wrong side.

I knew of Mike Masaoka because my employer, a Japanese trade agency, used the services of his Washington lobbyist office, Mike Masaoka & Associates, and I met him once for dinner. But I knew little else about him. So when his autobiography came out (he may have given me a copy), I had a great deal to learn about him and his life.

Only recently I learned that John E. Dahlquist was a poor military tactician and infamous for overusing the 442nd Regimental Combat Team.

Debunking America's "Good War" Myth

June 25, 2001, *Japan Times*

Pearl Harbor, a film directed by Michael Bay, may be copying what happened after Japan's actual assault: a spectacular initial success followed by a string of disappointments following the Doolittle Raid, although I must hasten to add that there won't be anything remotely resembling an unconditional surrender in store for the Hollywood venture.

Does the pattern seemingly shaping up for *Pearl Harbor* derive from the possibility that the movie is the reductio ad absurdum of the current boom in all things the Second World War, as Frank Rich, of the *New York Times,* put it? I cannot tell, because I haven't seen the film. But the easy patriotism that appears to form the core of the movie, as well as the boom, has spurred me to read a couple of articles.

In "The Real War" (*The Atlantic,* June 2001), Benjamin Schwartz takes on the popular historian Stephen Ambrose and finds him "littered with lofty cant." Ambrose, who has been providing narrative backing to the so-called Good War for some years now and who may well be the source of the current fad, has added a new title to his oeuvre: *The Good Fight* (Simon & Schuster, 2001), a ninety-six-page account of the Second World War "for young readers."

Schwartz sees at least two things "egregiously skewed" in Ambrose. One is the historian's flat assertion that American soldiers were "engaged in a sanctified crusade." They "didn't want to live in a world in which wrong prevailed," Ambrose says. "So they fought . . . and stopped Hitler and Tojo."

A world in which wrong prevailed? Racial discrimination was still the norm in the United States at the time. As some noted, U.S. officers often treated German POWs better than blacks. There were riots.

The other is Ambrose's suggestion that the Second World War was an American war for decency and democracy and that the United States is entitled to all the credit for defeating Germany and Japan. That's an odd view of the war, but just taking the German defeat, an honest history must give most of the credit to the Soviet Union, Schwartz says.

This self-righteous, "solipsistic" approach is troublesome. Ambrose is a popular historian who, among others, may have inspired the NBC news anchorman Tom Brokaw to write *The Greatest Generation* and its sequels, *The Greatest Generation Speaks: Letters and Reflections* and *An Album of Memories: Personal Histories from the Greatest Generation.*

Schwartz ends his essay by referring to Robert Penn Warren. Meditating on the Civil War's psychological bequest, Warren spoke of a "treasury of virtue" that the North has displayed to the South. Ambrose's kind of narrative does something similar, making the United States "insufferable to other nations." History, Schwartz concludes, must be treated as "tragic, ironic, paradoxical, and ambiguous."

At the *Atlantic* website, the Schwartz essay is linked to the article that Edgar L. Jones wrote for the magazine back in February 1946, "One War is Enough." As the monthly's editor explains, in May 1945, "Captain McGeorge Bundy, AUS, registered his vehement belief in peacetime military training, in his Open Letter to those college presidents who were opposing adoption of the measure in wartime." Early in the following year, as the debate came "to a head in Washington," so the *Atlantic* asked two of "those who feel that conscription in any guise is a war measure out of keeping with the peacetime policy of this republic" to submit their opinions. One of them was Edgar L. Jones.

What the magazine got from him was a full-throated *cri de cœur* against war and the military. Jones says of himself: "In the course of forty months of war duty and five major battles I was only an ambulance driver, a merchant seaman, an Army historian, and a war correspondent, never a downright GI," but he witnessed more than enough of barbarity to utterly debunk the image of American soldiers that Stephen Ambrose wants to project for future American generations: good-natured young men handing out candy to bedraggled but smiling children, avatars of decency and democracy who had no notion of "rape, pillage, looting, wanton destruction, senseless killing," of which, according to Ambrose, Soviet, German, and Japanese soldiers were the very vehicles.

"We Americans have the dangerous tendency in our international thinking to take a holier-than-thou attitude toward other nations," Jones begins his critical passage.

> We consider ourselves to be more noble and decent than other peoples, and consequently in a better position to decide what is right and wrong in the world. What kind of war do civilians suppose we fought, anyway?
>
> We shot prisoners in cold blood, wiped out hospitals, strafed lifeboats, killed or mistreated enemy civilians, finished off the enemy wounded, tossed the dying into a hole with the dead, and in the Pacific boiled the flesh off enemy skulls to make table ornaments for sweethearts, or carved their bones into letter openers. We topped off our saturation bombing and burning of enemy civilians by dropping atomic bombs on two nearly defenseless cities, thereby setting an alltime record for instantaneous mass slaughter.

Jones goes on to describe, among other things, how

> the Army and Navy had every opportunity to strike a clean blow for democracy by setting an example in non-discrimination against Negroes, but instead, both services insisted upon racial segregation wherever and whenever possible. The Negro in 'wellrun' military installations was not allowed to sleep in the same room with white men, eat at the same table, or attend the same churches.

"One War is Enough" is linked to Paul Fussell's 1989 article, "The Real War: 1939–1945," apparently a summation of his book, *Wartime*, which appeared in the same year. *Wartime* was panned so thoroughly for describing the bunglings and misconduct of the U.S. military during the Good War that the *New York Times* even did an article on it—though that is no reason to condemn the book. I read it and found it detailed and admirable.

Other than the *Atlantic* website, I must mention John Gregory Dunne's searing commentary in the *New Yorker*, "The American Raj: Pearl Harbor as Metaphor" (May 7, 2001). In the article, published in anticipation of the movie, Dunne, who, with his wife Joan Didion, often takes part in Hollywood movie-making, describes U.S. Navy life on Hawaii, pointing out, for example, how Saturday excursions of sailors "often ended up in the whorehouses on Honolulu's Hotel Street, where working girls might turn a hundred tricks through the day and night." That was no exception on December 6, the day before Japan's attack.

As Edgar L. Jones quoted in "One War is Enough," Gen. George C. Marshall's testified that Hawaii had "at least sufficient means so that it could have broken up the attack, so that it would have done only limited harm." Whoring on the Saturday night prevented that.

Edgar L. Jones' article, "One War is Enough", harked back to Gen. Smedley Butler's 1935 book, War Is a Racket, *and looked forward to President Dwight Eisenhower's farewell speech warning the military-industrial complex. "One War is Enough" may now be read as an independent pdf, not as part of the online* Atlantic *articles.*

The Japanese Sword I

High Price of Media-Fabricated Heroism

November 24, 2003, *Japan Times*

Good for her. Jessica Lynch, of the U.S. Army, finally given a chance on TV to have her say, punctured the notion of heroism concocted by the Hollywood publicist placed in Baghdad and the American mass media, ever the willing partner of their government when it comes to war.

Lynch is lucky, too. Unless something goes awfully wrong, she is unlikely to be punished for the fiction in whose creation she had no part. The core of the fiction was harmless, though some of the attendant allegations were repulsive.

Two Japanese soldiers during the Asia-Pacific War who were turned into unlikely heroes in a set of two newspaper accounts weren't so lucky. After Japan's defeat, they were tried, found guilty, and executed.

The story began with an article in the *Tokyo Nichinichi Shimbun*—the predecessor of today's *Mainichi Shimbun*—on November 30, 1937. A dispatch from Changzhou, a city between Nanjing and Shanghai, it had the kind of headline that was apparently created to delight the credulous of the day: "A Contest to Cut Down 100 people! Two Lieutenants Already Fell 80."

It told of two young officers who pledged to compete to see which could kill 100 people first: Mukai Toshiaki, whose sword was of the famous Seki no Magoroku make, and Noda Tsuyoshi, whose sword was no brand-name product but still "a treasure handed down from his ancestors."

"After leaving Wuxi, it came about that Sec. Lt. Mukai would move with his corps along the railroad for 26 or 27 kilometers to advance," said the dispatch, which was filed by Asami and two other special correspondents,

> while Sec. Lt. Noda would advance parallel to the railroad, so they were parted. The morning after the departure, Sec. Lt. Noda, finding himself in a nameless village eight kilometers from Wuxi, dashed into a pillbox and cut down four enemies to become the first to breach the enemy line. Hearing about this, Sec. Lt. Mukai worked himself up that night, jumped into an enemy camp with his men in Henlin Base, and cut down fifty-five.
>
> Following that, Sec. Lt. Noda cut down 9 in Henlin Base, 6 in Weiguan Base, and, on the 29th, 6 at Changzhou Station, a total of 25 people. For his part Sec. Lt. Mukai cut down 4 near Changzhou Station. When we reporters went to the station we happened upon the two being interviewed.

This article ends by quoting the two men. Sec. Lt. Mukai said, "At this rate, I expect to cut down 100 people by the time we reach Danyang, let alone Nanjing. Noda is the loser. My sword has cut down 56 but its blade is chipped in only one spot, I tell you." Sec. Lt. Noda said, "The two of us make it a rule not to cut down someone who tries to run. I can't raise my score because I'm working as a—t [censored] but I tell you I'll turn out a big score before Danyang."

The second dispatch two weeks later told the reader that by the time the two officers met next they had killed 105 and 106 people each with their swords but that since they couldn't tell which reached the goal of 100 first, they called it a draw and set out on a new round by raising the stakes to 150, or to a new total of 150—the original report isn't clear on this. The article ends with Sec. Lt. Mukai showing his Seki no Magoroku to the reporter, nonchalantly standing amid "incoming enemy bullets."

As we read this story today, the two officers' swordsmanship is just about as farcical as that of Uma Thurman in Quentin Tarantino's latest fare, *Kill Bill*. In comparison, a nineteen-year-old woman soldier in a horrible car crash "going down shooting" sounds like a model of truth-telling.

But some went on to believe the 1937 story long after the puerile militaristic fervor disappeared—most prominent among them Honda Katsuichi. The famous *Asahi Shimbun* reporter not only accepted it at face value in his recreations in the early 1970s of the atrocities the Japanese Imperial Army is said to have committed in China but he also went a few steps further. In retelling the story he changed those killed by Mukai and Noda from combatants to civilians, increased the numbers, and added details.

If Private Lynch felt "hurt and embarrassed" when she learned of the story made up for her, Sec. Lt. Mukai, when he returned to Japan and read the newspaper articles, was "astonished" and "ashamed"—the latter word used in the Japanese military's sense of ultimate condemnation. That is why Mukai willingly responded to a summons to go to the Chinese war crimes tribunal set up in Nanjing after Japan's defeat. He thought no sane person would believe such a fantastic story.

Yamamoto Shichihei, who noted the military sense of the word "ashamed" as Mukai used it, wrote a meticulous account of his own life in the Japanese Imperial Army to demonstrate the utter improbability of the killing contest: *The Japanese Military within Myself (Watakushi no naka no Nihon-gun)*. In it he marshaled an array of reasons—not just to annihilate the veracity of the original account but also to explain how such a story may have come about. One point he makes is simple: the Japanese Army in battle would not have tolerated the kind of activities the two lieutenants are supposed to have engaged in. Yamamoto, who died in 1991, was in a position to know.

Like the two men, he held the lowest commissioned rank of second lieutenant. More to the point, like Mukai, he was in an artillery division and, like Noda, he was an adjutant, two of the many facts that the reporter Asami deliberately obfuscated in creating two sword-brandishing killing machines. Mukai, commanding an artillery piece, would certainly have been court-martialed had he left the weapon he was in charge of in the heat of battle. Noda as adjutant couldn't possibly have left his unit to indulge in a personal competition, even if his aim was to kill as many enemy soldiers as possible.

Sad to say, when Mukai asked Asami from his prison cell in Nanjing to provide testimony that his account was a piece of fiction, the reporter refused. And he stuck to his guns to the very end.

In contrast, the Chinese defense attorney Cui Wenyuan was an astute, honorable man. He argued, though to no avail, that if Mukai and Noda told Asami and other reporters any kind of story of their samurai exploits, it was "an after-dinner joke," not a tale told amid "incoming enemy bullets."

The Japanese Sword II
Cutting an Ancient Myth Down to Size

December 29, 2003, *Japan Times*

The myth of the Japanese sword, which Quentin Tarantino plays to the hilt in *Kill Bill,* has several origins. There was a religious connection. The manufacture of the blade was linked to Shugendō, a form of nature worship that held that rough physical training is essential to enlightenment. There was the Japanese propensity to pursue anything, even sword brandishing, as a means of attaining "the Way." There was *bushidō,* which, in equating honor with death, found the very means of death in the sword. Edward Zwick deploys this ideal in *The Last Samurai.*

One might even add the ancient notion, which is probably universal, that the sword has magical powers. The Arthurian legend of Excalibur typifies it.

I don't know when I started believing in the myth. But if there was one thing that helped to congeal the amorphous sense I had developed while watching samurai movies during the 1950s and 1960s, it was Noel Perrin's 1979 book, *Giving Up the Gun: Japan's Reversion to the Sword, 1543-1879* (David Godine).

Perrin's short treatise was timely and important. In the days when horrible notions such as mutual assured destruction (MAD) still had intellectual currency, it argued cogently that military technologies did not have to advance unchecked. For a prime precedent, look at Japan. The Japanese accidentally gained knowledge of the gun in the mid-fifteenth century, but after perfecting its manufacture and use, they essentially abandoned it in favor of an inferior weapon, the sword.

Perrin made this point in a way that tickled a Japanese—yes, me—still suffering from the century-old sense of inferiority to the West. The prevailing view was that Japan was a backward country when the U.S. naval officer Matthew Perry forced it open, in the mid-nineteenth century. Perrin said that was not wholly the case. During the isolationist period, Japan had made progress that matched or was ahead of the West in such fields as waterworks, agriculture, mathematics, medicine, retail-merchandizing, and sanitary engineering. My favorite among his examples was Kleenex. If Americans think they were the first to invent it, they are wrong: the Japanese had invented its equivalent three centuries earlier!

Oh, yes, Perrin did not neglect to mention the superior quality of the Japanese sword. He quoted a Dutchman who observed that Japanese swords were "so well wrought, and excellently temper'd, that they will cut our *European* blades asunder, like Flags or Rushes." The twentieth-century arms collector George Cameron Stone took part in a test to check the Dutchman's word and saw a newly made Japanese sword "cut a modern European sword in two." It was the quality Walter Ames Compton called "a fantastic order of high efficiency in doing the work for which [it was] designed," when his collection of Japanese swords was shown at Japan House Gallery, New York, in 1976.

So tickled, I joined the credulous horde. Those who actually used the sword and those who had to deal with its consequences knew better, as I have recently learned.

During the Asia-Pacific War, officers of the Japanese Imperial Army, both commissioned and non-commissioned, wore "military swords" (*gunto*). The sword expert Naruse Sekitsugu toured the Chinese front at the Army's request to repair damaged swords. His detailed report, *The Fighting Japanese Sword (Tatakau Nihontō)*, published in 1940, was devastating. Not that Naruse, a modern-day swordsman, did not know the virtual uselessness of the Japanese sword as a weapon in a modern war before he was sent to the continent. Rather, he was disgusted, even amused, by the ignorance of those who carried the sword.

Of the 2,000 specimens he examined and repaired during the nine months of his tour in Northern China, seventy percent were those damaged as a result of mishandling. Naruse wrote of a major who inadvertently dropped his sword, scabbard and all, while on horseback. His horse stepped on it, creating a sword bent at two places for him. What!? A Japanese sword bent by a mere horse's hoof? Yes, and that particular sword was one made by the swordsmith Kanehira, no less.

(Most army blades were newly minted, a sizable portion of them, it was said, made from scrapped automobile springs imported from the United States. Many were also "real swords," some even made by fabled craftsmen like Kanehira.)

Bending, indeed, was one great flaw of the Japanese sword, as latter-day samurai quickly found out. The sword in most cases bent at the first strike, effectively becoming a non-weapon, like a gun that has run out of bullets. But, whereas a spent gun could be kept for further use without difficulty, a bent sword couldn't.

Another flaw lay in the hilt. The hilt, *tsuka*, of the Japanese sword is in effect a scabbard made for the part of the blade called the tang, *nakago*. It is fastened to the tang with one or more removable rivets. The fact that the tang receives scant attention in forging, in stark contrast to the blade itself, doesn't help. And since the hilt is an attachment that plays a pivotal role in brandishing a weighty blade, it easily comes undone, even breaks. In this, the Japanese sword was decisively inferior to the Western saber or the Chinese "blue-dragon" sword. In both, the hilt is a solid extension of the blade. A fully sixty percent of the damages Naruse inspected occurred at the hilt.

Some Japanese soldiers nonetheless believed in the invincibility of the Japanese sword, as actual samurai did not. Naruse tells of a soldier who possessed "a real and true Tadamitsu." The engravings on the sword said it was crafted by Tadamitsu, of Osafune, during the Bunmei era (1469–86), and it surely was made excellently.

Evidently having heard stories such as the one Noel Perrin tells of a Japanese sword slicing a machine gun, the soldier "suddenly cut at an iron plate two inches thick. Of course he created large chips in the blade and brought it to me. What he had to say then was, 'They say the

Tadamitsu is a superb sword, but this one was no good. It merely cut an iron plate by one inch, and chipped like this. It also bent. Do you think this is a fake?'"

Naruse, an admirer of the swords of his country, could only sigh: "A master's work died a dog's death." His simple word on the instrument is so commonsensical as to put all of us blind believers to shame: "After all, a sword is neither devised nor designed to cut iron."

Great Tokyo Air Raid Was a War Crime
"Scorched and Boiled and Baked to Death"

September 30, 2002, *Japan Times*

The Japanese government conferred the First Order of Merit with the Grand Cordon of the Rising Sun upon Gen. Curtis LeMay—yes, the same general who, less than twenty years earlier, had incinerated "well over half a million Japanese civilians, perhaps nearly a million."

The date was December 7, 1964. Earlier that year, in May, the general, now the chief of staff of the U.S. Air Force, had declaimed: "Tell the Vietnamese they've got to draw in their horns or we're going to bomb them back into the Stone Age."

I was reminded of the Japanese government's bizarre act when I read the responses of several readers of the *Atlantic Monthly* to the news that a museum was finally created in Tokyo to memorialize the Great Tokyo Air Raid. In the wee hours of March 10, 1945, 300 B-29s dropped 2,000 tons of incendiaries on one section of Tokyo—a space seven-tenths the size of Manhattan—and in two hours and a half "scorched and boiled and baked to death" 100,000 people. The quoted words are LeMay's.

No, "news" is not the right word. For his July-August column of the monthly, Jonathan Rauch mentioned the opening of a "small museum" and spoke of what lay behind it: an "obscure" air raid. "Few Americans have even heard of it," he wrote, "and few Japanese like to dwell on it."

Rauch met a survivor of the firebombing, a Japanese friend's mother, back in 1990. He admired her for her "matter-of-fact, detached manner." Her attitude was: "What happened happened, and war is always bad, and 1945 is ancient history." Still, "the Tokyo attack deserves the most introspection of all," Rauch decided, "even as it receives the least."

In sheer magnitude, the calamity brought by the firebombing surpassed both Hiroshima and Nagasaki, at least according to the U.S. Strategic Bombing Survey conducted shortly after the war. But the devastation of Tokyo, along with that of Hamburg and Dresden, was laid aside the moment an atomic bomb was dropped on Hiroshima, then on Nagasaki. With the advent of a weapon capable of snuffing out a large city in a flash, the sense suddenly took root that "the continuity of life was, for the first time, put into question," as Mary McCarthy put it.

In fact, one Japanese writer reported, in 1968, that "in the twenty-two years since the war the *Asahi Shimbun* has written only four times about March 10," while taking up Hiroshima a hundred times more often. At about that time, Saotome Katsumoto, a thirteen-year-old boy when he survived the firestorm, resolved to do something about it. It took him over three decades to create his modest archival center.

Was the raid justified? Rauch asked in his column. As with the dropping of the second atomic bomb, the question is legitimate.

First, before and during the Second Word War there were people who thought indiscriminate slaughter of civilians had to be avoided. Tacticians in the U.S. Army Air Forces themselves were split between those who believed in "precision-bombing" and those who were "area bombers."

Brig. Gen. Haywood Hansell, who was assigned to execute the first serious bombings against Japan, was of the former group. But he was duly relieved of his duty as ineffectual and replaced by Maj. Gen. Curtis LeMay. And LeMay, switching from high explosives to incendiaries, went on to carry out what Gen. Douglas MacArthur's aide, Brig. Gen. Bonner Fellers, called "one of the most ruthless and barbaric killings of non-combatants in all history."

Equally important, the victors of the Second World War did not just expand the definition of "war crimes" but introduced the new concepts of "crime against peace" and "crime against humanity." And these ideas have gained support in recent years. Probably with the latter development in mind, Rauch wrote: "I believe the firebombing of Tokyo should be considered a war crime."

Some readers did not like this. And the five responses the *Atlantic* has chosen to print in its October issue are yet another reminder: When it comes to Japan and World War II, some Americans are incapable of accommodating different viewpoints.

Blaine Browne, in Lighthouse Point, Florida, begins by taking Rauch to task for following "a convoluted path toward his goal of elevating the March 1945 U.S. firebomb raid on Tokyo to the historical prominence he feels it deserves," so you can guess the tenor of his letter. But in his determination to dismiss the importance of "an event that, as Rauch complains, has gone largely unremarked since its occurrence," Browne makes one point he may not have intended.

"By early 1945 the American public's willingness to support operations that might produce *any* significant casualties was increasingly strained," he tells us, and concludes: "The Truman Administration's decision to use the atomic bomb must be considered in this context."

I know Stanford historian Barton Bernstein has taken a somewhat different tack and argued President Truman used atomic bombs because American taxpayers would have revolted if they learned their government had expended $2 billion on the Manhattan Project but had not used what it produced. The amount was sizable at the time; the creation and maintenance of the large fleet of B-29's cost $3 billion.

But I don't know if Bernstein would go as far as to suggest what Browne does. By Browne's logic, Japan's invasion of China, for example, must be considered all right—in the context of the public's support.

Michael Franzblau, in San Rafael, California, writes: "Concern that Curtis LeMay's Army Air Corps committed war crimes in the firebombing of Tokyo has to be balanced by awareness of the despicable activities of the Imperial Japanese Army in China."

In other words, you murdered relatives of someone I know, so I murdered some of yours. This argument may have worked in the age of gunfighters of the American west. But it evidently wouldn't have worked in the military tribunals convened after the war. In any event, the countries that sat to judge Germany and Japan were careful to exclude their own deeds from consideration.

The shortest letter cited in the *Atlantic* comes from Devin Croft, in Littleton, Colorado. It reads in its entirety: "If the United States owed any debt to the dead of Tokyo, it was long since repaid through the reconstruction of Japan in the postwar years."

That is one conclusion some Japanese may accept, however ambivalently. But Croft, too, evades Rauch's point. Any deliberate mass slaughter of civilians is a war crime. And what happened in the early hours of March 10, 1945, was the greatest slaughter a single air raid produced in world history.

Indiscriminate Bombing and Legal Judgment
Inoue Yūichi and Okada Tasuku

February 27, 2017, *Japan Times*

Cultural geographer Cary Karacas asked me to translate some poems about the air raids on Japanese cities during the Asia-Pacific War, so I did. Later I found one of the areas he is studying is the civilian experience of aerial bombing.

For my translation, Karacas lent me an anthology, *Great Air Raids: 310 Poets (Daikūshū 310-nin shishū,* 2015). I knew of its compiler and editor, Saotome Katsumoto. A survivor of the night of March 9, 1945, that struck Tokyo with the biggest firebombing ever, Saotome was distressed by Japan's well-nigh disregard for the raid in comparison with Hiroshima and Nagasaka, so he decided to do something about it. After struggling for more than thirty years, he managed to found a museum to commemorate the calamity, the Center of the Tokyo Raids and War Damage. I mentioned him in these pages some years ago. ("Great Tokyo Air Raid Was a War Crime," September 30, 2002.)

However, one powerful piece describing that night that I found and translated, "Ah, Yokokawa Elementary School," was not in Saotome's anthology, maybe because it wasn't meant to be a poem. Inoue Yūichi, who wrote it, was on night duty at the school, in Honjo, where he was a teacher.

Like most schools that had been destroyed during the Great Earthquake of 1923, Yokokawa had been rebuilt with concrete and steel, and that proved fatal. After a thousand people evacuated into the school, incendiary bombs engulfed the building. "Ferocious fires around them / The old the young the men the women voiceless," Inoue wrote.

the school inside because of fire / is like daylight / iron-framed window glasses shattered in a single blow / in a single second / tearing sound at once school inside turns into fire / one thousand refugees / no place to run to / as if inside a strongbox / parents cover their beloved children who cling to them / "Papa" / "Mama" / children clinging to parents calling them / but parents respond only with groans / all the thousand piling one upon another. . . .

This piece, which you can see on the Internet, is written as if splashed on a piece of paper with a brush, writhing breathlessly like "the parents' and children's death screams." In fact, surviving this inferno, Inoue went on to become an outstanding avant-garde calligrapher who, some say, influenced Isamu Noguchi and Franz Kline.

Whenever I read about these air bombings—large-scale, methodical, and persistent—I often wondered: What happened when B-29s were shot down or crash-landed and crewmen survived? After all, from November 1944 to August 1945, Tokyo alone was firebombed 122 times, by one count. What awaited the surviving airmen? I never explored the matter.

I remember a Japanese TV drama from the end of the 1950s, I'd Like to Become a Clam (*Watashi wa kai ni naritai*). In it, a barber turned draftee is ordered to kill a survivor of a crashed B-29. After Japan's defeat, he is indicted on a war crime, found guilty, and sentenced to death. It was a fictionalized composite of actual incidents.

More recently, I'd heard that a film was made about a general who took responsibility for executing captured American airmen and was himself executed. His name was Okada Tasuku. Later I learned the film comes with the English title *Best Wishes for Tomorrow*.

This time, with little effort, I found a website called POW Research Network Japan. It devotes one section to "crash-landed U.S. aircraft during the air raids on Japan and crewmen POWs." Based on the documents of the Legal Section, GHQ/SCAP, it reports that, in total, about 570 crewmen of aircrafts shot down or crash-landed in Japan survived and were captured. About half of them were executed, died of wounds, or perished during air raids and the atomic bomb on Hiroshima. After Japan's defeat, those responsible for their deaths were tried at the Yokohama War

Crimes Trials. Lt. Gen. Okada Tasuku, commander-in-chief of the Tōkai Military District, headquartered in Nagoya, was one of them.

The Nagoya area was bombed thirty-eight times from December 13, 1944 to July 26, 1945, by a cumulative total of 1,973 B-29s. As many as 8,200 people were killed, 519,000 rendered homeless. During that period, crewmen of crashed B-29s were captured twice, thirty-eight in all, and they were beheaded. To defend his subordinates, Okada insisted he was fully responsible for the acts.

Okada, a devout Nichiren Buddhist, wrote that at first he thought of killing himself but that, as he "studied the U.S. military and found it was illegal / lawless (*fuhō*)," he decided to fight the charge of war crime, calling it a "legal / dharma battle" (*hōsen*). A number of Japanese ranking officers committed suicide upon Japan's defeat. Of those directly related to airmen's executions, there were Lt. Gen. Shimada Tomosaburō and Maj. Gen. Okada Chiichi, both judge advocates.

As the novelist Ōoka Shōhei, who as a historian chronicled the Battle of Leyte, points out in his detailed account of Okada's court battle, the Hague Rules of Air Warfare, 1923, states, in Article 22, "Aerial bombardment for the purpose of terrorizing the civilian population, of destroying or damaging private property not of a military character, or of injuring non-combatants is prohibited," but it was a rule made to be broken. The German bombing of Guernica in April 1937, which Picasso made famous, ignored it, so did Japan's "transoceanic bombings" of China from August 1937 to August 1943.

Okada made three arguments: the crewmen who carried out indiscriminate bombings were not POWs, but felons; Japanese military law required them to be executed; and no existing international laws and rules would apply now that the U.S. had dropped atomic bombs on Hiroshima and Nagasaki.

Dr. Joseph G. Featherstone, chief counsel for Okada's defense team, made similar arguments, to no avail.

Indiscriminate or otherwise, aerial bombing remains the preferred choice of warfare for the United States. Earlier this year, the Council on Foreign Affairs reported that America dropped 26,171 bombs in 2016.

Unending Ruthless Air Raids
"'We-Bomb-You-Die' Technology"

October 7, 2017, *Japan Times*

Where do the number of B-29s in each sortie, the tonnage of incendiary bombs they dropped on each Japanese city, from the end of 1944 to August 1945, come from? So I wondered when Cary Karacas asked me to translate a second round of air raid poems. Karacas teaches cultural geography at the College of Staten Island, with a stress on the civilian experience of aerial bombing during war.

In responding to his first request half a year ago, I was drawn to a teacher's experience and a military officer who put up a legal fight in a tribunal after the war. ("Indiscriminate Bombing and Legal Judgment," February 27, 2017). This time, Karacas made a selection of fifteen poems from Saotome Katsumoto's *Great Air Raids: 310 Poets*.

Saotome, a survivor of the air raid on the night of March 9, 1945, as a thirteen-year-old boy, cited in his earlier book *The Great Tokyo Air Raid (Tokyo dai-kūshū,* 1971) a wide range of figures for the number of B-29s that created the biggest firestorm in history, which burned to death anywhere from 80,000 to nearly 100,000 people—from 130 (Imperial HQ), 279 (U.S. Strategic Bombing Survey), to 334 (Len Giovannitti, Fred Freed).

In fact, I had vaguely assumed that the details about the air raids came from the bombing survey. But when I looked at it with some care this time, I found that its main report, filed on July 1, 1946, is a summary and that many reports related to the strategic bombing assembled in the Library of Congress and HathiTrust Digital Library are also summary assessments.

Then, I found what precisely gives the figures I wanted, and more: "tactical mission reports" that record the statistics, targets, etc., of each sortie. For example, No. 248 describes the biggest of the half a dozen air raids on Kōchi, which was executed in the early hours of July 4, 1945. Here are some salient points from it.

The 73rd Bombardment Wing under XXI Bomber Command carried out the bombing raid in four groups; target: Kōchi urban area; bomb load: three groups to "carry clusters containing M69 bombs and one group was to carry M76 bombs."

Report No. 248 comes with three other reports on air raids on July 3/4,1945: 247 (Takamatsu), 249 (Himeji), and 250 (Tokushima). Thus, Kōchi, along with Takamatsu and Himeji, was "typically highly built-up, densely populated, inflammable . . . highly vulnerable to an incendiary attack that would combine M47A2 bombs and E46 clusters. Because of the unavailability of M47A2 bombs, 1 Group was scheduled to carry the M76, 500-pound bombs."

The "average bomb load would be 17,000 pounds for the 73rd." The mission that early morning consisted of 12 pathfinders and 117 aircraft. Of these, 125 "actually bombed": E46 500-pound incendiary cluster bombs, released on targets, 748 tons; AM-M76 500-pound incendiary bombs, released on targets, 312 tons—a total of 1,060 tons.

"Air opposition was expected to be negligible from the 10 to 15 fighters," the report said. "The comparatively weak showing of Japanese fighters during recent operations was believed to be due to the commitment of many fighters to the anticipated invasion. Another controlling factor was believed to be the shortage of aviation gasoline." (The direct reason that Japan went to war with the U.S., Britain, and the Dutch East Indies was their embargo of oil in July 1941. As the war dragged on, the Japanese were forced even to try to extract oil from pine resin to make aviation gasoline.)

And "photographs of Kochi revealed only 2 heavy antiaircraft guns." As a matter of fact, the Japanese military's fight against the swarm of Superfortresses over Kochi proved "nil to negligible."

The assessed damage to the targeted urban area was "0.92 sq. mi.

or 40% of the built-up area of the city (1.9 sq. mi.)." The raid killed 400 people, wounded 300, and destroyed 11,800 houses.

That brings to mind another series called "target information sheets." The one on Okayama warned: "A raid on Okayama should serve as an additional notice to the Japanese people that they will not go unnoticed or unharmed, even in the smaller urban industrial areas, if their city is at all important in the prosecution of the war. If the future looks grey to the people of other small cities, this might add the tint which makes it black."

The biggest air raid on Okayama was carried out in the early hours of June 29, 1945, by a fleet of 140 B-29s that dropped 95,000 incendiary bombs (890 tons), burning down seventy-three percent of the city, destroying 12,700 houses, killing more than 1,700 people.

I should not overlook a point noted in a website of the Japanese Ministry of Internal Affairs to "commemorate" the victims of air raids on major cities. One on Fukui says: "Japan had already carried out urban bombings in Chongqing and other cities in China; but now Japanese citizens, non-military or otherwise, witnessed the brutalities of modern warfare firsthand."

At any rate, the brutalities of these airstrikes—enabled by what Robert Fisk has called "the new age of 'we-bomb-you-die' technology"—continued with ever more ruthlessness: in the Korean War (Curtis LeMay: "we killed off 20% of the population"), in the Vietnam War (more bombs dropped than "the amount during the whole of WWII"), and, since 2001, in the Middle East.

Foreign Policy reported on September 18: "U.S. Bombs Falling in Record Numbers In Three Countries"—Afghanistan, Iraq, and Syria. "American aircraft have dropped over 2,400 bombs in Afghanistan this year, far above the 1,337 dropped in 2016," it said, and added, "In Iraq and Syria, U.S. planes dropped a total of 5,075 bombs in August," more than in any month "since the campaign against the Islamic State kicked off in August 2014."

The source of the information is the Pentagon.

Condemnation Attributed
to "Utter Nonsense"

September 29, 2014, *Japan Times*

In mid-July, in Sugar Loaf, an idyllic village northwest of Manhattan, during a group lunch, someone asked me, "How about comfort women?"

I started saying, "If the question is whether or not the Japanese government forced women to prostitution for the military, probably it didn't." But our attention was diverted, as often happens in such a group gathering, and that was that. Like the Nanjing Massacre, anything less than an outright admission by a Japanese of the worst or the maximum assessment of the wrongs that Japan committed during the Second World War merely raises eyebrows.

Then, on August 5, the *Asahi Shimbun* announced that it had "judged the Jeju Island testimony to be false."

In sum, the paper was finally rejecting the assertion by a man named Yoshida Seiji that, back in 1943, he had "hunted out 200 young Korean women on Jeju Island" to provide the Japanese armed forces with "comfort women." By its own count, the *Asahi* had carried sixteen articles on Yoshida's words since September 2, 1982 when it reported his speech in Osaka.

The retraction raised a furor. (See, "Asahi Rivals Pile On over Sex Slaves Retraction," *The Japan Times*, August 8, 2014.) Why?

For one thing, Yoshida's "testimony" had been known to be false since at least the early 1990s. In fact, in 1989, when his book, *My War Crimes (Watashi no sensō hanzai*, 1983), detailing his claims was translated into Korean, a Korean reviewer for the *Jeju Daily News* had stated Yoshida's stories were "utter nonsense."

The reviewer went to a small village on Korea's largest island, where Yoshida had written he rounded up fifteen to sixteen young women, brandishing a wooden sword. But the villagers said that an abduction of so many girls in their village of 250 households would have been "a big event," yet no one remembered anything of the sort. A local historian, who said he'd been checking the matter since Yoshida's original book came out, dismissed the matter as "a product of commercial intent that shows Japanese evil-mindedness."

The islanders had reasons to remember such an incident—if it had happened. Three years after Korea's liberation from Japan in 1945, the residents of Korea's largest island rebelled against the U.S. Occupation. As a result, 8,000 people were killed. Many islanders fled to Japan, mainly to Osaka.

Yoshida nevertheless continued to play an outsize role in the "comfort women" question, with *Asahi*'s help.

On January 11, 1992, the news daily brought the matter front and center by splashing headlines suggesting, among other things, the government's cover-up, that it had hidden documents on "comfort stations" (*ianjo*), when in fact the documents had been open to the public for three preceding decades.

Asahi's efforts almost derailed Prime Minister Miyazawa Kiichi's impending visit to Korea and quickly worsened Japan's relations with Korea. But the matter went far beyond that.

First, it led to UN Special Rapporteur on Human Rights Radhika Coomaraswamy's 1996 report on "military sexual slavery in wartime." Eleven years later, on July 30, 2007, the U.S. House of Representatives passed a resolution that condemned "the 'comfort women' system of forced military prostitution by the Government of Japan" as "one of the largest cases of human trafficking in the 20th century."

Since then, statues to memorialize comfort women have been built in the United States.

In the 1980s, Japan's "mass media started to talk about the nation's crimes during the Second World War," as Chung Daekyun, the Korean-Japanese scholar on national identity questions, points out in *The*

Myth of Koreans Forcibly Brought to Japan (Zainichi kyōsei renkō no shinwa, 2004). If Yoshida didn't miss the bandwagon, you might say *Asahi* was one of the chief musicians on it.

Actually, the term "comfort woman" (*ianfu*) is a case where a Japanese attempt for euphemism misfired—many years later. A comparable English may be "daughter of joy" or even "camp follower." Faubion Bowers probably had this in mind in 1995 when he pooh-poohed the "comfort women" furor that was growing by the day by simply saying: "When Manila fell, in less than a day, 100 'comfort women' showed up near my barracks."

I had invited Bowers to my office to reminisce about his experience before, during, and after the war to mark the 50th anniversary of Japan's defeat. A Julliard graduate, he had taught in Japan before Japan's Pearl Harbor attack, studied Japanese at the Military Intelligence Service Language School, and was a translator/interpreter during the war. The war over; he served General Douglas MacArthur as an aide-de-camp and personal interpreter.

The existence of "comfort women" in wartime Japan was so utterly taken for granted that it remained a "non-issue" for several decades after the war until some people decided to turn it into a controversy, in a big way.

Was the Japanese government involved in "comfort women"? The answer will depend on how you define "involvement." If the Army Ministry's acceptance of the establishment of brothels for the military in war zones was "involvement," the Japanese government must plead guilty.

Yoshimi Yoshiaki, historian at Chūō University, who insists on the government's culpability, cites, in his 1995 book *Military Comfort Women (Jūgun ianfu),* the notification issued to the chiefs of staff of the North China Area Army and Central China Expeditionary Force as "one of the most important documents showing the involvement of the Army Ministry." Dated March 4, 1938, it has, among those who gave stamps of approval, Imamura Hitoshi, one of the few admired generals to come out of the Asia-Pacific War.

But the notification was a stern warning not to allow activities among recruiters or brokers that might "hurt the dignity of the military" and "create social problems." It asked that the Kenpeitai and the police authorities especially look out for anything "resembling kidnapping." Again, if you say the Army Ministry's acceptance of procurers of prostitutes proved "involvement," the government was responsible.

Were comfort women "sex slaves"? If you recognize that prostitution is largely a form of physical bondage, they were. But forcibly rounding up women for the work, as Yoshida said he did, would be a different matter.

A 1944 U.S. report based on interviews with Korean-Japanese POWs quoted them saying that "direct conscription" of Korean women for prostitution would have caused riots in Korea. Japanese police officers stationed in Korea made similar statements. They knew they had to be careful in governing Korea.

Redaction of a "Comfort Women" Story
The Life of an Alluring Woman

November 3, 2014, *Japan Times*

One of the Japanese stories sometimes mentioned in the "comfort women" controversy is *Shunpu den* by Tamura Taijirō (1911–83). That's because the story, written in the spring of 1947, depicted Korean comfort women but the U.S. Occupation "suppressed" it.

A few years later, when an attempt was made to turn it into a film, Occupation censors intervened again and ordered the rewrite of the script for a total of eight times. As a result, in the film, its main character was changed from a comfort woman to a singer visiting soldiers in a warzone.

Today, the *Asahi Shimbun* et al. might point to the story as yet another proof of the Japanese abuse of "sex slaves" during the war. Back then, though, it wasn't a matter of controversy. Prostitution was rampant in a devastated and occupied nation—as it had been before Japan's defeat. Also, standards of judgment were different, not least with U.S. policymakers.

How different? The reference to *Korean* prostitutes was judged to be "criticism of Koreans," though not the existence of prostitutes itself. GIs of the Occupation were making full use of Japanese prostitutes. Tamura's story was in romantic, Hollywood style, like the 1957 Marlon Brando film, *Sayonara*. But that didn't matter.

First, the title: It was translated *The Story of a Prostitute* for the Civil Censorship Detachment of the Civil Information and Education (CIE) Section of General Douglas MacArthur's GHQ. A more faithful translation may be *The Life of an Alluring Woman*, with the under-standing that *shunpu*, "alluring woman," is one of the many words for prostitutes.

The distinction *is* important for the story.

The heroine is an attractive, strong-willed woman known by her Japanese name Harumi. In her sexual dealings with a dozen men a day, she still can develop a passion for someone she likes. So, she falls in love with a low-ranking soldier named Mikami, who is naïve and timid. He is mortally conscious of the rigid Japanese military hierarchy that places an absolute value on rank.

In fact, one of Harumi's regular customers is Mikami's immediate superior, an arrogant lieutenant. When he finds out that his orderly is the man she really loves, he sends him away to a different company.

In a subsequent battle, Mao Zedong's Eighth Route Army captures Mikami. Though he is treated kindly and he knows he'll be court-mar-tialed and executed if he is sent back to the Japanese, Mikami, ever a Japanese soldier, insists on it. Upon his return, he is put in a stockade to await court martial. He decides to commit suicide and asks Harumi to steal a hand grenade for him.

Harumi, believing that he plans to escape with her, gladly steals one, but when she delivers it to him, he tells her to leave. When she refuses, Mikami removes the pin from the grenade. When she realizes what's happening, she finds herself "immersed in ecstasy" for the few seconds before the grenade explodes and blows apart the two lovers into a bloody mess.

In the finally approved film, the two lovers escape, but the vengeful lieutenant shoots both dead. It's titled *Escape at Dawn*.

No, U.S. Occupation's "suppression" did not mean what it normally means. *The Life of an Alluring Woman* was dropped from the April 1947 issue of a magazine for which it was intended, but the next month it was published in a collection of Tamura's short stories, with the direct refer-ences to Korea or Korean deleted or altered.

One important deleted passage was the author's heartfelt dedication at the outset of the story. It read:

This piece is dedicated to the tens of thousands of Korean Daughters
who volunteered to every battlefront, which Japanese women would not
approach with fear and contempt, in order to comfort the lowest-ranking
soldiers of the Japanese Army deployed to the interiors of the Continent
during the war, and who thereby destroyed their youth and bodies.

What I've given as "Daughters" is *jōshigun* (in Chinese, *niangzijun*).
Originally the word referred to the all-women unit that Tang Emperor
Liyuan's daughter Gongzhu is reputed to have raised to help her father.

Among the altered words or expressions was "Korea" or "the Korean
Peninsula" which was changed to "the land which is a corner contiguous
to this Continent." But such deletions and alterations would not have
duped any of the readers of the day. Then why did they bother?

Looking at the censor's decision (reproduced in its entirety,
along with an English summary of the story, in Vol. II of Tamura Taijirō's five-volume selected works, 2005), you see next to "Examiner:
Kunzman" a note saying: "Per check with Mr. W. H. Fielding, chief of
Ryukyu-Korea Division, officer of the Executive Officer, chief of Staff."

With Ryūkyū (Okinawa), it's easy to see why the matter came under
the purview of the Occupation's division chief. The archipelago had
been put under a special U.S. administrative rule even before Japan surrendered in the battle there. (The rule continued long after Japan was
made independent, until 1972, when the islands were "reverted" to the
country.)

With Korea, the matter was subtler. When Japan surrendered,
Korean people were declared "liberated." And some of those in Japan
turned into mobs. In *Encounter with Japan* (1983), Herbert Passin
describes the riotous mobs he witnessed in Hakata, the main junction
for those who wanted to go back to Korea. Passin later introduced the
idea of opinion survey in Japan as a CIE officer.

However, in U.S. policymakers' eyes, Korea wasn't really independent. Administratively, the country was more or less part of occupied
Japan. But every effort had to be made not to allow defeated Japanese to
offend Koreans in any way.

The U.S. view sixty years ago still holds in Japan today, at least in this instance. While reproducing examiner Kunzman's decision, the editors do not just print the story as censored by the U.S. Occupation. They do so, they explain, because "improper, discriminatory expressions toward those who were under colonial rule should not be permitted."

So this is a case of a Japanese publisher perpetuating the U.S. censors' old coverup, a dozen years after the allegation of the Japanese government's coverup became a matter of great contention in the early 1990s.

Censorship Distortion of "Comfort Women"

November 27, 2014, *Japan Times*

The U.S. Occupation censored Tamura Taijirō's 1947 story *The Life of an Alluring Woman (Shunpu den)* for describing Korean prostitutes in a war zone. The Civil Information and Education Section with censorship power decided that identifying the nationality of the prostitutes constituted "criticism" of that nation.

U.S. censors ordered Korean references expunged but not the description of prostitutes in a war zone—not initially anyway. They knew soldiers needed sex. "Whoring"—to use the word the New York cultural icon Lincoln Kirstein, for one, employed in one of his poems about his experience in the Second World War—was standard fare for them. The Japanese military at one time had done a study showing that soldiers in a war zone had a particularly high output of adrenalin.

In this regard, the Relaxation and Amusement Association and the network of "special comfort stations" under it that the Japanese government worked to set up for the occupying soldiers in the very month the nation surrendered, August 1945, which John Dower describes in *Embracing Defeat* (W. W. Norton, 1999), may elicit a sneer: Look how someone with a bad conscience behaves!

But the Japanese military was starkly aware of the conduct of its soldiers. After all, it issued the *Senjinkun*, the code of conduct on the battlefield, in January 1941, in the name of the then Army Minister Tōjō Hideki because military discipline on the Chinese front had broken down; insubordination, arson, pillage, and, yes, rape had gone out of control.

But in reality the move to set up RAA "comfort stations" was justifiable. Holly Sanders notes in *Prostitution in Postwar Japan* (2005) that, within ten days after Occupations soldiers started landing in Yokohama on August 28, more than 1,300 rapes were reported in Kanagawa alone.

The RAA brothels were shut down in half a year because of "a rampant spread of VD." During that six-month period 70,000 women are estimated to have worked in them, Tsukada Yukihiro, of Kwansei Gakuin University, has written. After they were abolished, most of those "sex workers" became "*panpan*" (a corruption of "pompom girls" perhaps), as prostitutes catering to the Occupiers were called. By the 1950s their number reached 150,000.

As journalist Ōya Sōichi put it with a touch of exaggeration in his 1953 book, "Japan had become a nation of prostitutes."

In April 1947 NHK did "street recordings"—interviews with men and women on the street. One of them, a *panpan* named Nishida Tokiko working around the Yamanote Line stations, sighed, in an aside, "Who's made me a woman like this?" (*Konna onna ni dare ga shita?*). The lament struck such a chord that it turned an existing song with that refrain into a hit. The song itself had been inspired by a former military nurse turned prostitute.

Behind it all was the devastation Japan had brought upon itself. The writer Nagai Kafū pinpointed one pressing problem when he wrote in his diary, on August 25, 1945: "food shortages are terrifying." The possibility of "10 million Japanese starving to death" was thought serious enough for four years after Japan's defeat. U.S. soldiers were a reliable source of money and food.

One reason Tamura Taijirō story *The Gate of Flesh (Nikutai no mon)*, published just before *The Life of an Alluring Woman*, became a runaway bestseller—then wildly popular as a stage drama and a movie—may well have been that it dealt with a small group of prostitutes in Yūrakuchō who pledged among themselves never to have sex with GIs.

So, *The Life of an Alluring Woman* was published with direct references to Korea or Koreans deleted or rephrased. But that was not the end of it. A year later, when the Tōhō Studio wanted to turn it into a film, the U.S. censors stepped in again, and again. They required eight revisions of the script, in the end forcing out the references to prostitution altogether.

In her *Mr. Smith Goes to Tokyo: Japanese Cinema Under the American Occupation, 1945-52* (1992), Hirano Kyōko, basing her report on her research in the National Archives, details how that happened.

A Tōhō producer's initial proposal to the CIE said the movie would aim "to show how the Japanese Army treated Japanese women during the war in China." The CIE returned the proposal, advising not to treat prostitution and sex provocatively, but to stress the causes of Japan's war.

The first script the director Taniguchi Senkichi wrote with Kurosawa Akira was rejected with "war and prostitution" noted and marked. Was the CIE saying the link between the two was too banal to take up? Probably not. The CIE also rejected the second script, with some other quibbles.

In the third script, Taniguchi provided a statement that he would stress the Japanese army's cruelty, adding how admirable love between a low-ranking soldier and "a woman of an ugly profession"—another name for prostitute—would have been in such a circumstance. The prostitute would not be depicted as "unnecessarily provocative." However, Taniguchi and Kurosawa changed the "comfort station" to a bar.

When the CIE rejected this, saying the matter would be discussed with its Civil Censorship Detachment, Kurosawa stepped down.

In the fourth script, Taniguchi, writing alone, emphasized his intent of dedicating the film to all the soldiers killed by Japan's war of invasion. He himself had been sent to the Chinese front during the war, taken prisoner, and repatriated to Japan two years after Japan's defeat.

But the CIE rejected it once again. Bringing in a comfort woman was "Oriental thinking." It would be sexually provocative and weaken the antiwar aim, the censors said. Obviously, Taniguchi thought dropping prostitutes altogether would have trampled upon what Tamura Taijirō had to tell.

There would be three more revisions ordered. It was in the seventh script that Taniguchi finally dropped the comfort woman and changed her to a singer visiting Japanese soldiers on the front. Yet U.S. censors demanded still another revision to take Chinese victims into consideration.

The resulting movie, titled *Escape at Dawn*, was a pure Hollywood melodrama: It does not leave a trace of what Tamura had written in *The Life of an Alluring Woman*—no trace of his dedication of the story to "tens of thousands of Korean comfort women who volunteered to the front and thereby destroyed their youth and bodies."

By all accounts, U.S. censorship of literature and film was mostly light, compared with Japan's own that had preceded it, as I discuss at some length in *Persona: A Biography of Yukio Mishima* (2012). I've brought this up in the context of the "comfort women" controversy again (see "Redaction of a 'Comfort Woman' Story," November 3, 2014, *The Japan Times*), because the "truth" in such matters is seldom straightforward.

Sex-Slave Wrangling Misses Human Picture

January 26, 2016, *Japan Times*

"These days bands of excitable people are making rackets on the streets, shouting 'Death to Koreans! Koreans, Get Out!,'" my friend in Tokyo, Ueda Akira, has recently written. "The other day some of these were marching down the conspicuous street of Roppongi where I live, saying unspeakably vulgar things."

"It may be true that an extremely small portion of Korean residents of Japan are doing some outrageous things," my friend continued, "but I'm horrified to imagine how I'd have felt if some group marched, shouting, 'Death to Japanese!,' while I lived in the United States."

Akira lived in Manhattan for a decade from the mid-eighties to the mid-nineties.

Still, he wondered: "The forces that insist that Japan did wrong and must remain contrite about it no matter what have grown too large, with no proper debate," until it has "now provoked this strong reaction."

Akira was talking about the *ianfu* (comfort women) controversy, but he also marveled, he said, how Japan and Korea have come to have such divergent views of the period from Japan's annexation of Korea in 1910 to the Korea-Japan Treaty of 1965.

The root problem lies in Korea's ineradicable contempt for Japan as an inferior culture that goes back to the beginnings of history, O Sonfa, the Korean scholar who naturalized in Japan, has explained. But with the *ianfu* question, wranglings have long ceased to be Japan vs. Korea, says Park Yu-ha, Sejong University professor in Seoul.

When a dispute arises between the two countries, the Koreans who most fiercely criticize Japan are "liberals," whereas the Japanese who criticize Korea are "conservative rightists." The serious 1990s confrontation between the two countries was touched off when Japanese conservatives condemned "liberal" politicians and citizens who tried to deal seriously with the *iafu* question as "traitors," accusing them of harboring a "masochistic view of history."

Japanese conservatives' opposition to the "postwar restitutions" for Korea that Japanese liberals advocated upset Korean liberals. And so forth. Thus the Korean-Japanese conflict has come to exist not between the two countries so much as between Korean liberals and Japanese conservatives.

That's how Park summarized the conflict in her 2005 book, *For a Reconciliation (Wakai no tame ni)*. In it, she discussed controversies over Japanese textbooks, *ianfu*, Yasukuni Shrine, and Dokdo (Takeshima, in Japan). The book won a prize both in Korea (2006) and in Japan (2007).

In her *Comfort Women of the Empire (Teikoku no ianfu)*, published at the end of last year, Park greatly expands on the *ianfu* question. To consider who or what was "responsible," she sets up a large framework.

First, there is imperialism—not the emperor system that may come to mind when you think of Japan until its defeat in 1945, but of the kind that prompts a state to expand its authority and control to other countries and territories. The Cold War world order that replaced imperialism is little different, in Park's view. Consider the United States in Korea, for example.

Then comes the state that necessarily controls its citizens in one form or another, as well as the patriarchal system that puts women at the lowest stratum, even allowing a father to sell his own daughters. Park cites some former Korean comfort women who said they hated their own fathers more than Japanese soldiers.

People in a colony are not exempt from responsibility, either. Most people in a colony more or less try to assimilate themselves to the system imposed by the colonizing state. Koreans were no exception. Their country annexed, most Koreans began to behave as Japanese citizens, which they were, officially.

Park cites former Korean comfort women who said they regarded some of what they did as "patriotic duties." I may refer to the diary of a Korean manager of "comfort stations" in Burma and Singapore, in 1943 to 1944, that was discovered in Korea in 2012.

The diarist begins by expressing his wishes for "the health and everlasting prosperity of the Imperial Family." On New Year's Day, 1944, he got up early, washed his face, and cleared up his soul, the diarist wrote, before "bowing deeply toward the Imperial Palace in the distant eastern sky." That's what all Japanese were expected to do on that felicitous day.

Korean activists ignore all this and more, their "collaboration and subservience" included. They believe that their country was pristine until the Japanese barged in and ravaged it. Thus they have "enjoyed their position of moral superiority." The resulting "moral arrogance" makes others cringe.

The bronze statue they built in front of the Japanese Embassy in Seoul, then in the U.S. presents an innocent girl in a traditional Korean dress. It clearly suggests that Korean virgins were kidnapped and forced into prostitution for the Japanese military, a distortion of what actually happened. Also, in successfully "globalizing" this particular plight of their own past, Koreans have made it impossible to contemplate why "so many comfort women were Korean," Park says.

For their part, the Japanese "supporters" of Korean comfort women are too busy insisting that "Japan did wrong and must remain contrite about it no matter what," as my friend Akira put it, to accept the actual acts of contrition of their government.

These include the Japanese House of Representatives resolution in 1995, the Asian Women's Fund set up the same year, and the monetary compensations offered to each Korean comfort woman with a letter of apology first of Prime Minister Murayama Tomiichi, then Prime Minister Hashimoto Ryūtarō. The activists reject all such acts as meaningless on the grounds that restitutions and atonements were not made "legislatively." It's as if they do not know that "politics is the art of the possible."

No wonder that a 2010 survey showed ninety-seven percent of Koreans thought Japan had "not apologized enough."

What prompted Park to study this subject in detail was this concern: As the dispute escalated since the early 1990s, "both in Japan and Korea, only the voices of the governments and citizens groups have grown louder, in the process drowning out the voices of those directly involved," namely, the Korean comfort women.

One thing Park found in the course of her exploration is that the retroactive term "sex slaves" actually deprives the Korean comfort women of their humanity. Some of them found Japanese soldiers kind and considerate, some commiserated their fate, some fell in love with them.

"Comfort Women" Question Is Far from Black and White

October 26, 2017, *Japan Times*

The dubious status some Koreans have sought overseas for what Sally McGrane fashionably calls "brutal state-run rape camps" has now won academic approbation in the United States, according to her report, "An Important Statue for 'Comfort Women' in San Francisco" (*The New Yorker*, October 12, 2017). McGrane quotes Harvard Professor Dara Kay Cohen and UC Berkeley Professor Elaine Kim to emphasize her point. But she doesn't even mention Sejong Professor Park Yu-ha who holds a contrasting, more considered view.

Park cast doubt on her Korean compatriots' campaign to sell the world the idea that "the comfort women" violated "the universal women's rights" as an expression of "moral arrogance." She explains why in her book *Comfort Women of the Empire (Teikoku no ianfu*, Korea 2013, Japan 2014).

"Colonization inevitably spawns a schism among the colonized people," she writes. But "Korea has lived by erasing the memory of its collaboration with and subjugation to the sovereign nation," Japan, since its "liberation" from the country in 1945—by refusing to see "the other face of Korea." In the process, those engaged in propagating the notion that "comfort women" embodied the evil that was imperialist Japan have lost the ability to talk about "why so many of the comfort women were Korean," even as they argued that "most comfort women were Korean."

To write her book, Park first focused on interviews with surviving

Korean comfort women. (There were more Japanese comfort women.) As a result, she confirmed that practically all those who "duped" or "forced" the women into prostitution, as well as those who managed the "comfort stations," were Korean, not the Japanese military. In some cases, their parents sold them to middlemen out of dire poverty. That was common in Japan, too, especially during its economic difficulties before the Second World War.

There were also "voluntary" comfort women, a la "sex workers" today.

As important, the recent Korean depiction that all Korean comfort women were "victims" of the incomparable tyranny of the Japanese military ignore what they actually said, Park found.

Some women sympathized with Japanese soldiers going to battle to "die" as they were told. Some fell in love with soldiers, as some soldiers fell in love with them. Some soldiers were kind, some came to spend time with them, not for sex, but for their company only. Some regularly passed them some of the special food meant for their officers. Some gave them money, pitying their fate, without touching them.

Some soldiers were coarse, of course, but most of them were not brutes as recent imaginations project them to be. Some took the women for horse rides or car drives. Horses were abundant in the Japanese military, but not cars. One woman remembered a woman almost wrecking a car, but the Japanese officers simply enjoyed the spectacle.

The Japanese military was also the protector of the women. One surprise in the interviews Park cites may be the Kenpei, the MPs. Contrary to their usual image, they acted as guardians of comfort women. They were tough on the soldiers who behaved badly to the women.

"Comfort women were not necessarily people that resisted the Japanese military as Koreans burning with nationalist awareness," wrote Yomota Inuhiko in his essay. An international intellectual at large, Yomota has taught in Korea and a dozen other countries.

Think of it: When another powerful country takes over your country and treats you, however superficially, as its own citizen long enough, you will begin to think yourself as part of the country, however unconsciously—unless you are a dedicated nationalist. This must have been true especially when only a certain stratum of society strongly thought of national identity.

Or suppose the U.S. Occupation of Japan lasted for twenty, thirty years, rather than seven. Even without a much longer occupation, the American influence on Japan was incalculable. Or recall the influence of Western culture on Japan since the nineteenth century. Park Yu-ha, known for her translations of the novelists Natsume Sōseki and Ōe Kenzaburō as well as the philosopher and critic Karatani Kōjin, received her Ph.D. on "Modern Japanese Literature and National Identity."

In fact, as the subtitle of Park's book, *Struggle with the Colonial Rule and Its Memory (Shokuminchi shihai to kioku no tatakai)*, says, her main purpose to write the book was to fill some of the willful lacunas in recent Korean accounts of Japan's rule—in particular, as regards "comfort women." And that put her in trouble. She may have quoted too many "testimonies" of comfort women that put the Japanese in a less than condemnable light.

Her book was favorably received at first. But not long afterward, a libel lawsuit in the name of former comfort women was brought against her. After several steps, the Seoul Eastern District Court dismissed the indictment by the District Prosecutors' Office in January 2017. The Prosecutors' Office appealed, and that's where the matter stands now.

For a Dialogue (Taiwa no tame ni, Crane, 2017), a collection of the arguments by twelve scholars, was put together and published in an effort to help ameliorate this legal impasse. Yomota is one of the twelve.

Park also addresses a larger issue. "'Comfort women' did not exist in wartime Japan alone," she points out. "They have existed since the ages going far back, and they exist now. The women [who do similar work] in the military bases all over the world are basically 'comfort women,' even if they are not conscious as such."

Limiting ourselves to the U.S. bases overseas, there are 900 of them. Of the countries that have them but not at war, Japan provides the "most valuable real estate" to maintain 39,000 U.S. troops—in Okinawa, Sasebo, Iwakuni, Yokosuka, Misawa, etc.—while Korea offers "the fourth most valuable real estate" to keep 23,500 U.S. troops—in Seoul, Busan, Daegu, etc. How do you suppose those American soldiers take care of their sexual needs?

By coincidence, this column appeared on the same day, October 27, 2017, that the Seoul Supreme Court rejected the Seoul Eastern District Court's dismissal of the Park Yu-ha case, imposing the penalty of 10 million won or about $10,000 on Park Yu-ha.

Earlier, in April 2007, Park had pointed out that Korea had created "special Korean comfort women" for American and UN soldiers during the Korean War. Aside from that, there is research and a number of books on the military and prostitution. Cynthia H. Enloe, for example, wrote a dozen books on this question—among them, Does Khaki Become You? The Militarisation of Women's Lives *(Pluto Press, 1983). In it she wrote, page 33, "By 1973, on the eve of the American military's withdrawal, between 300,000 and 500,000 women were working as prostitutes in South Vietnam," adding, "The precise number of women engaged in prostitution was impossible to calculate because thousands of Vietnamese women worked as cleaners and servants for American troops and thousand more raped by American soldiers."*

Blunderbuss Followup to the Invasion of Iraq

July 26, 2009, *Japan Times*

The *New York Times* editorial, on June 30, "The First Deadline," showed America's egocentrism at its worst. Dealing entirely with a single subject—the withdrawal of American combat troops from Iraqi cities, with 130,000 soldiers still remaining in the country—the lengthy commentary showed the blind hubris the United States often displays on the world stage. The declamation would have been comical were it not for the fact that the matter had to do with the slaughtering of thousands upon thousands of people.

The editorial simply rated George W. Bush's cowboy invasion of Iraq as "an unnecessary war," as if it were a board game with little at stake. It then, amazingly, went on to devote the rest of the large space to scolding Iraqis and their neighbor countries on their shortcomings.

Thus, the editorial blamed the Iraqi army for not being ready to take over for the invading troops—the American troops—that had bludgeoned into the country and torn apart its society. The Iraqi military is "plagued by corruption, discipline problems, equipment shortages and security breaches," the paper's indictment went, even as the commentary congratulated Americans for giving incompetent Iraqis "military training programs" that get "good marks" from "most analysts." What is the U.S. military doing training another country's military—is the question never asked.

The editorial then cautioned the Kurds on their "ambition." Here at least it admitted it was "often with Washington's blessing" that the

Kurds carried out their military and territorial expansion." One result has been the creation of "the most dangerous" situation in "the oil-rich, multi-ethnic city of Kirkuk."

Yet the United States must apply pressure on "Baghdad and the Kurds," the editorial advised, "not to stake out extreme positions." How can a mere editorialist take such a high-handed, moralistic stance after his country threw a remote, foreign region into turmoil? Why is the presumption always that the United States must be the destroyer and preserver?

Even with "an estimated four million refugees" that George W. Bush's blunderbuss war has created, the *Times* editorial barely suggested that the responsibility lies squarely with the United States. The help must be both "international and American"—in that order. The only thing America must pay greater attention to, the editorial indicated, is those Iraqis "who risked their lives to work with the Americans." Otherwise, it's not America's sole responsibility. Ah, yes, the United Kingdom is also responsible, I admit, but what can you expect from America's poodle?

Then, the *Times* told the Iraqis to come up with "competent, inclusive government." What cheek! Whatever happened to the Biblical injunction: "first cast out the beam out of thine own eye"? It may be the kind of high-handed "advice" the self-regarding media entity of a country that can readily destroy another country is prone to proffer, but its solipsistic disregard of realities still boggles the mind. Is the U.S. government competent?

Was it evidence of competency to allow a feckless boy king to declare "war on terrorism"—the term, by the way, the editorial still uses—and make a mess of two countries, Afghanistan and Iraq, and endanger a third, Pakistan? What about allowing its treasury secretary, its central bank chairman, and a free-market diehard in Congress to promote financial shenanigans to multiply until they brought down the global economy?

Will the U.S. government be competent enough to devise some way to rectify the exorbitant healthcare system? What about global warming?

When it comes to inclusiveness, is it not precisely inclusiveness that renders democracy that America arrogantly promotes often unworkable, except when the president declares to take his country to war? I am constantly amazed how so many Americans are eager to bomb another country—say, for the moment, Iran.

The *Times* editorial, in its peroration, committed the ultimate brazenness. In complaining that Iraq's neighbors are not doing enough to help the country, it accused Iran and Syria, among others, of having "meddled constantly—driving up the violence and backing off only when it looked as if the war could spin out of control." Surely the *Times* was talking about the United States.

The editorial's main aim was to assert America's "strong strategic interest" in the region, of course. It offered no apologies to Iraq, let alone Afghanistan, "the real front." Naturally, it gave nary a hint on the possibility of taking George W. Bush to the International Criminal Court for war crimes.

So, it was not the "unnecessary war" itself that the *New York Times* had objected to, but the man who started it, George W. Bush.

Several days later the *Times* confounded the matter by printing an article with the headline, "A Treasured Bush Memento, Once the Property of a Foe, May Be Put on Display" (July 6, 2009). The article, by Don Van Natta Jr., reported, with what could only be described as "fond respect," on the likely disposition of George W. Bush's most coveted of the 40,000 gifts he and his wife received while they occupied the White House: the nine millimeter Glock 18C that once belonged to Saddam Hussein. The gun represents "the pinnacle moment of the Iraq war" for Bush, Van Natta said.

If there was any saving grace to this article, it was quoting the Rice professor of history Douglas Brinkley. Bush's attitude toward the captured gun "represents this Texas notion of the white hats taking out the black hats and keeping the trophy," Brinkley said. "It's a *True West* magazine kind of pulp western mentality."

There were different accounts of the manner of Saddam's capture, suggesting that it may not have been the generally accepted one that put him in the Hollywood-style self-humiliation of an evil man, but never mind. The feckless former president will go on believing whatever he wants to, with the *Times* encouragement.

> *On September 1, 2021, Brown University's Costs of War project estimated that the "20 years of post-9/11 wars" that Bush started have killed more than 900,000 people.*

Terrorism Brouhaha, Then and Now

April 21, 2017, *Japan Times*

For a talk at the University of Massachusetts, Amherst, I was searching the Internet to see what I could find about Fukue Shinpei, one of the Japanese generals who were sentenced to death for war crimes after the Asia-Pacific War. Lt. Gen. Fukue had left a couple of remarkable "fare-well-to-the-world" haiku before facing a firing squad on April 27, 1946.

Among the several items I readily found on him was a *Straits Times* article, "Jap General Executed in Singapore," that began with "A red patch of sand on Changi beach early yesterday morning marked the spot where a Japanese General met his death as a war criminal." But, just below it was a one-paragraph dispatch with the headline, "Dutch-Indonesian Clash":

> Batavia, Apr. 27.—Referring to the reported clash of Dutch and Indone-sians outside Batavia, an official Dutch report today stated that Allied troops attacked a concentration of terrorists near Tjiteureup, south of Batavia, yesterday killing 19 and taking 150 prisoners.—Reuter.

"Terrorists"?

My father, an officer of the Special Higher Police, was stationed in Java during the war, so he, like many of his fellow officers, was detained on suspicions of war crimes when the Dutch came back on the heels of Japan's defeat in August 1945. He was released by next summer, but the Dutch revanchism was not just to "deal with all of the 'war crimi-nals' who had collaborated with the Japanese, to hang 'traitors' like the nationalists Sukarno and Hatta"—the idea that struck Laurens van der Post as "incomprehensible and frightening" as he wrote in *The Admiral's Baby* (1996). He knew that meant a new war for the Netherlands to regain its glory as a colonial power.

Van der Post had written *The Seed and the Sower* (1963), which was later turned into a film, *Merry Christmas, Mr. Lawrence* (1983), so some of the readers of this paper may know. As a South African officer under the British army, he had become a Japanese POW in Java. Upon Japan's surrender, he was thrust into the role of liaison between the Dutch, British, and Japanese forces in the power transfer, becoming Admiral Louis Mountbatten's aide: hence The Admiral's Baby.

As he explained in the "secret" report he wrote at the end of 1946 for the Foreign Office, which is included in the book, even while in a Japanese POW camp with little contact with the outside world, he had learned of "a tremendous legacy of nationalism" the Japanese would leave. After all, Japan's ostensible aim of invading the region was to liberate it from Western colonialism—just as, you might say, the United States invaded Iraq in the name of democratization.

In the ensuing war, the Dutch and their allies killed 6,000 Indonesians in the one month from October to November 1945 alone, as Van der Post noted in his report. But they would persist in revanchism for four more years, killing up to 200,000 Indonesians. For the Dutch, the natives were "these yellow apes."

So, I shouldn't have been surprised by "an official Dutch report" labeling the anticolonial Indonesians as "terrorists," but I was. That's because I didn't know that by the mid-1940s the word "terrorist" had apparently shed its meaning deriving from one etymological strain tracing its origins to Tsarist Russia in the nineteenth century.

In Japan, for example, the poet Ishikawa Takuboku used it in that sense in 1911 when he wrote the poem "A Spoonful of Cocoa," with famous lines: "I realize a terrorist's / sad, sad heart." He wrote this evidently thinking of An Jung-geun, who had assassinated the Japanese statesman Itō Hirobumi in Harbin, in 1909. An Jung-geun regarded Itō as the avatar of Japan about to annex Korea, as it did several months after his execution.

So, the current application of the word "terrorist" may have to an extent reverted to its "classical" sense. But what brouhaha the U.S. media makes, so disproportionate to the havoc the country makes, foreign and domestic!

Take the "2017 Westminster Attack" on March 22 or the "2017 Stockholm Attack" on April 7. In both, four people were killed. For both, U.S. media has given maximum coverage for days on end, even while giving short shrift to other killings and destructions. On March 23, for example, a U.S.-led airstrike killed more than two hundred civilians in Mosul, Iraq, but how much attention did the media give it?

You might say "terrorist attacks" are different from attacks made in battles. Then you may compare the deaths caused in so-called "terrorist attacks" with the deaths caused by other, let's say, regular attacks in the United States.

In October 2016, CNN, heeding President Barack Obama's urging, published an article tallying the numbers of "Americans killed through terrorist attacks" versus those killed in gun violence, finding that "for every one American killed by an act of terror in the United States or abroad in 2014, more than 1,049 died because of guns."

CNN also found that, from 2001 to 2014, a cumulative total of 440,095 people were killed by firearms in the U.S., whereas the number of U.S. citizens killed in terrorist incidents was 3,412—369 overseas plus and 3,043 on U.S. soil. The latter figure includes 2,990 people who died in the 9/11 attacks in 2001.

Taking a different tack, New America looked at "deadly attacks by ideology" from 2002 to early 2017 to assess "Terrorism in America after 9/11" and came to the sum of ninety-five by jihadists (including forty-nine killed in an Orlando nightclub in June 2016), fifty-one by right-wingers, and five by left-wingers. The think tank's conclusion: "the threat is not existential."

When it comes to "mass murders," which the FBI defines as "murdering four or more persons during an event," there have already been five such killings so far this year (as of April 20), but they have hardly made any news.

Indefensible Costs of Military One-Upmanship

February 27, 2011, *Japan Times*

I was recently surprised to learn that Singapore has 72,500 troops on active duty and plans to double the number of "combat-ready aircraft" to more than two hundred. It also plans to have ten more submarines to add to the four it has today. Or so the *Wall Street Journal* reported ("Asia's New Arms Race," February 12, 2011).

In fact, Singapore has "one of Asia's most modern armed forces," according to a U.S. military site proudly announcing the country's purchase of twelve more F-15 fighter jets for $1 billion (October 2007). The island nation is smaller than New York City (ninety percent in land and sixty percent in population). Yet its annual military expenditure of $9 billion is 3.4 times as large as that of Vietnam (population eighteen times as big) and seventy percent larger than that of Indonesia (population fifty times bigger).

All this was a surprise to me, because the proud and prosperous Lion City strikes me as eminently indefensible in any serious military confrontation. I do not have to bring up the Japanese army overrunning the British Empire's "impregnable fortress in the Far East" in six days, back in early 1942, with a troop size less than half that of the defenders. Imagine New York City as an independent nation having to defend itself from surrounding enemies.

No, I do not mean to advance any argument on geopolitics or regional military strategy. It's simply that when the *WSJ* article came out, I had just read Andrew Bacevich's essay "The Tyranny of Defense

Inc." (*The Atlantic*, January/February 2011). I was also thinking about Mishima Yukio's novel *Silk and Insight (Kinu to meisatsu)* that I had translated a dozen years earlier.

Bacevich, a retired army colonel who teaches international relations at Boston University, for some years now has been highly critical of U.S. foreign policy, especially in the military field, writing books such as *The Limits of Power: The End of American Exceptionalism* (2008) and *America's Path to Permanent War* (2010), to name only the latest two.

In the *Atlantic* article, he revisits President Dwight Eisenhower and his warnings on the military running amok "in the councils of government." It is of course his famous farewell speech, in which he said, "we must guard against the acquisition of unwarranted influence, whether sought or unsought, by the military-industrial complex."

But Bacevich also discusses Eisenhower's speech eight years earlier, the one he gave soon after he became president. The speech, before the American Society of Newspaper Editors, shows the military commander's thinking hadn't changed over the years. It is particularly notable for the concrete examples illustrating the high costs of military hardware.

"The cost of one modern heavy bomber is this: a modern brick school in more than thirty cities," Eisenhower said. "It is two electric power plants, each serving a town of 60,000 population. It is two fine, fully equipped hospitals.

"It is some fifty miles of concrete highway. We pay for a single fighter with a half million bushels of wheat. We pay for a single destroyer with new homes that could have housed more than 8,000 people."

Direct cost comparisons between six decades ago and today may be difficult to make, but let me try.

Each B-2 "Stealth Bomber" costs $1.01 billion. The "flyaway cost"—the whole cost minus R&D—of each F-35, the product of "the most expensive arms program" of the U.S. ever and for now the source of Congressional hubbub, is somewhere between $89 million to $200 million.

The CIA's *World Factbook* puts the 2010 U.S. per capita income at

$47,400. This means a total of 21,300 people—men, women, children—must work one whole year to produce a single B-2, and 1,900 to 4,200 people to produce a single F-35. Japan, whose per capita income is way below that of Singapore, plans to buy 100 F-35's.

The biggest issue in education in New York City now is Mayor Bloomberg's threat to "eliminate" 6,000 teaching jobs because of a budget shortfall. These teachers are new hires, so suppose their average salary is $30,000. The elimination of a single F-35 at the higher cost estimate should make the firing of those 6,000 teachers unnecessary.

St. Vincent's, the most valuable hospital in my neighborhood, shut down last year because of a monthly deficit of $7 to $10 million, according to the *New York Times*. To maintain a U.S. soldier in Afghanistan just one year costs "a cool one million dollars," Bacevich puts it. The United States now has 100,000 troops, at the monthly cost of $8.4 billion.

The main purpose of the U.S. invasion and destruction of Afghanistan is now obscure, but if it is to force its own idea of government on it, it goes against Eisenhower's observation: "Any nation's attempt to dictate to other nations their form of government is indefensible."

As to Mishima Yukio's 1964 novel *Silk and Insight*, it was based on Japan's "first human rights strike" at a textile manufacturer ten years earlier, in 1954. Mishima does not seem to have explained it, but the puzzling title he gave to the novel harked back to the phrase "silk and warships" that dated from the Russo-Japanese War.

For decades before Japan attacked Pearl Harbor, silk was Japan's principal export product, so it was silk that enabled the country to buy and build warships, hence the phrase. But the Yamato, the greatest battleship Japan ever built, and its twin, the Musashi, were both sunk ignominiously before engaging in any worthy battle. Of the two, the Yamato was sunk in the country's biggest and, yes, "stupidest," suicide sortie.

And what was the cost of building the Yamato? As I have remembered it since my junior high school days, the same amount would have enabled Japan to electrify its entire railway system at the time, in 1940.

Has any of the expensive weapons systems, much of which Japan has been buying from the United States since it was coerced into rearmament despite the "no-war clause" of "the MacArthur Constitution," served any real purpose in defending the country? I don't know.

I do know that F-86s were used for years to slaughter Steller sea lions. They ate too many fish near the Japanese coast. Partly as a result of that operation perhaps, their number has dropped from 20,000 in the 1960s to 5,000 today.

A Breed Apart
Liberal Hawks Who Buoyed Bush

June 30, 2014, *Japan Times*

Frank Rich's "Iraq Everlasting: We are still stuck in 2003, and it isn't (only) George W. Bush's fault" (*New York Magazine*, June 4, 2014) is a laundry list, however partial, of those in "the liberal Establishment" who "enlisted in the stampede" that would slaughter many hundreds of thousands of Iraqis in the next decade.

Rich's list begins with Senate Democrats—Hillary Clinton, Joe Biden, John Kerry—and extends to those of "the so-called liberal media, much of which cheered on [Bush's] war with a self-righteous gravity second only to Dick Cheney's."

That covered "the East Coast liberal media cabal," as Bill Keller, the *New York Times* op-ed writer whom Rich quotes, put it in his column, "The I-Can't-Believe-I'm-a-Hawk Club" (*The New York Times*, Feb 8, 2003). The self-disbelieving members of the "hawk club" were "op-ed regulars at this newspaper and the *Washington Post*, the editors of the *New Yorker*, the *New Republic* and *Slate*, columnists in *Time* and *Newsweek*."

Among them were Paul Berman, Thomas Friedman, Matthew Yglesias, Fred Kaplan, George Packer, Dan Savage, Jacob Weinberg, and Andrew Sullivan.

Berman was a cultural commentator turned advocate of "liberal interventionism" in *Terror and Liberalism* (2004) who decided that bombing and blasting people into bits would help "foment a liberal revolution." Friedman is a *NY Times* columnist who wrote with a knowing condescension, a few weeks before Bush's "ultimatum" to Saddam Hussein: "Mr. Bush's audacious shake of the dice appeals to me" ("The Long Bomb," *The New York Times,* March 2, 2003).

Or, as Tony Judt put it in "Bush's Useful Idiots" (*London Review of Books,* Sept 18–21, 2006), Friedman's "pieties are always road-tested for middlebrow political acceptability." Hence his durability.

Actually, Rich's essay is a journalistic followup on Judt's historical assessment, and Judt, who died four years ago, was scathing. These "'tough' new liberals reproduce some of that old left's worst characteristics," the historian, whom I admire, wrote. They "display precisely the same mixture of dogmatic faith and cultural provincialism, not to mention the exuberant enthusiasm for violent political transformation at other people's expense."

How could that have happened?

Keller concluded: "We reluctant hawks may disagree among ourselves about the most compelling logic for war—protecting America, relieving oppressed Iraqis or reforming the Middle East—but we generally agree that the logic for standing pat does not hold."

True, liberals are suckers for conceits such as "reform" and relieving other peoples of "oppression," but did they truly believe, at that juncture of history, that their country needed protection from a puny country in a faraway Middle East? By then it was known that Iraq had suffered a great deal under the victor's imposition of no-flight-zone and other clampdowns since the Gulf War, was it not? There were academic reports that more than half a million babies had died as a result.

More practically, did Keller and other liberal hawks believe that Saddam Hussein had intercontinental missiles capable of delivering nuclear bombs or any other WMDs to a land 10,000 kilometers away? Didn't they wonder, as Richard Dawkins did: "Why did Bush suddenly start threatening to invade Iraq when he did, and not before?" ("Bin Laden's Victory," *The Guardian,* March 21, 2003).

The English ethologist and biologist asked that question, apparently after listening to George W. Bush declaim, on March 18: "Saddam Hussein and his sons must leave Iraq within forty-eight hours. Their refusal to do so will result in military conflict commenced at a time of our choosing." Wasn't it clear that Bush was drunk fancying himself to be a lawman in Hollywood moviemakers' Wild West?

"The United States Has Gone Mad," another Briton, John le Carré, had decided two months earlier: "America has entered one of its periods of historical madness, but this is the worst I can remember: worse than McCarthyism, worse than the Bay of Pigs and in the long term potentially more disastrous than the Vietnam War" (*The New York Times*, Jan 15, 2003).

Frank Rich was moved by Michael Hastings' posthumous book, *The Last Magazine* (2014), to write "Iraq Everlasting." The book describes how the bloviators at the author's employer, *Newsweek*, and elsewhere shifted their stance *en masse* to support Bush's war, from 2002 to 2003.

John R. MacArthur was similarly moved by the same book to write "In Praise of Michael Hastings" (*Harper's*, June 19, 2014). In doing so, he quotes another mindless pronouncement: Fareed Zakaria writing in the "real" *Newsweek*: "I believe that the Bush administration is right: this war will look better when it's over. . . . Weapons of mass destruction will be found." MacArthur notes "some omissions" in Hastings' account. One of them is David Remnick, editor of the *New Yorker*, and that reminds me.

In the fall of 2004, I went to Town Hall when the *New Yorker* held an event for the publication of Seymour Hersh's *Chain of Command: The Road from 9/11 to Abu Ghraib*. In the book, Hersh, only too famous for his 1969 exposé of the My Lai Massacre, meticulously describes Bush's willful ignorance, indifference, swagger, and the resulting brutality that led to the Abu Ghraib torture.

Remnick served as MC on that occasion. Did he admit to his error on stage? No. Worse, what he said in his introduction to Hersh's book was patently contradictory and absurd. "No one was able to expose in fact and in full, before the war," he asserted, "what the Administration's critics were rightly asserting as a matter of possibility and likelihood—that the White House's claims of an imminent threat were false or exaggerated."

Frank Rich wrote his piece before the swift rise of the Islamic State of Iraq and Syria (ISIS) in the past few weeks, and that makes it all the more timely.

The suddenly expanding turmoil, some suggest, may scrap the Sykes-Picot Agreement of 1916. It was that imperialist act that created the oddly shaped national borders of the region and the unnatural ethnic and sectarian divides. The Balfour Declaration that would spawn Israel three decades later followed a year after the agreement.

Perhaps those tough liberal hawks a decade ago secretly wanted to nullify those one-sided actions a century ago.

II

Birds and Other Animals

The Gall of Those Gulls

March 30, 1987, *Mainichi Daily News*

Geraldine Little, a singer and haiku poet friend of mine, has concluded her recent letter to me by saying: "The Canada geese at the school where I teach are beautiful on the lake there at the moment. I hear they're a plague—how lucky the world would be to have only that kind of plague!"

This has prompted me to take out a somewhat dated clipping from the *New York Times*. On September 28, it reported on a conference held by the National Academy of Sciences and the Smithsonian Institution where scientists warned strongly on the accelerating destruction of nature by human beings and its consequences. As a result of paving, plowing, logging, overgrazing, flooding, and draining, not to mention the introduction of toxic substances into the environment, animal and plant species are vanishing fast—10,000 each year in one estimate.

At the same time, human beings, though only one of at least five million species on earth, are consuming an inordinate proportion of the energy converted into food for living organisms through plant photosynthesis. The share at present is thirty percent, but if the population grows at the expected rate, it will reach eighty percent within the next 100 years. Paul Ehrlich, Stanford professor of biological sciences, who made this observation, called for "a quasi-religious transformation of contemporary cultures" to prevent such an overkill.

Is it possible for us to transform ourselves culturally? Is it possible for us to start regarding ourselves, not the Canada geese, as a plague? Probably not.

Though I didn't clip them, I have seen a couple of newspaper accounts confirming my friend's point: that Canada geese are regarded as a plague—not only in the United States but in the land from which their name derives, Canada, as well. In one seashore town in Connecticut the residents have devised ways, an article reported, to keep these magnificent birds off their lawns and beaches to prevent them from sullying their valuable properties. In Toronto, another article said, the residents, perhaps to maintain their reputation, which the *New Yorker* sadly misses, of keeping their city clean, are irked because the geese congregate in numbers considered excessive and, yes, sully their public parks and waterfronts.

Neither on the Connecticut seashore nor in Toronto do people appear to have started outright killing of Canada geese because of their habit of messily trampling on man's aesthetic sensibility. Seagulls are less lucky. In yet another article, which I saved, people of the same city of Toronto are said to have "anti-gull workers" whose task it is to destroy "thousands of eggs (of gulls) each spring."

When I read this in the *Wall Street Journal,* I recalled the carnage reported in Farley Mowat's book, *Sea of Slaughter* (Atlantic Monthly Press, 1984), that was wrought upon the large colonies of seabirds on the northeastern seaboard of Canada and the United States in the seventeenth and eighteenth centuries. When you think of it, though, there is some difference then and now. In the earlier periods the destruction had some gainful purposes, such as getting eggs to eat and (with gulls) feathers to sell, even if those purposes were achieved in sickeningly wasteful ways. Now the destruction has no other purpose than destruction itself.

Some of us, thinking of the gull's gloriously effortless flight, may wonder why. The reason is that gulls, after they were nearly annihilated in this part of the North American Continent, have made the mistake of recovering themselves since a U.S.-Canadian treaty to protect them was signed in 1916. How human beings have begun to regard these birds is captured well in the heading of the *Wall Street Journal* story: "Brazen Sea Gulls Are Capable of Filching A Guy's Pork Chops."

And many are the complaints: they sully public docks and thus hurt tourism; damage rooftops; attack tomato farms and cherry orchards; and collide with airplanes. At airports, "Gulls are Public Enemy No. 1, worldwide," as JFK's "bird-control supervisor" is quoted as saying.

So, man and the gull have collided. Naturally, it is the gull that must beat its retreat. If you become affluent enough to buy a sailboat, you don't want it dirtied by gull droppings. (And believe it or not, many of us are becoming affluent.) Rooftops are not made for gulls to peck at. Tomatoes and cherries are grown for human consumption, not for the gulls. If you fly, you want to show that you do it better than the gulls. Gulls may not be completely wiped out, at least for some time. But their fate is again up in the air. And I have a suspicion that a similar fate awaits Canada geese.

Since I mentioned Mowat, I should note that the foremost advocate of gull "control," at least in this part of the world, is the Canadian Wildlife Service—Mowat's nemesis since he was commissioned by it more than twenty years ago to "prove" that the wolves were reducing the number of caribou. He found that man, not the wolf, was the cause of the decline, but the Canadian Wildlife Service ignored his findings and raised the amount of bounty paid for each wolf slaughtered. The result was his book of stirring protest, *Never Cry Wolf*. In *Sea of Slaughter*, he says the situation hasn't improved at all.

Paul Ehrlich is famous for his book, The Population Bomb, *from 1968.*

On January 15, 2009, a US Airways jetliner with 155 people that had just taken off from the LaGuardia Airport had to ditch in the Hudson River, because, it was judged, its engines had sucked some birds. That strengthened "the bird-killing programs at the New York City area's three major airports." As a result, "nearly 70,000 gulls, starling, geese and other birds have been slaughtered" in the eight years since then, AP reported on January 14, 2017, with the headline, "'Miracle on the Hudson' legacy."

Bird Bashing

April 27, 1987, *Masamichi Daily News*

I used to butcher and devour sparrows.

For several years after the war my family lived on a small island called Tobishima, in Nagasaki. My late father tended to have a couple of young men working for him as informal henchmen, as it were, and while we lived on that island a handsome carpenter played the henchman's role. His name, if my memory doesn't fail me, was Yoshikatsu, affectionately called Yoshikatchan.

From time to time he would take me around, shooting sparrows with an air gun. He didn't do it for the fun of it, though. He gave them to us to eat. I did the feather-plucking. The denuded birds were then broiled and basted, and became a delectable part of our evening meals.

I thought of the sparrow butchery in my boyhood as I watched the couple who recently bought the co-op downstairs have all the trees in the backyard cut down. As far as I can tell from my bay window, they haven't much advanced into their thirties, but they appear quite well-to-do. They bought the basement floor, which consisted of two separate apartments.

That alone must have cost them a fair sum. They then employed a group of several carpenters, removed the existing partitions to merge the two apartments, and renovated the whole thing. Though the carpenters were, my wife observed, Irish immigrants and their wages may have been much lower than the regular New York carpenters whose rates, determined by their union, are quite stiff, the renovation too must have cost a considerable amount.

Anyway, they had all the trees cut down—all six of them. The trees are of the species called *Ailanthus altissima*, popularly known as the tree of heaven. Simon and Schuster's *Guide to Trees* says *Ailanthus* comes from the *Moluccan ailanto*, "tree that can grow up to the sky." Indigenous to China, the species was introduced to Europe and America in 1751 (whether the introduction to the two continents was made in the same year isn't clear from the text). The tree is "hardy and very adaptable" and "thrives in cities in meager soil," the *Guide* says.

Indeed, when we moved to this apartment at the end of 1973, the six trees were no more than shoots. But they grew quickly, and for the past ten years or so provided cool shade during the summer, in every season extending convenient perches for all the many birds that visited our backyard.

Now they lie stacked in one corner of the yard, cut to firewood size, and our avian visitors have nothing to sit on close to our bay window, except the metal support for our birdfeeder.

Watching the trees being cut down brought back the memory of killing and eating sparrows probably because, if you live in a city long enough, you develop a selfish pity for non-human forms of life. So, even though I once happily ate sparrows, I was quite disbelieving several years ago when I read in the *New Yorker* that for some period before the turn of the century this city offered money for the slaughter of these birds.

The sparrow was introduced to this city from England in the mid-nineteenth century to help eradicate a certain type of caterpillar that was ravaging the trees in this region. The bird turned out to be a spectacular natural enemy of the caterpillar, and the defoliation was halted not long afterward. The bird was also a good adapter, and proliferated fast, in a few decades prompting the city to equate it with the rat as a vermin to be exterminated.

Now, for most New Yorkers, it would be nearly impossible to imagine that at one time many residents here regarded the occasional chorus of the sparrows as an intolerable din, attributing some other unfavorable traits to these birds, besides. A number of people in this section of town

put out birdfeeders, apparently thinking, as I do, that having small flying and singing creatures around isn't a bad thing. Yet, if putting out a
birdfeeder is some manifestation of our love of nature, it is selective,
willful, and in the end not quite helpful.

We are selective, because we still do not tolerate, for example, the
pigeon. The bird is too large to be cute, and its unabashed appetite,
constant horniness, and messy excretion remind us all too well of some
of the more unsavory aspects of ourselves. For this reason, it must be
assumed that our care for sparrows and other small birds may readily
vanish if they mess up the place where we feed them.

We are willful. We sometimes forget or otherwise fail to fill our
feeder. This can wreak havoc among the birds, though we seldom see
its consequences. For one thing, small birds' metabolism is so high that
they can't go hungry for too long.

Finally, our bird-feeding may not necessarily be helping the cause.
The birdseed industry in this country took off in the 1960's largely as a
result of rapid urbanization. As we cut down more trees and otherwise
destroyed more of nature, we began to buy food for the birds. Not long
ago the U.S. birdfeed industry was put at $200 million a year—far larger
than the Gross National Product of such countries as The Gambia and
French Guiana. As we feed birds in cities and suburbs, we are killing
birds elsewhere.

To Keep the Fairway Fair

October 17, 1988, *Mainichi Daily News*

Martha Hill, the picture editor of *Audubon*, recently remembered me and sent a copy of the November 1987 issue of the famous bird-conservation magazine. I became acquainted with her many months ago when she asked me to do her the small favor of translating a letter to a Japanese ornithologist.

Evidently she decided to send me this particular issue because it carried a one-page report called "Why the Japanese Will Save Cranes But Not Their Habitat," which summarized a survey conducted by Prof. Stephen Kellert, of the Yale School of Forestry and Environmental Studies, about Japanese attitudes toward nature. It appears that one aim of the study was to posit Japanese views against those of the Americans, for the summary contained such comparisons as: "While 69 percent of Americans interviewed said they were willing to pay higher prices for tuna if fewer porpoises are killed in nets, only 34 percent of Japanese were similarly inclined."

But what interested me far more greatly was another, much fuller article in the same issue, entitled "Hazards of the Game." It was the first article condemning golf courses I ever read, and I was happy with it. I am prejudiced against golfing and golf courses.

I began to have a despairing sense of golf and things people do to play the game in 1975, when I went back to Japan for my first visit since coming here twenty years ago. In town after town I passed through by train or by car, I saw ugly-green structures soaring above the roof-lines.

Puzzled, I asked what they were, and was told they were driving ranges. In trying to satiate the golf craze that seized the country in the late 1960s or early 1970s, entrepreneurs began to build them right in the middle of towns and cities because Japan doesn't have enough space. The result was those sickening giant nets erected to catch golf balls. The collective mental laxity that allowed such eyesores to be built was enough to trash any illusion I might have had about my compatriots' vaunted aesthetic sensibility.

At about the same time I began to have doubts about golf courses in the United States, but the reason was just the opposite: the spectacular attractiveness of those "flawlessly manicured, ultragreen playgrounds," as the *Audubon* article puts it. There's something wickedly wrong, I felt, about messing so constantly with what's better left alone. Obviously the strong sentiments for environmental protection then prevailing shaped my attitude, but I also read somewhere that messy-looking under-growths are vital to a great variety of small creatures. Needless to say, I also began to harbor grave doubts about the American passion for the lawn.

As if to drive that point home, a man became a news item for having let the garden of his suburban home go wild. He explained that by doing so he could have, as he actually did, insects, birds, and other forms of wildlife in his backyard. But precisely because of that his neighbors sued him. They also complained that his negligence of his lawn marred the uniform suburban presentability of the neighborhood and reduced its real estate value. I don't know what became of him in the end, but I secretly applauded him.

Still, until I read "Hazards of the Game," I didn't know the case against the "fairways" went far beyond the simple clearing of under-growths and trees. To be sure, that action itself is one of the two prin-cipal reasons cited to illustrate the damages done by the building and maintaining of golf courses. The scale of the land transformed to accom-modate this seemingly innocuous sport is considerable. On the average, 110 courses, each consuming about 150 acres, are built every year in the United States. That's 16,500 acres of land cleared or otherwise tampered with annually. And, like any kind of development in non-urban regions, building a golf course means "certain death for the existing ecosystem."

Death, however, does not occur only through the simple change of the natural environment. After a course is built, a great variety of pesticides, herbicides, and fertilizers is used to keep the fairway fair, the green green.

"Hazards of the Game" reports some of the killings that have occurred as a result of the use of such chemicals. One day in May 1984 a common pesticide called Diazinon was used on three fairways in Hewlett Harbor, New York. A flock of brant flew in and fed on one of the fairways. By next morning a couple of hundred of these geese were found dead, the number rising to 700 over the next three days. In an incident in October 1986 a college toxicologist by the name of Ron Kendall knowingly killed a total of eighty-five wigeon on a golf course to prove what was already known: the toxicity of the same pesticide. For the experiment he was funded by its manufacturer, Ciba-Geigy.

Earlier, in August 1982, a navy lieutenant played golf on a course at the Army Navy Country Club, which had been freshly treated with Daconil—"a compound particularly effective in eradicating brown spots." He developed a nasty allergic reaction to the chemical and died of a heart attack.

"Hazards of the Game" tries to be fair, citing such observations as "We won't know the whole story until another decade from now." Meanwhile, I am heartened to know that a range of people are lined up against the builders of golf courses.

An NPR report of June 2019 says that the golf-course building mania started in the 1980s, as "the National Golf Foundation encouraged the industry to build a course a day for 10 years." As a result, now "about 2 million acres of green space" are given to golf courses." But the boom peaked in the early 2000s, so about "800 golf courses have closed in the last decade."

Emotion Trumps Logic in Whaling Debate
Moby-Dick and *A Whale Hunt*

December 25, 2000, *Japan Times*

Over a sushi lunch with Scott Latham, I mention "whaling," and Scott, my trade consultant friend, doesn't miss a beat: "The Whaling Wall."

I brought up the topic because the first secretary of the Embassy of Japan, in Washington, had come to New York a few days earlier to discuss whaling, and he had done so because the U.S. government was preparing to put into effect sanctions against Japan. As he explained, one of the enabling laws is the Pelly Amendment, which is part of the Fishermen's Protective Act of 1967. It authorizes penalizing "nationals of a foreign country" for actions that "diminish the effectiveness of an international fishery conservation program" and "any international program for endangered or threatened species."

I was curious to learn what the first secretary had to say, though I mainly felt a foreboding.

Like most of my generation of Japanese, I grew up when whale meat was an important source of protein. Also, by some fluke, my college graduation thesis was on *Moby-Dick*.

On the other hand, I arrived in the United States when the focus on cetaceans was swinging from their utility to their intelligence (and, yes, their cuteness in the case of dolphins). And not long after my arrival, an international moratorium on commercial whaling was instituted in 1972, with Japan as the main target. The change in American attitude and the international decision would make, I expected, any defense of Japan's whaling a Sisyphean task—if that was what the first secretary had in mind.

I'm afraid the secretary's talk was a failure.

Apparently exasperated by the prevailing sentiment in Washington that whaling is a "crime," not to mention the environmentalists' willful disregard for science (or common sense or what have you), the secretary did not explain well the purpose of his talk: to persuade the audience that commercial whaling, which is the ultimate goal of what Japan is doing (though with the sneer-provoking pretext of "scientific research"), is justifiable.

As a result, when, after his talk, a gentleman in the audience asked what would be the merit or demerit of stopping the whaling, the secretary's response raised many eyebrows, I think. He said it would save the Japanese government money. The number of whales captured today doesn't make Japan's whaling "commercially viable."

(A friend of mine in Tokyo, Ueda Akira, did a quick Internet search for me. The price of whale meat listed on a website would "knock you out," he reported. When he was growing up, whale meat used to be served for school lunch!)

Now, my young colleague at work, Donald Howard, warned he wouldn't speak to me if I wrote an article *for* whaling. So, here I'd like to limit myself to the few things I learned along the way.

The International Whaling Commission (IWC) is unlike most other international bodies: it accepts as members nations that have no whaling business, such as Switzerland. In addition, many of its members are dead against whaling. That would be like a World Trade Organization made up of non-trading nations and nations that are against international trade.

The political and intellectual shenanigans the IWC is forced to play as a result is eloquently described in an *Atlantic Monthly* article called "Flouting the Convention." Written by three professors, William Aron (fisheries science), William Burke (law and marine affairs), and Milton Freeman (anthropology), the May 1999 article can be easily read on the Internet. (If you read it, you might also want to take a look at another one in the same magazine, "To Whale or Not to Whale." The poet Mark Derr wrote the October 1997 piece.)

In "directing that Japan be denied future access to fishing rights in

U.S. waters," President Clinton said: "Strong international cooperation has allowed the recovery of many whale species once pushed to the brink of extinction." That, various reports suggest, appears to be true. With some species, the recovery may have pushed their populations above the levels before large-scale commercial whaling.

One example is the gray whale (*kokujira* or *kokukujira* in Japanese). That's the species famous for migrating up and down the West Coast of the United States and breeding in Baja California where people go to "pet them and touch them and be with these giant creatures"—to quote someone quoted in Robert Sullivan's *A Whale Hunt* (Scribner, 2000).

"The National Marine Mammals Laboratory released figures today showing the latest estimation of gray whales at 26,600," a UPI dispatch of March 19, 1999, said. "The population was down to around 4,000 at the end of the 19th century, when commercial whaling thrived. The number was up to an estimated 23,100 when the whales were removed from Endangered Species Act protection in 1994."

The figures 23,000 and 26,000 are "within the range (20,000 to 30,000) estimated in 1850 before Yankee whalers' counts made at a central California shore station during the whales' southern migration," as another report put it. The recovery was such, in fact, that various U.S. reports in 1999 said that 800 to 1,000 gray whales were washed up dead, probably from starvation, during the season of that year alone.

And yet, when the Makah, the Native Indian tribe at "the most northwestern tip of America," tried to kill a single gray whale to revive their tradition, what a glorious whale of a fuss Americans made! It is the subject of the book I've just mentioned, *A Whale Hunt*—which, incidentally, uses *Moby-Dick* as a curious backdrop.

No, I am not out to persuade anyone. I know there is Scott's "Whaling Wall." I can't help wondering nonetheless: Banning the slaughter of *all* whales for human consumption because humans once drove some of their species close to extinction—wouldn't it be like banning the slaughter of all quadrupeds because humans once did the same with the American bison?

Depredation of Species That Get in Our Way

July 25, 2005, *Japan Times*

"Protected Birds Are Back, With a Vengeance: Cormorants Take Over, Making Some Enemies"—this headline in the *New York Times* earlier this month, inset in a photo showing a few black birds atop a tree, struck me with the thought: So it has come to pass. Hadn't the same daily some years back carried a story very different in content and tone, which nonetheless portended this outcome?

It indeed had, seven years ago, as I quickly confirmed. With the headline "A Slaughter of Cormorants in Angler Country," the August 1, 1998 story had told the reader of a "massacre" of double-crested cormorants on the uninhabited Little Galloo Island, on Lake Ontario, which "left 840 birds dead and more than 100 others injured [and] transformed the local issue into an extraordinary environmental crime." As the newsletter *The Federal Wildlife Officer* put it one summer later, "the shotgun slayings," which were the result of the conflict between local fishermen and the birds, "are considered by the U.S. Fish and Wildlife Service to be one of the largest mass killings ever of a species protected by Federal laws."

The front-page article came with a photo of a few dead cormorants lying on the wet, foggy ground, as I remember vaguely. The report, by Andrew Revkin, quoted Clifford Schneider, who worked for the New York State Department of Environmental Conservation: "You see a young chick still laying there alive among all the others that had been wiped out, and you can't help but be moved emotionally." It appropriately ended with David J. Miller calling for "a swift investigation and aggressive prosecution of the shooter or shooters." Miller, the head of the National Audubon Society's New York State chapter, said, "The message has to be strong that people really can't take the law into their own hands."

It took eight months, until April 1999, for nine perpetrators of the killing to plead guilty.

Cormorants are migratory and are protected by the Migratory Bird Treaty Act (MBTA), originally of 1918. But they did not come under special protection until 1972 when they were added to the list of birds whose "killing and harassment during their annual cycle" was prohibited, says a 2001 report prepared for the United States Fish and Wildlife Service (USFWS), "Status of the Double-crested Cormorant (*Phalacrocorax auritus*) in North America." The MBTA lists six subspecies of the cormorant: Grant's, double-crested, great, neotropic or olivaceous, pelagic, and red-faced.

The year 1972 also saw a ban of DDT and a regulatory reduction of other pesticides. DDT and other toxic chemicals had drastically reduced the number of double-crested cormorants by 1970. Increases since then have been contrastingly spectacular. The "massacre" occurred in the midst of that recovery. This largely explains why Lisa Foderaro, writing "Protected Birds Are Back, With a Vengeance" a few weeks ago, did so as though cormorants are now the enemies not just for some people, such as fishermen, but for the reporter herself.

Just a year after the arrest of the nine men, Foderaro writes, the USFWS acceded to "complaints from fish farmers, anglers, landowners and biologists" and effected a "depredation order." What does "depredation" consist of? According to a March-May 2004 "statement of findings" by the New York State Division of Fish, Wildlife, and Marine Resources, it includes "egg-oiling, nest destruction, hazing, habitat modification, exclusion techniques, and limited lethal removal of birds." As a result of that order and another one that "authorizes shooting at farms and nearby roosting sites," in 2004 alone a total of 21,000 cormorants were killed nationwide. But the problem remains, both locally and nationally, according to Foderaro. And she doesn't like what she sees on Four Brothers Islands, on Lake Champlain.

"The double-crested cormorants perch like conquerors at the top of the spindly white pines, their driftwood-gray branches devoid of needles," Foderaro opens her story. "The trees were killed off, along with much of the other vegetation . . . by the birds' highly acidic droppings." Killing of cormorants on the small cluster of islets, which are located toward the southern end of the lake between New York and Vermont, has yet to begin; the Nature Conservancy's Adirondack chapter, which owns them, has declined to give permission to "manage" the birds.

The result violates Foderaro's sense of what "birds" should be like, her notion of their place on this planet. Four Brothers Islands "constitute a strange sanctuary," she says, "a smelly, noisy, barren landscape, seemingly plucked from a Hitchcock film," where "the ubiquitous black birds can be seen stretching out their wings Dracula style to dry their feathers."

Dracula style! But, darling, cormorants can't help that!

Seriously, Foderaro's "strange sanctuary" reminds me of what I should have said upfront: I am an armchair nature lover. In Sunset Beach, North Carolina, where my wife and I vacation every summer, I kayak in the marsh. There, when the tide goes out a sand bar emerges and collects a gaggle of waterfowl—pelicans, oyster catchers, skimmers, royal terns, curlews. Not a whole lot of them, no: The resort is too developed for that, but sizable enough to give off a stiff whiff of odor as you slide toward it. That delights me, real nature! But could I live right next to such a sand bar, let alone a colony of cormorants, all year round? I doubt it.

And yet, and yet. What has happened to cormorants is yet another story of humans overpowering animals whenever they see them getting in their way. Neither the population size of a particular animal nor what the animal does (more often, does not do) matters.

One estimate puts the number of double-crested cormorants in North America at two million, less than a quarter of the number of humans in New York City. On Lake Champlain there are two nesting sites for the birds, six-acre Young Island and eighteen-acre Four Brothers Islands, a total of twenty-four acres or one-tenth of a square kilometer. And though the "management" of the bigger space is on hold, Vermont has been "aggressively" practicing "depredation" on the smaller one. Why can't we leave both places alone?

As to fishermen's claim that cormorants are depleting certain fish stock, it remains unproven. That is why the Canadian government objected, at least initially, to the USFWS's "depredation order." But Canada, too, has buckled under pressure. For a few years now it has been killing sizable numbers of cormorants to see whether their varying population sizes affect fish populations. Animals don't have a chance.

"Good Old Days" Dispensed
with Body Counts

September 29, 2008, *Japan Times*

Driving back from Sunset Beach, North Carolina, where we spend two weeks every summer, we hugged the coastline. After crossing the forty-kilometer Chesapeake Bay Bridge-Tunnel, we for the first time stopped at the Eastern Shore of Virginia National Wildlife Refuge visitor's center. The center turned out to be more like a museum, with several exhibits. One, with some blown-up old photos, was arrestingly called "The Outlaw Gunner."

No, the display was not about a soldier run amok, as I learned soon enough. "Gunner" here is the same as "hunter," and the story is the wholesale slaughter of wildfowl with "mass production methods" that were practiced in Chesapeake Bay and its tributaries even after the Migratory Bird Treaty Act of 1918 made them illegal.

The Outlaw Gunner, by Harry M. Walsh, MD, which the visitor's center carried for sale, details the weapons and other devices that the "market gunners"—those who engaged in mass killing for a living—had at their disposal. Central to them all was, of course, "the fowling piece": the gun. There were a range of those pieces: swivel gun, punt gun, battery gun, etc., and what was simply called "the big gun."

How big was the big gun? A list of "names and addresses of owners of big guns in the vicinity of Susquehanna Flats, Maryland," dated January 1, 1914, that Walsh reproduces in his book notes: "These guns are all about the same weight, —100 to 125 lbs.; length, 12 feet; diameter of bore from 1– ½ to 2 ins." In other words, they weighed forty-five to fifty-seven kilograms and were 3.7 meters long. No wonder each such gun required a special skiff or rig. Walsh shows a photo of an old market gunner, a Sam Armstrong of Delaware City, who referred to the big gun as his headache gun. He said, Walsh writes, "he took two aspirins before and after firing."

A skiff whose bow is equipped with a three- to seven-barreled battery gun looks like a miniaturized battleship, and must have been equally deadly, in a scaled-down way. Not that a regular, non-outlandish gun was ineffective. Walsh shows a photo of a former market gunner named Atley Lankford, of Elliott Island, Maryland, with his Model 11 Remington automatic, "which has killed over 35,000 ducks." No, that isn't a typo.

Walsh wrote his book in the late 1960s, when the consequences of the ill treatment of nature were quickly coming to the fore. So one aim of his writing about outlaw gunners, he said, was to plead for an end to "the slaughter we have brought about."

But as someone who once "apprenticed" with a former market gunner, Walsh could not hide his nostalgia for "the good old days" when unchecked mass killings were "a way of life." Indeed, he sounds a little forced when he argues that such slaughtering was an economic necessity—a way of helping "to feed a hungry America that was living off the land." A good part of it must have been our killing instinct. Vice President Dick Cheney's occasional gunning sprees suggest it; so does *Seashore Chronicles*, by Brooks Barnes and Barry Truitt (1997), a book I also bought at the visitor's center.

A collection of writings about the Virginia Barrier Islands from 1650, when Henry Norwood, the "treasurer" of Virginia, wrote an account, to the early 1990s, the book gives ample glimpses into the kind of "way of life" Walsh had in mind all right, but also one in which people killed, regardless of needs.

To take one example from an appropriately named writer, Alexander Hunter (1843–1914), a frequent visitor to the island resorts, described how he went hunting one morning on the shore of Cobb's Island. It was Christmas 1895 when "earth, air and water harmonized in one grand anthem in honor of the Nativity."

"On this sandbank the snipe were feeding in countless numbers, and I was not exaggerating when I say that the bar running into the sea was so thick with them that there was not a bare spot discernible. Creeping up on my hands and knees to within forty yards, I sighted along the fluttering mosaic-looking ground and pulled trigger. A long swath of dead and dying marked the track of the shot."

After gathering up the dead snipe and piling them "in great heaps," he was ready for "further sport," but his guide distracted him for a greater "thrill" of killing the brant. The visitor's center lists the snipe as "uncommon" today. The brant is "common," but only in winter, and "common" just means that the bird is "likely to be seen or heard in suitable habitat."

On Sunset Beach, North Carolina, a barrier island that turned into a developers' dreamland in the 1970s, no wildfowling is possible. There are too few birds. Aside from gulls and grackles and, yes, brown pelicans, the only bird that forms a sizable flock is the ibis, at least during the period of summer we are there. Sandpipers, plovers, and curlews are so few they always look like stragglers.

Still, our killer mind never rests, even in the kind of inlet Sunset Beach forms. Each year, more people are out to catch minnows, for bait. Each year, we see minnows, in schools, break the surface of the water less often, kingfishers and herons and egrets fly in for them less often.

August 24, Sunday, was our last day. In the morning I kayaked out of the canal into the inlet for the summer's farewell. The tide was low, and some of the sandbanks were out of water. Several men were already out working with cast nets. Several were fishing with poles. On one sandbank a Great Blue Heron, the ever-wary bird that prefers to be camouflaged, strutted on its spindly legs, uncertain, lost.

No Country for Millions of Canada Geese

August 29, 2010, *Japan Times*

The State of New York plans to "gas" or otherwise kill 170,000 Canada geese to reduce the number from 250,000 to 85,000.

This news item, tucked away in the *New York Times*, struck me as yet another sign of human willfulness toward flora and fauna. After all, when it appeared, the BP oil spill off the coast of Louisiana had only recently been stopped, and images of oil-soaked pelicans and those cleaned and released, were still fresh. The efforts to save oil-damaged pelicans and others were made despite the warning: the survival rate of animals so "rescued" is a mere one percent.

Why then plan mass killings of another species of bird?

Brown pelicans are common south of Virginia, I learned when my wife and I started spending summers on the Carolina shores three decades ago, but the first time I saw one remains as my first taste of "wilderness." In the summer of 1966, a friend took me out on a fishing boat, overnight off the coast of Redondo Beach. Perhaps it was near Santa Catalina Island. Against the crags rising out of the choppy dark blue sea flew a solitary pelican. Right then it ceased to be the odd creature confined to pictures I had known.

I began to see Canada geese near Manhattan about ten years ago. That was when a friend and I started taking an occasional ferry ride from midtown across the Hudson. There, next to the New Jersey terminal, resting on a small patch of lawn or swimming along the shore, was a family or two of these large birds, with yellowish juveniles almost the size of a regular duck. Being so close to them gave me a great sense of comfort.

More recently they showed up near my home. After years of work, the Hudson River Greenway started to be completed. As that happened, the length of it from about West 10th Street to Gansevoort Street, with two abandoned piers turned into attractive waterborne parks, as it were, became a favorite place for me and my wife to take a walk in.

There, a few years ago, we saw Canada geese. For all the annihilation of the shoreline with stone, steel, and concrete, they must have done something right, I thought, although it may just be that enough time had elapsed for seaweeds to grow on the below-waterline part of the esplanade. Geese and ducks come to peck away at the weeds.

Not that I had not seen Canada geese before; I had, large congregations of them, in Union County, Illinois. My wife's mother, Florence, lived in Cape Girardeau, on the Mississippi, and we would visit her during Christmas. At times, my wife drove me across the Old Man River to a wildlife refuge—the one on the road to Carbondale, Illinois, where her brother and his wife live. There, invariably, were a great many of those great birds. Sometimes a large flock would fly in, in the famed wedge formation, sinuously undulating.

For that matter, though only several times, I saw, from the window of my apartment, a flock flying away high in the sky. My apartment is on the twelfth floor and, for all the tall sprouts of buildings around us, it faces the open air to the north.

It must have been in the same space I see from my window, in fact, that in January 2009 a flock of Canada geese were sucked into the engines of a jetliner that had just flown up from LaGuardia Airport, forcing it to splash down into the Hudson River.

The *Times* indeed said that the plan for cutting down the Canada goose population by two-thirds, "according to a high-level official at the United States Department of Agriculture, was a result of five months of meetings between February and June 2009"—that is, after Canada geese downed the jetliner.

As it turns out, the *Times* report was somewhat misleading, said a follow-up on the website Your News Now (YNN), "Controlling the

Canada geese population." What the *Times* called "a doomsday plan for New York's geese" has been "in place for a long time" and it has not been "all that successful."

True, a 2006 U.S. Fish and Wildlife Service document says the idea for a "strategy to reduce, manage, and control resident Canada goose populations" was hatched in February 2000. Yes, they make a distinction between those birds that fly back and forth between the arctic and subarctic regions and temperate zones and those who stick around all year long.

The document, titled "resident Canada goose management," poses the question: "What would happen to resident Canada goose populations without management?" The answer: In the Atlantic Flyway, of which New York is a part, the number would increase to 1.25 million; in the Mississippi Flyway, to 1.5 million; and, in the Pacific Flyway, to 400,000—a grand total of 3.15 million, by this year, 2010.

A question: Can't this vast land of the United States that continues to allow human beings to increase—now 310 million—accommodate 3.15 million Canada geese? Is one bird for every 100 human beings far too many? New York State is pretty large, too, with 141,000 square kilometers or 35 million acres, nearly twice the size of Hokkaidō. Is a single Canadian goose for every 140 acres one too many?

The YNN article quoted Dr. Guy Baldassarre at the College of Environmental Science and Forestry, the State University of New York, as saying, "When you see geese, they're eating or they're defecating." Isn't that what we human beings do as well, too well?

Baldassarre suggested one alternative to "mass euthanasia": "You let the grass grow up a little bit and maybe get into growing native wildflowers or some other habitat type, you won't see the geese there because they don't eat those things." But this is a country where the lawn and grass cutting remain supreme.

In her famous 1962 book, *Silent Spring*, Rachel Carson wrote: "The 'control of nature' is a phrase conceived in arrogance, born of the Neanderthal age of biology and philosophy, when it was supposed that nature exists for the convenience of man."

Despite all the environmental talk ever since, nothing has changed.

The Transient Rasping That Captivates the Poets

May 27, 2013, *Japan Times*

"And there it was, its beady, blood-red eyes glaring up from the sidewalk, a threat of shrieking hell to come."

That's how Ashley Halsey III reported the re-advent of seventeen-year cicadas (*Magicicada*) for the *Washington Post* ("Those beady-eyed bugs are back: Cicadas spotted in Northern Virginia," May 12, 2013). He went on to call cicadas "ugly bugs."

Do cicadas create a shrieking hell? Are they ugly? Halsey III was describing the periodical cicadas whose "incredible ability to merge by the millions," Richard Alexander and Thomas Moore observed in their 1962 paper, "within a matter of hours after having spent 13 or 17 years underground as silent, burrowing, solitary, sedentary juveniles is without parallel in the animal kingdom."

So I asked three Japanese—one relative and two friends—what comes to mind when they hear the word *semi*, "cicada."

Atsuko, my niece who lives in Mamaroneck, north of Manhattan, because of her husband's assignment to New York, wrote: "Experiencing the summer here for the first time last year, I remember thinking, Ah, unlike London, there are cicadas here." She and her family lived in the British capital for over seven years. "They weren't as rambunctious as they are in Japan. In the Japanese summer, cicadas' cries are so noisy as to be annoying." What she heard were annual cicadas (*Tibicen tibicen*) whose short rasping can be musical as the Latin name suggests.

"Flavorful, crisp. That's what pops in my mind," Ueda Akira, a friend in Tokyo responded. "Come season, their shells dot the ground, and their light amber appeals to my tactile sense. Before I know it, I find myself picking them up crushing them between my fingers. (Their contents are screaming up in the trees.) Once they die, they are dead, rolling about supine here and there, drily unconcerned about it all."

"Empty cicada," Kakizaki Shōko, a friend in Aomori, said. "A poetic image. They live only for a little while, hence transiency. Because I live in a relatively cold region, when I hear cicadas cry, I feel all the more that the short summer will end even before I have the time to sigh."

The word she used for "empty cicada" is *utsusemi,* the cicada shell. Because of homophones, early Japanese poets equated it with "the human in this world," another short-lived being.

The cicada shell as a symbol of the vanity of life—as in the Biblical "vanity of vanities"—is expressed well in an anonymous poem in *Kokinshū,* an anthology from the early tenth century:

> Though the shells of empty cicadas stay on every tree
> not seeing where the souls are gone saddens me

> *Utsusemi no kara wa ki goto ni todomuredo*
> *Tama no yukue wo minu zo kanashiki*

In the original, *ki,* "tree," also means "coffin," it is noted.

But the word *utsusemi* most likely reminds the readers of classical Japanese literature of the chapter with that word of *The Tale of Genji.* That is where Genji the Shining Prince, still in his late teens, tries to seduce an old, low-ranking courtier's young second wife, and fails. He fails because the married woman, sensing his approach in the darkness of night, slips away, leaving only her garment behind.

Not that Japanese poets forgot about the first thing my Mamaroneck niece thought of: the great noise cicadas can make. In fact, those who look into such matters tell us that the *Man'yōshū,* the large anthology of 4,500 poems from the eighth century, has just one poem using the word *semi,* and it describes the creature's impressive sound-making power:

Listening to the cicadas' voices roaring like rock-rushing waterfalls
    I can't help thinking of the Capital

Iwabashiru taki mo todoro ni naku semi no
    koe wo shi kikeba miyako shi omoyu

"The Capital" here is Nara, not Kyoto. The poet, Ōishi no Minomaro, composed it on Kurahashi Island, in Hiroshima. He was saying he missed the noisy crowds of the big city.

The most famous haiku on cicadas may be:

Quietness: seeping into the rocks the cicada's voice

Shizukasa ya iwa ni shimiiru semi no koe

This poem, by Bashō, prompted a scientific controversy, as it were, in 1926, when the psychiatrist-cum-tanka-poet Saitō Mokichi asserted that the cicada here has to be *aburazemi*, "oily cicada" (*Graptopsaltria nigrofuscata*). It is this species' persistent, sizzling shirring that is said to "amplify" the oppression of the hot, humid Japanese summer.

But the German scholar Komiya Toyotaka objected. Considering the time and place Bashō wrote the piece—mid-Seventh Month 1689, at Risshaku Temple, in the northern prefecture of Yamagata—the cicada has to be *niiniizemi*, "tremulous cicada" (*Platypleura kaempferi*), Komiya judged. It makes a low-key yet penetrating sound. Komiya won the argument.

Bashō also wrote this:

Not showing it's soon to die: cicada's voice

Yagate shinu keshiki wa miezu semi no koe

There is, for that matter, a striking difference between English and Japanese Wikipedia entries on the cicada. The English entry is detailed enough, but the Japanese entry lists a number of subspecies, which are then linked to sub-subspecies, each described with care.

And, speaking of differences, Ashley Halsey III's "shrieking hell" and "ugly bugs" are the antithesis of how Takamura Kōtarō viewed the cicada. Takamura, the sculptor-poet, captivated by Auguste Rodin and "Western ideals" in his youth later came to appreciate the traditional sculpting skills of his father, Takamura Kōun, which he had initially condemned as "artisan's," not "artist's." One such skill was carving wood with a single knife.

"The way the Japanese cicadas rasp as loudly as they can, with child-like abandon," he ended his 1940 essay on carving the insect, "the way their rasps pierce the core of my brain, is very pleasant. "Indeed, what's described as *semi shigure*, 'cicada shower,' or the competitive perfor-mance of cicadas in the woods, is a gift of summer, as beautiful as a dream. When I carve a cicada, I feel as if a breeze dripping with the green of such woods fills up my room."

Takamura's essay was titled "The Beauty and the Plasticity of the Cicada."

Kōtarō's essay is included in my translation A Brief History of Imbecility: Poetry and Prose of Takamura Kōtarō *(University Press of Hawaii, 1992).*

"Where to Go to Survive the Day?" the Corbies Say

July 28, 2013, *Japan Times*

"Our 'jungle' crows are disappearing," my Buddhist-scholar friend Gene Reeves wrote from Tokyo.

"For years, if I looked out my living room window I could see at least a dozen or two of crows. And, once upon a time, when they were quite plentiful, one would walk into our dining room, take a taste of one or two house plants, and walk out."

I at once became apprehensive. Did Tokyo start "dealing with" crows? Several years ago a Japanese friend in the same city had written to grumble: "The crows are menacing us. There are too many of them. Something must be done about them." He lived near Meiji Shrine at the time.

I checked the Internet. Sure enough, some municipalities had websites "dealing with" crows. So I wrote back to Mr. Reeves: It would be terrible if Tokyo had indeed begun to "manage" crows, American-style. But Tokyo already had, he responded.

"I have a vivid memory of taking a ride through Zenpukuji Koen, a long park in Suginami-ku that runs along the river by the same name. For the first time, on the other side of the river from where I was, and not far from a major crow breeding area, I saw a large tent-like affair made of netting. It was made such that crows could get into it, but not out.

"On the inside were half a dozen screaming crows desperately trying to find a way out, and on the outside were another eight or ten trying, equally desperately, to help them. I felt it was a gruesome scene, and probably never will be able to forget it."

I checked the matter further, and this time learned that it was Ishihara Shintarō who, as governor of Tokyo, announced, back in the summer of 2001, that he set up "a project team on anti-crow measures." The team published a report with alacrity—just a month later.

And there it was: the proposed "crow-capturing trap." The diagrams with dimensions showed a pretty large trap, at 3 x 3 x 4 meters. Initially 100 such traps were set up in parks throughout Tokyo, a later report said. Evidently Mr. Reeves saw a "gruesome scene" in and around one of these.

I also found that earlier, in March, the Environment Ministry's Nature Conservation Bureau had published a 135-page "Manual on Anti-Crow Measures for Municipal Officers." The Wild Bird Society of Japan had written the report.

So what? you might ask. Why should a New York city dweller care about what's happening to the crows in Tokyo—or in Japan?

Well, for one thing, precisely because I am a big city dweller, I seem to notice, almost every day, how willful we human beings are to animals, plants, and birds.

Just now, for example, reading the two anti-crow reports, I see it's over the past three decades that "jungle crows" (*Corvus macrorhynchos*) increased and have come to outnumber "carrion crows" (*Corvus corone*) in Japan's urban areas. The cause? The food waste surfeited humanity creates.

The illustrated book on Japanese birds I have says that jungle crows, called *hashibuto-garasu*, "thick-billed crows," are far fewer than carrion crows, called *hashiboso-garasu*, "thin-billed crows." The book was last revised in 1980, so that's what prevailed back then. Also, the actual damage and harm crows are said to bring to humanity strikes me as too insignificant to fuss about.

Most complaints about crows are about their cawing. But whether it is the *kah-kah* of the thick-billed crow or the *gah-gah* of the thin-billed crow, those calls should be music to the ear of those living amidst urban din. How is it that they, of all people, have become so intolerant of "nature"?

For another, I've had a soft spot for crows since I read Konrad Lorenz's descriptions of jackdaws in *King Solomon's Ring* forty years ago. The jackdaw is a member of the crow family (*Corvus*).

"I like crows," Mr. Reeves wrote, "for their intelligence, but also for the way they like to amuse themselves by playing with their voices, sometimes mimicking a dog or a cat or even a truck."

I can attest to that. Some mornings, a flock of crows flies in from New Jersey, across the Hudson River, and engages in aerial frolicking before my eyes. I live on a twelfth floor facing a roof garden and a large open space.

There is also the splendor of the crow.

Five years ago I saw crows—Japanese crows—for the first time in many years, and I was impressed. I was in Tokyo and had a chance to visit, with a friend, the "nature education park" in Shirokanedai, the last remnant of the Musashino Plain preserved as it once was. The crows there practically gleamed in their blackness, and were dignified as they sharply looked around.

And they were big. They are, in fact, one size larger than the American crow (*Corvus brachyrhynchos*).

Looking at them, I recalled what the haiku poet and translator Bill Higginson had said years ago: The "crows" described in Bashō's famous haiku as perched on dead branches in the autumn evening should be "ravens" in English. In truth, as I've learned since, Japan also has a raven (*Corvus corax kamtschaticus*), but its range is limited to the northern end of the archipelago.

Speaking of such things, Miyazawa Kenji wrote a number of poems referring to crows, among them "Crows in a Hundred Postures." It simply describes the way some members of a flock on a snowy rice paddy act. My translation is quoted in full, and compared with Wallace Stevens' "Thirteen Ways of Looking at a Blackbird," in the blogsite *Isola Di Rifiuti*.

I wish those Japanese who complain about crows will read

Miyazawa's original. After all, many of their compatriots regard him as a saint.

No, not all Japanese are out to get the crows. The urban ornithologist Karasawa Kōichi, for one, has written two books on the bird, *The Crow Is a Genius! (Karasu wa tensai!)* and *How Clever Is the Crow? (Karasu wa dorehodo kashikoi ka).*

In another book, Karasawa tells us how he was once called upon to explain why crows came to peck at one outdoor exhibit at a Flower Expo. He could not puzzle out the cause, but gently suggested that it may well be man's fault.

The slogan of the Flower Expo was "Harmony between Man and Nature." Then why do so unnatural a thing as assembling thousands of different flowers in a single spot? Perhaps the crows were warning about the folly, Karasawa said.

Kenji's crow poem is in my translation Miyazawa Kenji: Selections *(University of California Press, 2007).*

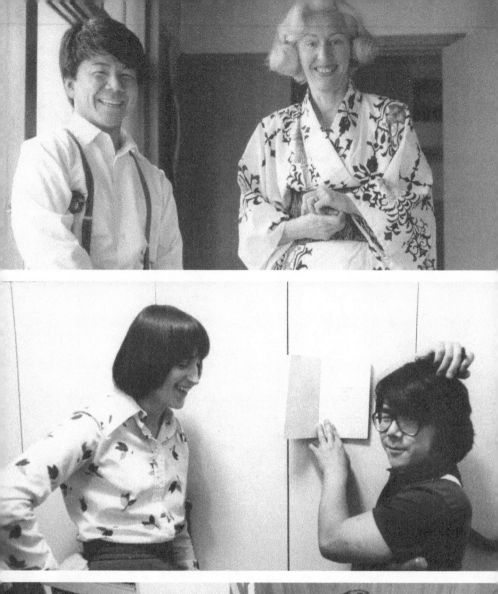

COUNTERCLOCKWISE FROM TOP LEFT: With poet Edith Shiffert, circa 1966; first book party, with then girlfriend Nancy; party for my second book of translations devoted to a single modern poet, *Poems of a Penisist*, 1975, from left: Jorge Perez (who kindly shared his apartment with me when I arrived in New York in 1968), Jeannine Ciliotta (my editor and collaborator), Rand Castile, and Hiro; with John Ashbery, 1991; at the northern end of what would later become an abandoned railroad turned into a park called The High Line, 1987; with Michael O'Brien, 1979.

Rooting Out the Purplish, Yellow Perils
Search-and-Destroy Missions

May 28, 2007, *Japan Times*

The plant, of the pea family, has been appreciated in Japan, poetically, dietarily, and medicinally, since ancient times. So, in the oldest extant anthology of Japanese poetry, the *Man'yōshū*, it is used as an epithet for "without interruption," "for a long time," and so forth, because its most impressive attribute is "vitality," as a photo-packed Japanese website for "seasonal flowers" (*kisetsu no hana*) puts it. Its vines grow not just fast but also unendingly.

For example, in the early eighth century, when Prince Yamasaki wrote an elegy upon Prince Ishida's death, he referred to the plant to lament, "I had expected to come to visit you forever and ever." Similarly, Lady Sakanoue cited the plant in replying to a man who had sent her a poem saying days had passed without his seeing her—noting in her reply that she had wondered if something had happened to him because his messenger who used to come "without interruption" had "faltered."

The autumnal coloration of the plant didn't go unnoticed either. An anonymous poem says he noticed the plant turning color after "the geese honking sounded cold" to him. Later, as poets developed more elaborate conventions, it was the underside of its leaf—"densely whitish pubescent," a botanical dictionary describes it—fluttering in the wind that attracted their attention.

The luxurious vitality of the plant did not put off the haiku poets of the Edo Period. Kagami Shikō, for example, named his treatise on poetics of the Bashō School in a way that suggested a pine grove covered with that plant.

The plant puts on reddish purple, butterfly-shaped flowers in the fall. Ishihara Atsushi, the theoretical physicist who studied with Einstein, wrote a tanka describing the sadness he felt looking for those flowers as he took a morning walk "in a faint mist, along a vague trail." He had been forced out of his university as a result of an extramarital affair with a beautiful poet, Hara Misao.

The vines of the plant are so packed with fiber you can make cloth from them, as they do in Kakegawa City, Shizuoka. Its roots are so rich with starch that various cakes are made from them. The hot drink made with it can work against cold, too. And, yes, the plant is among the *aki no nanakusa*, "seven grasses of autumn"—wildflowers selected to represent that season.

By now, you may have guessed which plant I'm talking about. It's *kuzu* or, in its Anglicized spelling, kudzu (*Pueraria lobata*). Yes, that which is the scourge of the American South, the nemesis of the horticulturalists in the ever-widening regions of the United States as the earth warms, something no gardener in her right mind wants to see in her backyard. And all that because the U.S. government once decided to spread the gospel of kudzu, and then changed its mind.

I had such thoughts when the summer issue of *The Nature Conservancy* arrived—along with its New York supplement—blaring "Declaring War on Invasives," with talk of "invaders at the gate" of New York. So, the entity whose aim I had taken to be to "conserve" as much of "nature" from development and other forms of human destruction was also engaged in war—to destroy the plants and animals that are already in this country or fight off those trying to come to it.

I have always thought America's naked hostility toward "alien species" puerile, but I find *The Nature Conservancy*'s talk of war and invasion at this time simply mindless. This country is about to pulverize a country it assaulted without provocation four years ago, even as much condemnation goes around of the people who want or need to come to this country, the so-called nation of immigrants.

So, Scott McMillion, reporting on the "war on weeds" in Hells Canyon, between Oregon and Idaho, gleefully talks about the deployment of poisons and fire, bioweapons, search-and-destroy missions, etc., happily telling us, besides, that the team engaged in it is called SWAT, though in this case it stands for "strategic weed action team," not, thank goodness, "special weapons and tactic." The targeted weed? Yellow star thistles.

The arrival of these thistles on this continent is as old and, shall we say, as innocuous, as that of kudzu. They came to California during the Gold Rush with clover seed or alfalfa imported from Mediterranean countries, McMillion tells us. Kudzu happened to adorn the Japanese pavilion during the 1876 Centennial Exposition in Philadelphia. Unlike kudzu, yellow star thistles were never, apparently, promoted by the U.S. government as beneficial to Americans at any time, but no matter. They both ended up on the government's lists of "noxious and nuisance plants," "invasives," and such.

The New York supplement of *The Nature Conservancy* at least remembers to tell us: "Beginning with the first colonist that set foot in America, human development has drastically changed the plant communities in New York and across the country." That is Eurocentric, but it is a reminder that biospheric change, manmade or otherwise, is nothing new. As far as Homo sapiens goes, you can readily trace it to those people who migrated from Asia to this continent many thousands of years ago. When it comes to the migration of flora and fauna on their own, the transformations have been going on since time immemorial.

What's basically unsettling about this talk of war, threat, invasion, SWAT, and so forth in relation to certain plants and animals (mostly insects, obviously because now no big mammals come here to roam with measurable effects) is the sheer willfulness of it all. One plant the New York supplement calls a "threat" is purple loosestrife, a plant introduced to add "a welcome burst of color" to the garden, then found undesirable. I remember someone saying all the brouhaha about alien species is undemocratic. That branding, too, is apt, especially in the context of the latest vituperation against immigrants.

With kudzu, fortunately, it has not been a story of total betrayal. Some Americans have found uses for the plant other than that of preventing soil erosion, "The Amazing Story of Kudzu" reports. Some make quiche, syrup, and a range of other dishes from it. Some make baskets and paper. Some even raise Angora goats on the plant—reminding us that one of the Chinese names for kudzu is *luhuo*, "deer peas."

Don't Destroy That Invader, It Was Here First!
Asian Carp, Lionfish, Yellow Jacket

March 27, 2011, *Japan Times*

Among the most recent invaders of the United States to be exterminated that I learned about is the red lionfish. Before then the Asian carp got all the attention. About the time the carp scare was quieting down the yellow jacket—yes, the wasp—came forward as a heinous invader to be destroyed.

I thought of these animals when I read T. Coraghessan Boyle's *When the Killing's Done.* The novel fictionalizes the consequences of the National Park Service's decision to exterminate two invasive species on the Channel Islands of California: the black rats and feral pigs.

Actually, the lionfish as an invasive species to be destroyed may not be that new a topic. I first read about it in the *Wall Street Journal* last fall ("The Lionfish Creates an Uproar, Bringing Out the Hunters," November 15, 2010). But NPR had talked about the fish as a marine menace a year earlier, I see now, and lionfish hunting "derbies" had started in 2008.

How is the lionfish an "invader"? Because it's native to the warm waters of the Indo-Pacific seas. But its colorful and fanciful body—the name comes from the mane-like display of its fins—turned it into a popular aquarium item in this country. During the 1992 Hurricane Andrew a Florida aquarium tank broke and some fish escaped into the Atlantic Ocean. A dozen years later it was found to have multiplied in the seas around Florida.

How can a sedate, coast-hugging fish that doesn't grow larger than forty centimeters, according to *National Geographic*, and doesn't form schools as, say, the bluefish does, prompt a call for "extermination"? Because it is "voracious" as it "hoovers up nearly everything in its path," as the *Wall Street Journal*'s video version puts it. But Americans do not call for the extermination of the pelagic bluefish that grow to be eighty centimeters and are so voracious as to devour their own children and kin as they move in great schools at high speed, do they?

The Asian carp dominated the U.S. talk of "invasive" species for months until a Chinese company offered to buy all the catch. The fish, it was said, threatened to destroy the Great Lakes. That outcome, at least for now, was a happy one for me. As I read the news articles on the potentially dire consequences of an inability to kill off Asian carp, I kept wondering: Why not simply catch and eat them? They are big and delicious. Why are Americans so choosey about the kinds of fish they think fit to eat?

In contrast, the authorities began with the fact that the lionfish is edible. Even though the slogan the superintendent of the Florida Keys National Marine Sanctuary devised, "Kill it! Grill it!," is an American-style overkill, I have fondly remembered that a family member of this species, also called the scorpion fish, was prized on a small Nagasaki island where I grew up. Its Japanese relative is called *okoze*, the name coming from a word meaning "sharp pain." The fish has poisonous spines.

So, the lionfish and the Asian carp at least were found to have a saving grace: edibility. No such luck with the yellow jacket discussed here. As its Latin name *Vespula pensylvanica* suggests, it is not an invader from Asia, but from Pennsylvania, and the place where the insect is targeted for annihilation is Hawaii. It obviously has no ameliorating quality, as far as human beings are concerned.

It was, in any case, in disbelief that I watched on one of PBS's *Nature* programs a couple of people in chemical warfare garb running around in a grassy, foliage-covered land to kill masses of yellow jackets (each colony these insects build can house 5,000 workers). The program was "Kilauea: Mountain of Fire: Hawaii's Vulnerable Biodiversity" and it mostly had to do with the impressive volcanic activity, the forces that gave birth to the island cluster that is Hawaii. But what stuck in my mind was the destruction of the insect.

I have long been suspicious of a set of people, whatever expertise theirs may be, deciding a particular species harms humans or the environment and calling for its extermination or "control." With "invasive species," one doesn't need a special insight to see all kinds of fauna or flora have been moving from place to place since time immemorial, with human beings greatly aiding the process since they started walking on this planet.

And non-native species in time become native. In *When the Killing's Done*, T. C. Boyle sets up a scene where the NPS environmental scientist Alma Takesue (yes, her father was a Japanese American) tries to educate people on the need to kill off the black rats on Anacapa with poison to protect the Xantus' murrelet and other species. That's when the animal protection activist Dave LaJoy sardonically asks:

"Those rats have been there for a hundred and fifty years!" The black rats are thought to have started inhabiting the island when a shipwreck occurred in the mid-nineteenth century. The deer mice, on the other hand, are regarded as indigenous to the island. "What's your baseline? A hundred years ago? A thousand? Ten thousand?"

Not that Boyle takes obvious sides. After all, he gives the irascible, unbending LaJoy a fictional divine punishment, as it were. Still, he explains well the absurd complications that arise when you try to tamper with the already tampered environment.

In fact, on the online site for "Kilauea: Mountain of Fire" PBS flatly tells you what is the main destroyer of the "delicate balance" of the most biologically diverse Hawaiian islands: "human colonization." Because of it, intentional and unintentional introduction of new species to Hawaii now occurs "at a rate that is 2 million times more rapid than the natural rate."

Is there any hope or remedy? PBS is neutral or at least seems to counsel against the cry of "Exterminate all the brutes!"

"Every day, as fresh lava spills into the ocean, new land is formed—land that will someday be new habitat for Hawaiian plants and animals, both native and invasive," the PBS site says. "Just as the geography of Hawaii is always changing, so is the shape of life on these islands."

Anthropocentric Bent of "Alien" Fish

Destruction of Ecosystem?

July 28, 2014, *Japan Times*

Are Japanese researchers of fauna and flora becoming more like their U.S. counterparts? They may well be. Some now talk about the environment, ecology, and biodiversity only to disguise their anthropocentric expediency.

This thought occurred to me recently when I was checking a couple of things to revise a translation for publication. One of them had to do with the carp.

At one point in his childhood memoir *The Silver Spoon (Gin no saji),* Naka Kansuke (1885–1965) describes *yoka-yoka-ameya,* "yummy-yummy candy vendors," who went about in couples. With the man-and-woman duo who used to visit his neighborhood around 1890, Naka recollected, the man wore a yukata with the design of a carp leaping up a waterfall splashed across it.

Ah, a carp leaping up a waterfall! The image is a familiar one in Japan. *Koinobori,* the carp-shaped streamers hoisted in the early-May sky, are the most colorful, lively representation of it.

Like many such traditional customs, the idea behind it comes from China—in this instance, from the *History of the Later Han Dynasty* of the fifth century. One episode in it says that every year thousands of fish and turtles gather at the downstream end of the torrents called the Dragon Gate in the Yellow River, but only a few succeed in leaping up them. The Japanese thought those successful ones were carp.

But something is wrong with this, I had long thought. The carp is a sluggish, bottom-feeding fish, isn't it? How can it swim up a violent flow like the salmon?

My vague wonderment continued until another "invasive" species grabbed the headlines several years ago. The Asian carp in the Mississippi River was multiplying so fast that they threatened to take over the Great Lakes, endangering America's, nay, the world's greatest freshwater ecosystem!

What made me pause was not the species "invasion," however. In the United States nowadays, every organism that grows and moves is suspected to be "invasive." Rather, the news came with an arresting bit of information: this sizable fish jumps up into the air as a school, sometimes injuring people on a boat.

So, when the time came to revise *The Silver Spoon* once more, I thought to upgrade the footnote on "a carp leaping up a waterfall" and checked to see what the Japanese Wikipedia entry on the carp has to say. And what I read made me wonder.

As environmental concerns have extended to waterways, the entry says, communities have started stocking "natural" rivers with carps, utterly unaware that could drive to extinction "the endemic species that have developed over tens of thousands of years." Could that be true? Most Japanese rivers are heavily tampered with and seem unlikely to maintain "endemic" species. Am I wrong again?

Not entirely, it seems. The entry mentions, briefly, "the destruction of ecosystem" resulting from "river improvements," and says that's one reason the International Union for Conservation of Nature added the carp to the "vulnerable" list in 2008.

If the concern for endemic species is so great, what about the artificially improved variety known as *nishikigoi*, "brocade carp," that appears to have made the word "koi" part of the English language? The Wikipedia entry sets aside a section for it, listing all the color variations, but the only negative thing it mentions is the "koi herpes virus" that could kill thousands of carp. The koi is important not just for the Japanese market but for foreign markets as well. Hugh Hefner and Larry Ellison, among others, are known to keep them in their gardens.

The entry says the carp is "omnivorous" and eats "aquatic plants, shellfish, earthworms, insects, crustaceans, frogs, and the roe of other fish, and small fish, most anything that can enter its mouth," so it is "an evil eater." By that standard, Homo sapiens is the evilest of them all.

The carp's "greediness," along with its tolerance of low temperature and lack of potential natural enemies when fully grown—again the attributes of the Homo sapiens—led the IUCN to put the fish on its list of "100 of the World's Worst Invasive Alien Species," the entry adds. It does this by way of bringing up the black bass as Japan's top "invasive" species.

And that brings us back to this quintessentially anthropocentric term.

I didn't think it existed a couple of decades ago. Back then, the term was "alien." So I checked. Sure enough, a National Oceanic and Atmospheric Administration site says 1999 Executive Order 13112 defined "invasive" as a category within the "alien" category.

But, be it alien, invasive, exotic, or nuisance—words on the NOAA list—such categorizations strike me as all wrong. Species started propagating the moment they came into being. In the Anthropocene, humans have aided and abetted the process. A great many among the IUCN "worst 100" were and continue to be deliberately introduced or else migrated to non-endemic places because of human movements.

The kudzu, for instance, was brought to the U.S. for the Philadelphia Continental Exposition in 1876 and farmers were paid to plant the vine in the 1930s and 1940s. Its rapid growth in amplitude was regarded as a godsend to stop soil erosion. The Asian carp was introduced to the U.S. in the 1970s "in hope that they would control weed and parasite growth in aquatic farms," as the National Park Service puts it.

Conversely, the black bass was introduced to Japan from the United States in 1925 and it continued to be stocked until the end of the 1980s. It wasn't until 1992 that steps to control it began. Americans, in fact, may be shocked to learn eradication programs are now in place in Japan for one of their favorite species in sport fishing. For that matter, the brown trout and rainbow trout are also in the IUCN list.

Oh yes, the Japanese Wikipedia entry does say that the carp is a bottom dweller who prefers to live in slow-moving waters. But it also says that the smaller ones can jump up as high as two meters.

It goes on to add that the fish doesn't "climb a waterfall." But that may be taking a metaphorical imagining too literally. An unrelated video shows a bunch of carp trying to swim up a spillway.

Don't Exterminate the Zebra Mussels, Ruffes, or Gobies!
The Tragedy of the Common

June 3, 2016, *Japan Times*

One surprise I had during the fracas in the Malheur National Wildlife Refuge in Oregon early this year—a group of armed men led by an anti-government protester took over a federal building—was the existence of a large-scale plan to eliminate carp from Malheur Lake.

The "five-year plan" was set last year, but the effort to get rid of the fish had started earlier. The common carp was introduced to the lake in the 1920s (or in 1951; depends on who's talking) for its food value. Now "millions" of fish abound in the lake 3.4 times larger than Manhattan, so it has been a success.

Then, why eliminate them? Because the carp, an "invasive species," changed the character of the shallow body of water from a lake to a marsh, the elimination advocates argued. But is it that simple? Is the ominous, belligerent term "invasive" right?

A study of some species "invading" areas not of their original growth appears to have been established by Charles Elton's book, *Invasion Ecology*, in 1958. But the term "invasive species" became part of U.S. law with the National Invasive Species Act of 1996 which amended the more benignly named Nonindigenous Aquatic Nuisance Prevention and Control Act of 1990. It specifically listed three small animals, the zebra mussel, the ruffe (a freshwater fish also known as "pope"), and the round goby.

In 1999, President Bill Clinton issued Executive Order 13112 that established the National Invasive Species Council with its members made up of representatives of federal departments and agencies. Still, the council's "invasive species definition clarification and guidance" that came out in 2006 was, in retrospect, rather circumspect, for it said, "many *invasive species* are examples of 'the tragedy of the commons.'"

That "tragedy" is an economic theory proposed by the British writer William Forster Lloyd in 1833. Put it simply, it says "how actions that benefit one individual's use of resources may negatively impact others." In other words, the determination of an "invasive species" is circumstantial.

But the anti-invasive movement that began in the mid-1980s had become, by the mid-1990s, "a growing threat to biodiversity conservation efforts," the California seedsman J. L. Hudson wrote in his online bulletin. Hudson may have a stake in promoting various seeds, but isn't biodiversity indeed one important purpose of nature conservation?

Evidently, *The Nature Conservancy* doesn't think so, judging by its splashy special, "Declaring War on Invasives," some years ago. As I wrote in "Rooting out the Purplish, Yellow Perils" (*The Japan Times*, May 28, 2007), the main enemy of that war, waged with "poisons, fire, bioweapons, search-and-destroy missions, etc.," was, of all things, the "yellow star thistle"! Scott McMillion, who wrote the article, didn't mention it, but this thistle is an important source of pollen and, like so-called "weeds," plays a great role in restoring "abused" land.

In the meantime, animals were not spared, either. In a span of several years around 2010, the yellow jacket, the carp (yes!), and the lionfish, among others, were marked for destruction in this country, as I reported in "Don't destroy that invader, it was here first!" (*The Japan Times*, March 27, 2011).

One of these creatures saw the awesome power of the U.S. government raise its sledgehammer ready to strike: Asian Carp Prevention and Control Act of 2010. Shortly afterward, the "bighead" carp was added to the federal list of "injurious wildlife." The fish can be "harmful to either the health and welfare of humans, interests of forestry, agriculture, or horticulture, or the welfare and survival of wildlife or the resources that wildlife depend upon," it was explained.

The penalty for raising this fish is six months in prison or $5,000.

When something like "anti-invasive mania" occurs, there's usually some profiting body behind it. In the case of the insistence on the sanctity of native species or "natives," it is Monsanto. The seedsman J. L. Hudson had pointed out the giant herbicide manufacturer's influences two decades ago, noting, for example, that it was a sponsor of the 1994 California Exotic Pest Plant Council meeting" and had "an employee on the Council's board of directors."

In "Weed Whackers: Monsanto, Glyphosate, and the War on Invasive Species" (*Harper's,* September 2015), Andrew Cockburn describes Monsanto's insidious and powerful sway on politics in some detail. For example, it pressured the Clinton administration, which, obligingly, overpowered France's objection to the company's GMO corn that is closely related to the most widely used herbicide glyphosate.

In his article Cockburn also mentions two evolutionary biologists, Stephen Jay Gould and Edward O. Wilson. To my surprise, they had opposite views on "invasive species."

Gould, who was proud of his 300 consecutive monthly essays for the monthly *Natural History,* dismissed the arguments for the sanctity of natives as "romantic drivel." Natives are no more than "those organisms that first happened to gain and keep a footing," he wrote, Cockburn says. I had forgotten Gould's point if I'd read it, but I agree with him.

Wilson wrote, with a group of other biology professors, that "a rapidly spreading invasion of exotic plants and animals not only is destroying our nation's biological diversity but is costing the U.S. economy hundreds of millions of dollars annually." That was in a letter to Vice President Al Gore in 1997.

To me, that argument seems to contradict the "island biogeography" for which Wilson is famous. To demonstrate the theory, he once killed off all the animals on a Florida isle with methyl bromide to see how recolonization occurred, an experiment he describes in his *Naturalist* (Shearwater, 1994). Aren't recolonizers tantamount to invasive species?

The nativist argument reminds me of Robert Frost's 1941 poem, "The Gift Outright," that begins: "The land was ours before we were the land's." As Derek Walcott, the Saint Lucian-Trinidadian poet who won the Nobel Prize for *Omeros* (Farrar, Straus & Giroux, 1990), pointed out, this simply ignores the "colonization of Native Americans" and says "nothing about the dispossession of others."

I'd like to see "invasion" and "invasive" dropped and the old earlier biological term "alien" restored. It is not satisfactory, either, but in *A Field Guide to Wildflowers* (Houghton Mifflin, 1968), Roger Tory Peterson and Margaret McKenny defined it as "foreign, but successfully established in our area by man, or as an escape."

Belatedly, I've learned that for some time now there has been a considerable number of people opposing the notion of animals and plants "invading" spheres virgin to them. In The New Wild: Why Invasive Species Will Be Nature's Salvation *(Beacon Press, 2015), for example, Fred Pearce rejects "invasion ecology." Yes, the idea of "pristine ecosystems" may have existed since the beginning of Judaic and Christian traditions ("the Garden of Eden") and, in more recent centuries, people like George Perkins Marsh (1801–82) have been pushing such ecosystems forward as ideal, but it's all wrong, argues Pearce.*

To make his point, the environmental reporter cites a wide range of examples, beginning with Ascension Island. In 1836 Charles Darwin found the mid-ocean land formed by a volcano, long extinct, to be a clump of "naked hideousness," but now it's covered with lush greenery. Why? Because over the past two centuries, human beings have brought a great variety of plants from all over the world, among them Japanese cherry trees!

In fact, with or without human invention, the ideal natural equilibrium such as imagined by some (and an increasing number of) "scientists" may well have been a phantom. Nature has been in perpetual motion since time immemorial. Didn't Lao Tzu say that?

Seagulls
A Poem by Hiroaki Sato

Seagulls, the rare birds
that have bucked the tides
of man's advance
and increased spectacularly
in the past two hundred years,

fly from right to left
like leaflets
dropped into a gentle wind.
There are many of them,
apparently disturbed.

As I turned into 22nd
more of them appear and keep appearing
above the uptown-side rooftops
near Ninth
and cover the whole block,

moving southeast. Evening
clouds, generous melons of summer,
rise to the west.
An airplane enters the scene.
It is the size of a seagull.

III

Teachers and Friends

Lindley Williams Hubbell / Hayashi Shūseki

November 22, 1994, *Japan Times*

In the early 1960s, not long after I became a student at Doshisha University in Kyoto, I began to notice an elderly gentleman in the courtyard of what was then the new building for its English Department. With or without a beret, he would walk in the gate with a slight rightward stoop and in that posture traverse the distance from the gate to the entrance of the building. He was short, and there was mild smile in his large, limpid eyes.

Someone told me he was a scholar of Shakespeare, Professor Hayashi Shūseki. Much later, I learned that he had naturalized only a few years earlier, in 1960. Hayashi Sensei's original name was Lindley Williams Hubbell.

The first course of Hayashi Sensei's that I took, "Writing Poetry in English," turned out to be nothing like any I had taken before or since. When he came back to class with the results of his first assignment, he called each student to his desk. The small envelope he handed over was chosen with evident care, and it had in it the poem the student had composed in the specified form—say, the heroic couplet—and a letter, neatly typed on onion skin, commenting on the poem.

Sensei did the same for each of the seven poems in seven different verse forms he assigned during this yearlong course, selecting an envelope of a different size and shape each time. And each time he said what he had to say gently, limiting, we all felt, to some of the more flagrant grammatical errors or nonidiomatic expressions, which, if changed, might make the poem slightly clearer in meaning. Sensei never showed irritation or condescension.

He was also humble, a great scholar with the readiness to say, "I do not know." One of the poems he read in "Writing Poetry in English" was Ezra Pound's "Hugh Selwyn Mauberley." It is where Greek, Latin, and French pop up and lines such as "Bent resolutely on wringing lilies from the acorn: / Capaneus; trout fir factitious bait" occur. To explicate the poem, Sensei prepared a mimeographed list of translations and allusions, which ran to nearly ten pages. In reading it with us, however, he would say he was unable to find the source of allusion whenever he came to such a spot.

In graduate school I found in the library an anthology of world poetry in which I saw Sensei's translations of Sappho and ancient Egyptian verse. This did not surprise me; by then I had read some of his books in which notes were given in the original Sanskrit, Greek, and so forth. So I plucked up my courage, perhaps in his next seminar, and asked him how many languages he knew. He blushed and said, "Perhaps half the English language."

Lindley Williams Hubbell was born in Hartford, Connecticut, in 1901. As he noted in "Autobiography in Fifty Lines," his "seven times great grandfather" was Thomas Hooker, the founder of the Connecticut Colony and the father of American Congregationalism. He "left Hartford forever on August 20, 1953," he said, "'Vomiting out of the train window,' to quote Stephanie Terenzio." In six weeks he was in Japan. "The Japanese are just as lousy," he said, adding, "But what oh the difference to me."

I do not know when he started it, but every year Mr. Hubbell would send a congratulatory poem to the Emperor on his birthday, such as the one when the Emperor, a marine biologist, turned seventy-seven:

The long grasses of Sagami Bay
Wave slowly in the tide.
The fish dart on their secret errands.
The crabs teeter on spindly legs.

The sea anemones bloom
In the deep gardens of the oceans.

Mr. Hubbell published his first book of poems in 1927. Entitled *Dark Pavilion* and issued as the 23rd volume in the Yale Series of Younger Poets, it is a crystallization of lyricism tinged with gentle irony, as may typically be seen in the first lines of "Warning," a sonnet:

Because I loved the way the candle-light
Caressed your hair while someone played Ravel,
You need not think by that one tender sight
I shall be swept into the usual hell.

This clear-eyed lyricism was to give a light, lilting touch even to his most complex poems, such as "Long Island Triptych," and most erudite prose writings, such as "The Rig Veda and Robert Herrick."

Mr. Hubbell loved Shakespeare, whom he said he read every day. His *Lectures on Shakespeare*, published in 1958, is surely among the most inspired guide to the Bard, and the fourth and final edition of his "Notes on the Shakespeare Apocrypha," published in 1977, lists seventy-five plays attributed to the English poet that "he could not possibly have written."

He was also a dedicated student of nō. By the time he wrote "Autobiography in Fifty Lines" in the late 1960s, he had seen 186 of the 240 plays in the classical repertory, although here his respect was so profound that he wrote only a few short articles and a few simple odes to some actors.

A life-long admirer of Malevich and Mondrian, he was equally devoted to several Japanese popular singers, among them Hashi Yukio and Misora Hibari. He loved a story about the latter: After he became a member of the Misora Hibari fan club, a yakuza would show up whenever he arrived to hear her sing and, calling him Sensei, guide him to a special seat.

In "A Poem About Japan," he wrote:

On Sunday in Kurashiki
walking through busloads of Japanese tourists,
looking at the groups plodding through the museum,
following their guide like cattle,
seeing nothing caring for nothing,
and the high school girls
giggling in front of the El Greco and the Cézannes,
I said to myself:
No country in the world
is as vulgar as Japan.

Then I turned into a side street
and from the second floor of an old house
I heard voices *Hagoromo...*
Azuma Asobi no kazu kazu ni...
and I knew that they were a group of young men
who come there every Sunday to sing yōkyoku
for their pleasure,
and I said to myself:
No country in the world
is as refined as Japan.

After reaching Japan, he did not once go back to his native country. Still, in one of the poems he typed out and enclosed in a letter to me, he wrote:

If I could relive
one musical experience
of my whole life

I would choose the evening
in the late winter
or early spring

of 1919

at the Lexington Opera House
in New York

when I heard
Mary Garden sing
in Pelléas et Mélisande

I was 17
now I am 69
in Kyoto

and Mary Garden
dead at 92
in Aberdeen

that night
still shines
like a star.

Mr. Hubbell died on October 2, in Kyoto, at age ninety-three. Around the time I saw him for the first time, he had written:

Coming home in a taxi
after the day's heat
the cool air poured in the window

and over the city in the west
Venus and the new moon
brighter than I had seen them.

There is no end, I said,
of love and beauty
and fulfillment,

and my dust
will be part of Japan
forever.

Eleanor Wolff
How I Came to "Teach" Haiku in Manhattan

What follows is my tribute to Eleanor Wolff (1907–95) when her niece Priscilla Meyer, professor of Russian literature at Wesleyan College, held a memorial service for her at The Stanhope Apartment Hotel on Fifth Avenue, on December 9, 1995.

Eleanor Wolff was my personal teacher of English and editor of my translations and writings. Had I not become acquainted with her, it is doubtful that I would have ever started publishing books.

It was during the winter of 1969 or 1970 that I was introduced to Eleanor and her friend Carmel Wilson. They were looking for someone with whom to work on Japanese haiku. As a graduate student in Japan a few years earlier, I had majored in English literature, and my knowledge of haiku certainly was no greater than that of any man on the street. But I was young and brash then, and agreed to take on the weekly tutoring work.

Memory, however, often plays self-serving tricks. A dozen years later when I set out to write a book on English haiku in Japanese and naturally decided to include Eleanor, I gave her this account of the way we had met. Thereupon, she corrected me. She and Carmel were looking for someone who could work on tanka, a very different genre of poetry. According to Eleanor, I told her and Carmel that I knew practically nothing about tanka, but I might be able to do something with haiku.

Eleanor and Carmel had taken Harold Isaacson's course on haiku at the New School. Prof. Isaacson evidently had strong views on haiku, and Eleanor and Carmel—but especially Eleanor—must have had deep misgivings about turning to an obvious amateur like me not long after receiving Isaacson's observations, which were dogmatic but which Eleanor found persuasive. They took me on nonetheless. Their decision would prove exceptionally fortunate for me.

On the face of it, I was to select a few haiku every week and provide word-for-word interpretations, along with their backgrounds, so that Eleanor and Carmel might work out their own translations. But this exercise was always followed by dinner and I soon learned to wine and dine like an American. Both Eleanor and Carmel also threw a string of dinner parties where I was introduced to the kinds of people I would never have met otherwise.

Also, Eleanor soon began to look over my translations. She was a considerate and scrupulous editor. Considerate because she would do her best to honor my translations and, later, writings—staying close to the way I had chosen words and cast them. She would never automatically rewrite them as many editors are prone to do. As for her scrupulous approach, I remember her once taking out a map of England and spending a couple of hours to learn whether or not a place the poet I translated mentioned was a village as the poet said it was. She had remembered it as a town.

One day Eleanor showed me the notice of a new literary magazine, *Granite*, inviting submissions. It was started by one George Young, who taught Russian at Dartmouth, and Priscilla had forwarded the notice to her. A few weeks after mailing my translations, I received a long letter from Mr. Young saying he had not known such a wide range of poems were written in Japanese and that he would accept a large number of them. That was the way my translations began to see print.

Thank you, Priscilla.

Eleanor generously continued to read my manuscripts until a few years ago, returning each with a stack of pages in which she, in her elegant handwriting, wrote out her comments or typed them. The last one she read for me was a 600-page manuscript, which came out finally a few weeks ago, in November, under the title of *Legends of the Samurai*. I am sorry I was not able to show the book to her.

I am even more sorry that she cannot see my next book, which I have dedicated to her. It is a translation of *Oku no hosomichi,* the famous travel diary by the haiku master Bashō; Stone Bridge Press published it as *Bashō's Narrow Road: Spring and Autumn Passages*. I came to know Eleanor by way of haiku and she became my teacher through haiku. The travel account ends with a haiku:

Hamaguri no
   futami ni
      wakare yuku aki zo

A clam
   separates lid
      from flesh as autumn departs

I wish to conclude by citing two haiku Eleanor wrote herself. The first one she composed, she said, when she had surgery in the eighties.

Two dark rivers
of my city soon under
the autumn moon

Eleanor said she meant this as her farewell-to-this-world haiku.

The other one she wrote for my book, *One Hundred Frogs* (Weatherhill, 1983), a history of haiku which started out as a compilation of English translations of the most famous haiku of all time:

Furuike ya kawazu tobikomu mizu no oto

Eleanor's haiku was a tribute to the more than 140 English translations that I assembled of the ephemeral poem describing a frog leaping into an old pond.

Voices of frogs
As if to accompany
All those stars

Thank you.

Eleanor Wolff published a book of poems, Spaces, *in 1972, and edited her Russian-born art historian friend Léo Bronstein's* Romantic Homage to Greece and Spain, *in 1993.*

Ronald Homer Bayes
On the Movie *Mishima*

March 3 and 24, 1986, *Mainichi Daily News*

I've known Ron Bayes, a poet who teaches English at St. Andrews Presbyterian College, in Laurinburg, North Carolina, since he asked me to translate Mishima Yukio's play My Friend Hitler *(Waga tomo Hittorā) for his magazine,* St. Andrews Review, *in 1980. This spring he was in town when Paul Schrader's film* Mishima: A Life in Four Chapters *was being shown, so when he saw the movie I had a chat with him.*

"Eroticism and Sacrifice"

SATO: What was your impression of *Mishima*?

BAYES: *The Village Voice* compared it unfavorably to the Ōshima movie *Merry Christmas, Mr. Lawrence,* as far as capturing the feeling of the time and the Japanese pride and frustration at the war's end. I thought that was a valid point. Still, I want to have a little time to reflect on it because I didn't know quite what to expect from what I've read in reviews. I've never seen Ogata Ken in a movie before and I wasn't sure how much he looked like Mishima. It affected me more than I had expected it to, having known Mishima briefly. But I've never seen anything about *Kyoko's House,* which I don't think has been translated into English. It takes up one-fourth of the movie, and its pain-and-pleasure theme reminded me a little bit of another movie by Ōshima, *In the Realm of the Senses.*

SATO: Poet Takahashi Mutsuo saw it here and said that Mishima's fictional world was intended to be *artificial,* and that the movie was successful in presenting that artificiality. What do you think of that?

BAYES: I was very shocked and surprised when right after the *seppuku* I read Donald Richie's column in the *Japan Times* where he referred to it as a "coup de theatre" ultimately, rather than a major, passionate statement. I had a hard time with that because I didn't sense a great deal of artificiality with Mishima. Very unscientifically, I go by a person's laugh among other things; I was very impressed with the depth and sincerity of his laugh.

SATO: Takahashi was a good friend of Mishima's in the last six years of the latter's life, and evidently Mishima was a very considerate fellow. But Takahashi thinks that Mishima's fictional world, or whatever he did, existed only on the strength of his personality. As soon as he died, the whole thing collapsed.

BAYES: That's fascinating. It's an unlikely comparison perhaps, but Mishima's work reminds me of T.S. Eliot's in that I can take his work apart and put it back together and it seems stronger every time. With many writers, if I take the work apart, it's like if I took a watch apart and put it back together, it would never work for me again. I am particularly thinking of the *Sea of Fertility, Death in Midsummer,* and *Five Modern Noh Plays.*

SATO: Vincent Canby, of the *New York Times,* gave a rather long review of the movie and said something like, "This is all very well done, but I still don't understand all the fuss about Mishima."

BAYES: Mishima was one of the last idealists. There was a part of him that I didn't understand, but then I read a review in which Paul Schrader was quoted at length, talking about his Calvinist repression or semi-repression and the ability to identify with Mishima's being thwarted from early childhood by the strictures of Grandma. I grew up as a Calvinist kid. And what Schrader said put me on a different track of self-investigation. Mishima may be such a smash in America, because there are so many people who come out of secondary, if not primary, Calvinist families and perhaps identify with him on a very deep level there.

SATO: What do you mean by Calvinist in this context?

BAYES: I guess suspicion of the senses; if anything is sensually pleasurable, there must be something wrong or evil lurking behind it. It heightens the fantasy world of such things, because of the damming up of the natural curiosity, instead of the playing out of the natural curiosity in childhood, let's say.

SATO: Did that shape the later life of Mishima?

BAYES: Yes. Robert Frost, whom I don't very often quote, said that every single human being has one metaphor in him or her and how it takes one whole life to spin out that metaphor. But actually we are just continuing to expand on the metaphor which is essentially ourselves. I think early childhood effects every artist. Even if overcoming it is part of it, still there is that obstacle to be overcome.

"A Surge toward Paradise"

SATO: Would you explain more about being an idealist and a Calvinist?

BAYES: Playing amateur psychologist again, I would suppose that out of the repression and in spite of the fantasies, the Calvinist figure might strive mightily to do something to turn society toward a purity it doesn't have, maybe sacrificing himself in the attempt. Something like that. You have perhaps the emergence of the pleasure and pain principle, the erotic fantasies on one hand, and on the other the idea of sacrificing oneself for the pure cause or the pure nation. I think the film did an awfully good job in one section where it pointed out that he was against the left wing and, as well, against the right wing. So many people were so quick to say he was a right-wing fanatic. But I never believed that.

SATO: Taylor Gregg, Asia area specialist for *National Geographic*, reviewed the film for the *Washington Post* and said, "The real danger in

Mishima . . . is that it offers Americans an opportunity to misunderstand Japan on an even grander scale than was heretofore imaginable." Do you agree?

BAYES: If that's the case, you've got a paradox: most of the Americans who met Mishima that I've heard of and the few that I've met always felt that he understood America and he understood better than any Japanese writer and conversely they felt a sense of empathy and understanding with him more than any other Japanese writer.

SATO: Gregg takes a historical view and says Mishima's life was an extreme manifestation of the Japanese-American confrontation that has existed since Commodore Perry went to Japan in 1853. He says there was an idealist position that regarded Japan's opening its door to the West as a spiritual failure, and that's the sense Mishima had. He took his own life to show that, Gregg says.

BAYES: I've seen people make reference to it, but not in depth, or people comparing him to, in his last years, Tanizaki [Jun'ichirō's] going back to the old ways, renouncing the western ways that he embraced as a young man. I've never felt comfortable with that.

SATO: Gregg ends by quoting the dictum, "To know and not to act is not to know." This is Wang Yangming philosophy.

BAYES: It is really hard to put together for a non-Japanese, but we have the saying, "Put your money where your mouth is." That comes out of both cultures, I suspect: if you mean it, prove it. It's exciting, awe-inspiring, like the suicide by the Jews at Masada. Outside of the ritual of *seppuku,* the very idea of "I meant it and I'll prove it by dying for it" may be universal.

SATO: How did you meet Mishima?

BAYES: When I was in Okinawa, some boys stoned an old farmer to death on New Year's Day. He had been an old drunkard and had threatened them if he caught one of them alone he would do them physical harm. So they were meaning to discuss what to do about that on the New Year when the old farmer came staggering home from a neighbor's. They adjourned their committee with amazing objectivity and stoned him to death. Well, I read this article and it was so amazingly close to his *Sailor Who Fell From Grace with the Sea* that I clipped the article and sent it to him. He responded by return mail quoting Oscar Wilde: "Often the fiction precedes the fact." That is how we met.

It struck me later that his own suicide was so much like Steiner's in *La Dolce Vita*. If you remember, the wife comes home to find the apartment surrounded by reporters. It is the reverse situation, Steiner is the intellectual, a lovely human being who for unknown reasons commits suicide after murdering his two children. It is just a horrible scene. I couldn't help but think of that when I heard of Mishima's having his wife pack the kids off to school; apparently it came as a similar shock to her. I know he was a fan of Fellini's. Thinking back to his "Sometimes fiction precedes the fact" it is a little on the bizarre side. The idea of being in somebody's shoes like that is scary.

SATO: How about the persistent view that *The Temple of the Golden Pavilion* is too contrived to make a good novel?

BAYES: I agree to that. I think some people told him that this was his masterpiece and you still hear that quite a bit. On one of the few occasions we had dinner, he asked me what I thought of it and I sinned bravely and was honest and said that it moved rather slowly and seemed somewhat contrived and I wasn't sure if it was the novel, the translation, or the lady's introduction. That introduction was a bit tedious, I thought. I think one of the ones that pushed him toward the Nobel was *After the Banquet*. I think that's a very delicate, lovely, light-handed touch—the opposite of heavy-handed—perceptive.

SATO: What did you think of his political stance?

BAYES: It reminded me of the fact that in the West people like Ezra Pound, T. S. Eliot, and W. B. Yeats all had their flirtation with fascism when they became disillusioned, but again, they would be the first to say that Hitler was an absolute crumb and swine. Still there was the attraction of the "purism" of fascism.

Eliot's flirtation, however brief, resolved itself into turning almost totally to the church in the conviction that nothing on earth would ever really rectify itself and there is nothing rectifiable this side of heaven. Of the three poets, in fact, Eliot is apparently the only one who totally resolved it to his own satisfaction at least. Pound paid his dues of suffering in the long haul instead of a short dramatic surge like Mishima. There is a lot in common, looking for the paradise on earth and trying to find the means to it.

Ronald Homer Bayes, born on July 19, 1932 in Milton-Freewater, Oregon, joined the faculty of St. Andrews Presbyterian College in 1968. He invited me to the Poetry Forum that he set up there, every year, from 1980 until he retired in 2008. He died on December 11, 2021.

Michael O'Brien

"Elation of the Original"

November 3, 1986, *Mainichi Daily News*

Michael O'Brien became my friend in 1970 when he began helping me to put my English translations of Japanese poems into shape. Whenever I had a bunch of translations ready, I would go uptown and walk up five floors to get to his apartment on 123rd Street and go over them with him.

Two things about him soon struck me. First, he had a delightful way of illustrating his felicitous comments with quirky line drawings. In time it became our joke that the manuscripts we worked on ought to be part of some university archives. Second, he was modest; through all the evenings he spent with me, he never once imposed upon me his choice of words, phrases, his will. The fruit of these jolly evenings was Spring & Asura: Poems of Kenji Miyazawa *(Chicago Review Press, 1973).*

Michael has recently published two books of his own imprint, Cairn Editions: Veil, Hard Rain, *a book of poems, and* The Ruin, *a selection of translations. So I asked him a couple of questions.*

SATO: As you may recall, Miyazawa published his book of poems at his own expense. There are quite a number of poets who take the same route. But in your case, it's somewhat puzzling. You have been published by regular presses and your poems have appeared in magazines. What prompted you to take this step?

O'BRIEN: Miyazawa published *Spring & Asura* himself, that's such a

175

disgrace! There are two lists you can keep: one of the great poets who published their own work—Rimbaud is another—and one of the perfectly awful poets who did so.

Obviously the second list is much longer than the first, and one does not want to be on it. Though what is one to do: be silent out of caution? I published *Veil, Hard Rain* and *The Ruin* myself because none of the presses I submitted them to would publish them, and because I was tired of being refused and behaving well. It seemed to me this was something I could take care of myself—it's not hard to do, the knowledge is not arcane, it didn't even cost that much, I had a steady job. I was tired of fidgeting with the manuscripts, sandpapering my ass. I wanted to be done with them so I could get on with something else. I know poets who can simply put a manuscript away, but I can't. I fret, I make little changes. You can wear yourself out with perturbations invisible to the naked eye. I knew who I wanted to get the book into the hands of, and I knew I could take care of it myself.

SATO: You spend long hours translating poems. What does translating poems mean to you?

O'BRIEN: Translation is like hoping for a miracle: most likely one won't occur, but it's hard to proceed if you rule it out. I made my first translations as a desperate schoolboy trying to keep a line or two of Virgil ahead of someone who could make my ignorance of those lines seem very humiliating indeed. How little we would know without translations, though what we know by means of them is a deceptive kind of knowing. There's a humbling difference between getting into the habit of watching French movies with subtitles—the illusion of fluent comprehension that affords—and bumping into someone speaking French to you. "A Translation," a prose piece in *The Ruin,* addresses itself to this difference.

Poets are often predatory in their relations to other poets, and translation is one of the forms this takes. We all know instances of expropriation, aggrandizement of the ego. I mean, it's tempting to pretend you wrote the *Duino Elegies,* which are probably immeasurably better than whatever piece of your own you happen to be working on. Immeasurably.

Translations can convey other things than information about their originals. Part of what's attractive about Rexroth's translations, for instance, is the quality of his own passionate curiosity that they convey. And it's a way of remembering that something happened before you were born. There's much to be said for living the life of one's time. But translation reminds you that there were other ties, which resist being brought up to date. The *resistance* of a poem to being translated is one of the most attractive things about the endeavor. For it's not a resistance you can overcome: the poem eludes your will. The words remain themselves. The past is more foolproof than the present, and harder to trash. You can ignore it, but it's not malleable. I was very struck when I first went to the south of France by the surviving Roman inscriptions—not by what they said but by the fact of them, the nature of the carving.

SATO: In translating poems, there's one question I constantly ask: what is one to do with phrases that are awkward in the original? An American translator of German poetry once praised your translations as "perfect." What do you think of this schism between faithfulness and readability?

O'BRIEN: Phrases that are awkward in the original have never been my problem. Sometimes an awkward *translation* is useful, as an enticement: behind someone's clumsy English you sense something much greater, and decide to go look for it.

Translation doesn't lend itself to perfection. Keeping the elation of the original, as in Olson's lovely "Variations Done for Gerald Van De Wiele": for *that* to come across, that's the thing.

Other than those two self-published chapbooks, Michael's books of poems after that came out of regular presses, and Sleeping and Waking *(Flood Editions, Chicago, 2007) became a finalist for the National Book Critics award that year. It was that book that the poet-lawyer David Orr selected to discuss for "On Poetry," his one-page column for the* New York Times Book Review, *on December 9, 2007. Orr quoted from three "one-liners" from "Another Autumn" but did not mention this, so I should point out that these twenty-two monolinears are in fact seventeen-syllable haiku. The first one reads:*

slenderest of new moons, surfer's sail transparent as an insect's wing

Speaking of one-liners, the first book of his Michael gave me was Conversations at the West End, *and it contained this unforgettable line:*

I think I'll go home and date all my poems.

Michael was born in Granville, New York, 1939, and died in Manhattan, in 2016.

Herbert Passin
Modesty Marked This Great Man of Letters

March 31, 2003, *Japan Times*

Herbert Passin, whom I had the honor of knowing, died on February 26. Like Faubion Bowers, whom I also knew, he was a top graduate of the Military Intelligence Service Language School that was established in 1941 in preparation for the coming war with Japan. Both did wonderful things under Supreme Commander for the Allied Powers Gen. Douglas MacArthur and went on to do more. Both were decorated by the Japanese government. But they were so self-effacing that you wouldn't have had an inkling of such things in their presence.

My first encounter with Herb was startlingly memorable, however. (After thirty-five years in the United States, I remain a quintessential Japanese in certain matters of social protocol. I feel discomfited referring to a much older man of such illustrious accomplishment by his first name, let alone an abbreviated one. But "Herb" is the name he used with me.)

Sometime in the late 1970s a very unassuming gentleman appeared in the library of the trade agency where I work. After examining statistical and other books, he wondered if I could get some information from Tokyo, especially from a professor friend of his. He was giving a talk to the Tanners Association the following week, in Florida, and he needed certain information on Japan's "untouchables." His Japanese professor friend was the greatest authority on the matter.

At the time, one big trade "friction" between Japan and the United States was the fact that Japan imported quantities of leather from the

179

United States but few leather products, exporting shoes and handbags instead. If an American could clarify the whys and wherefores of that lopsided situation to an important American trade group, that would be more than a Japanese trade agency could hope for. So I was more than happy to oblige. I asked him to leave his name and address so I might get in touch with him as soon as I had responses to his list of questions. His name was Herbert Passin, and he was a professor at Columbia University.

The moment I reported to work the next morning I was summoned to the executive officer's room and grilled. Our Tokyo headquarters was in an uproar. Why had I sent a message without clearing it with him? Sir, you were away on a business trip. Well, then, why did I use a term that didn't exist? I was stumped. A term that didn't exist? In any case, said the executive officer, the designated authority on the question disavowed any knowledge of the matter.

The mistake lay entirely in my inept and impolitic approach. I should have submitted the Columbia professor's inquiry, itself a supremely legitimate one, through an unofficial route.

Some years later I became friends with the trade consultant Scott Latham. As someone in the business of consultancy, he soon proved unusual. He refused to submit himself to the usual practice of creating a "them against us" dichotomy. For example, he took exception to characterizing the Japanese as "conformists."

One sticking point with Scott in that regard was the oft-quoted (and, I might add, mostly misunderstood) proverb, "The nail that sticks up gets hammered down." If you are to cite it as indicative of the conformist society that is supposed to be Japan, Scott pointed out, how about expressions such as "Keep your head down," "Cover your ass," and "Don't make waves" in America? Are they indicative of Americans' vaunted individualism, rugged or otherwise?

I admired Scott for his stance. I had long harbored doubts about facile differentiations of societies and peoples, but in trade disputes people willfully resort to them. The reason is simple. It's easier to accuse someone of doing certain things if you ignore you do the same things. Scott refused that easy recourse.

So I wasn't surprised when Scott told me Herb was his stepfather. As he later wrote in a magazine, since he was a young man, he'd been meeting and talking to Japanese academics, politicians, businessmen, and artists who came to visit the great sociologist and international counselor. Scott may not have learned the error of social and cultural stereotyping entirely from Herb, but I'd venture Herb's genial, knowledgeable presence helped.

As he recounts in his short autobiography, *Encounter with Japan* (Kodansha, 1982), even before going to the military language school, Herb had had firsthand experience with "the prejudice of minority groups toward each other." Working for the War Relocation Authority in Detroit, a city in great racial and ethnic turmoil in 1943, he saw black and Polish workers turning their anger toward re-relocated Japanese Americans, who, in turn, expressed contempt for "dirty Jews." Herb was a son of Ukrainian Jewish immigrants, and his job was to find employment for those Japanese Americans let out of the relocation camps in the West.

Assigned to Fukuoka after the war ended, Herb witnessed another type of racial strife. Fukuoka was an important port for Japanese repatriates from former colonies and battlegrounds. At the same time it became an important departure point for the majority of Koreans brought to Japan for forced labor during the war, now returning to their homeland. Gangs of Koreans and Japanese pitched against each other. Fukuoka also had a sizable concentration of the U.S. military, and the segregated black soldiers' anger against their white counterparts was always ready to erupt, and often did.

Among the MISLS graduates, Faubion Bowers received "the most glamorous assignment," as Herb put it: Gen. MacArthur's personal interpreter and aide-de-camp. Bowers then did something unusual. He resigned the military commission as major to take on the theater censor's job to de-censor kabuki. Later he was called its "savior."

Herb's assignment after Fukuoka, at the Tokyo GHQ, wasn't that glamorous, but it was a dream come true. He headed SCAP's Public Opinion and Sociological Research Division, the sociological research part of it added at his own suggestion. Before the war with Japan started, he, a fledgling anthropologist, had done a year's field work with the Tarahumara Indian tribe in Mexico.

"In my wildest dreams, I could never have concocted a better job for myself at that particular stage of my life," he wrote. He was thirty years old. His career as a great sociologist lay ahead.

One of the books Herbert Passin wrote as a sociologist was Society and Education in Japan (*The Teachers College Press, Columbia University, 1965), later reprinted by Kodansha International.*

Earl Miner
Japanese Poetry Loses a Gentleman-Scholar

June 28, 2004, *Japan Times*

Princeton professor Earl Miner, who died on April 17, at age seventy-seven, was the one gentleman-scholar I had the honor of knowing. No, I wasn't his student in the usual sense, though I'd have loved to be. He is reputed to have considered every student part of his extended family. I met him only twice, in 1979 and 1994. But between the two meetings he amply proved his courteous self.

In 1979, the year I became president of the Haiku Society of America, I invited Professor Miner to speak to the group's annual meeting. (For the rest I'll call him "Earl" as he always so signed in our correspondence.) My heading the HSA, as the society is affectionately known by its members, had come about in an unexpected way. A few years earlier, when asked to discuss haiku as a translator of modern Japanese poetry at one of its meetings, I had given a somewhat unflattering assessment of the poetic form: it is too short to make it as a poem on its own, its origins suggest it requires a larger context, and so forth. An English major a dozen years earlier, I did not have a high regard for this itty-bitty thing. Not a propitious way of assuring presidency of an organization specializing in the genre!

Not long after I became president, however, Earl's book *Japanese Linked Poetry: An Account with Translations of Renga and Haikai Sequences* (Princeton University Press, 1979) was published. Though before then there certainly were some attempts to explain *renga*, "linked poetry," it was the first book to take this sequential form head on, on

183

its own ground. The earlier efforts, in fact, were either dismissive or wrong-headed.

The redoubtable English student of things Japanese Basil Hall Chamberlain (1850–1935) had observed that the rules of *renga* are at once so complicated and trivial as to be "puerile." Octavio Paz and three European poets simply took the notion of linking poems to produce *Renga, A Chain of Poems* (Braziller, 1971). The form, in any event, was one from which haiku was born. So here was the chance for HSA members to learn the historical background or "the larger context," if you will, of their beloved form, in a most authentic way.

Actually, inviting Earl required a good deal of temerity. Princeton University was an august institution of higher learning. HSA at the time was a puny body, its membership fluctuating at around 150. I can't even remember whether we were able to scrounge up an honorarium—enough money for him to travel from Princeton to New York. But he kindly accepted the invitation and came with his wife, Virginia, whom he called Jinko. I remember him saying that she grew up in Japan as a missionary's daughter and spoke Japanese far better than he. One good thing was that the Japan Society, New York at the time was generous and allowed us to use their rooms, as well as their address. Earl spoke in its auditorium.

For many years afterward all I remembered from his talk was his encounter with haiku: a Japanese steel executive inviting him to dinner and, over sukiyaki, telling him about the mystery of a small poem about an old pond and a frog. In fact, his was a full-length presentation, titled "Japanese Linked Poetry, Its Rules and Freedom." Cor van den Heuvel, the author of *The Haiku Anthology* (Anchor Books, 1974) and my predecessor as HSA president, found his talk printed in *Frogpond*, the HSA magazine, and made a copy for me.

As he said in the talk (and I had forgotten it), the encounter occurred in 1947, when he was "at the redoubtable age of twenty" and "a civilian in military government in Nagoya." I wish I had asked him what his function was, though the Princeton online bulletin made upon his death suggests he was at the time a student of Japanese at the University of Minnesota. After earning a BA in Japanese, he went on to earn an MA and Ph.D. in English, famously enabling him to span two distinctive literary fields.

The Journal of the Association of Teachers of Japanese then asked me to review *Japanese Linked Poetry*—or I was perhaps brash enough to propose the idea to its editor. Whichever the case, by then I must have been wearied of one-sided "reviews," especially of the academic variety: I proposed to do it in Q&A format. The editor, then Earl, agreed.

For a long time again, all I had remembered from that Q&A was Earl's expression "a bee in your bonnet"—until Amy Heinrich, director of the East Asian Library of Columbia University, kindly and promptly acquired a copy of it for me. Then I realized that my "questions" had been, shame on me, a series of grudges and complaints. To all that, though, Earl was courtesy incarnate.

The "bee" flew in only when I remonstrated, "Both the tanka and haiku are regarded as one-line poems in Japan. Then why translate them as five and three lines?" Earl's advice: Go right ahead whatever you want to do, but make sure to buy a bottle of skin thickener. He might as well have recommended a bottle of anti-brain-addler. The bee has since so addled my brain that academics have seized every occasion to gleefully point out my brain damage. But not Earl.

In the late 1980s I received a letter from an editor of *The Princeton Encyclopedia of Poetry and Poetics*—Alex Preminger. He and his coeditors were updating the tome, the first edition published in 1965, and Earl recommended me to rewrite his entry on haiku. Earl had taken a classic classicist position: "haiku is too reduced a form and grows too complexly out of its cultural background to be adaptable as a whole into Western languages" and actual haiku written in non-Japanese languages are "almost invariably . . . trivial."

In 1994, I received a letter from the Japanese Consul General in New York: Professor Earl Miner, being decorated with the Order of the Rising Sun, asked me to attend the ceremony. I was honored to do so, and I did, doing my sartorial best. He looked frail.

Earl Miner had a simple aim in discussing and interpreting

literature, beginning with his monumental work with Robert Brower, *Japanese Court Poetry* (Stanford University Press, 1960): Try to understand what the original poet was trying to do. He liked to remind me how his work affected this or that person, even while telling me about those who objected to his approach.

Here I am happy to report that Michael O'Brien and Maureen Owen, among my poet friends, have been following his approach to *renga*: to repeat each stanza to move the "disjunctive" narrative forward.

Robert Anthony Fagan

The following are my remarks at the memorial service at St. Marks Church, New York, on December 17, 2009.

Of all the people assembled here today, I am probably the most indebted to Robert Anthony Fagan in the matter of writing in general and translating in particular. In writing, Robert told me, among other things, that I should try not to write sentences that go beyond fifteen words because not many people can. (The preceding sentence contains twenty-six words.)

In translation, Robert was the reader, corrector, and editor of my translations for almost forty years. In any literary annals, this must be among the longest periods of time one person helped another. As long as I live, I will remain grateful to him for his generosity and tolerance.

Here, I wish also to thank Michael O'Brien. After working for months on my miserable and worthless translations of Miyazawa Kenji's poems, spanking them into shape, Michael introduced me to Robert. That was in 1971 or so. Considering what happened for the next four decades, Michael's choice of Robert was most inspired.

One indelible memory I have of Robert Fagan in our early days was the way he made steaks. As soon we finished working on the batch of translations I had prepared for the evening—in his studio in Washington Square Village—he would go to the kitchen, take out a large, black frying pan encrusted with years of grime (he kept the act of washing pans and dishes to the bare minimum). He would then make us two steaks of gigantic proportions, which made me of think of a hippo's straw sandals—assuming hippos have ever worn sandals, of straw or anything else. I loved those steaks and looked forward to them. Lately, I am amazed to remember how both Robert and I would devour those huge chunks of meat, without leaving a scrap of anything. Time flies.

Robert accepted literary ideas as they came. So he accepted without demurral the point that most Japanese haiku and tanka writers regard what they write as one-line poems and that, accordingly and therefore, I translate them in one line. The result has won only disbelief, derision, and dismissal among academics, prompting some to go miles to denounce me.

Luckily, the world of literature does not consist only of academics, and practicing poets are unlike academics. Among the poets who have accepted the one-line idea of haiku, I am happy to say, is Michael O'Brien.

Robert readily, easily, accepted any poet I chose to translate. One poet some other editor-helpers might have shied away from is Yoshioka Minoru (1919–90), an addict of striptease and a great admirer-friend of Hijikata Tatsumi, the leader of Butoh, or *Ankoku butō*, "Dark Dance."

Many of Yoshioka's poems are hard to translate, especially after you learn that each line is written to make sense with the preceding and following lines. I'd like to read one of his poems that I worked out with Robert so many years ago.

Still Life

Within the hard surface of night's bowl
Intensifying their bright colors
The autumn fruits
Apples, pears, grapes, and so forth
Each as they pile
Upon another
Goes close to sleep

To one theme
To spacious music
Each core, reaching its own heart
Reposes
Around it circles
The time of rich putrefaction
Now before the teeth of the dead
The fruits and their kind
Which unlike stones do not strike
Add to their weight
And in the deep bowl
Behind this semblance of night
On occasion
Hugely tilt

Thank you.

Kyoko Iriye Selden

January 25, 2013, *Japan Times*

Kyoko Iriye Selden, a scholar and teacher at Cornell University much admired and beloved by her colleagues and students, died in Ithaca, NY, on January 20, 2013. She was seventy-six. The cause of her death was pneumonia.

Born on October 2, 1936, in Tokyo, Iriye graduated from the English Department of the University of Tokyo with top honors, in 1959. She then went to Yale University on a Fulbright scholarship. Among her teachers there was Cleanth Brooks, the proponent of the New Criticism. There she met Mark Selden, the future Marxist historian and sociologist.

She earned a Ph.D. on the Elizabethan text *Gismond of Salerne* (1965). Her studies in English literature bore fruit in her close annotation and explication for Japanese readers of Thomas Kyd's play *The Spanish Tragedy* (1972).

She became an able translator of Japanese literature into English while translating English into Japanese. Among her first English translations was *Japanese Women Writers: Twentieth Century Short Stories* (1982), which was followed most recently by *More Stories by Japanese Women Writers* (2010). Among the books she translated into Japanese was Liza Dalby's *Geisha* (1983).

Her most recent translation into English was one of the books by the Chinese scholar teaching in Japan Cho Kyo (Zhang Jing), *The Search for the Beautiful Woman: A Cultural History of Japanese and Chinese Beauty* (2012). With extensive references to classical Japanese and

Chinese literature, it was the kind of book only someone like Iriye, who was versed in both fields, could manage. She also translated into Japanese the posthumously found English autobiography of Inukai Kyōhei (1886–1954), the Japanese painter who won fame for his society portraits in the United States.

She taught at Dean Junior College, Taipei (National Taiwan) Normal University, Tsuda College, and Washington University, before she reached Cornell University in 1987. As a senior lecturer at Cornell, she taught classical and modern Japanese literature, classical Chinese, and reading of handwritten classical texts. She won a distinguished teaching award in 1993.

An accomplished calligrapher who played the piano, alto recorder, transverse flute, and shakuhachi—for a while a translator of Japanese articles for *Talent Education Journal*, the magazine for the International Suzuki Association—she regularly entertained students, scholars, and artists, with her husband, Mark. Her students often honored her as their favorite teacher.

Daughter of the journalist and later professor of international law Iriye Keishirō, she is survived by Mark, editor of the online magazine *The Asia-Pacific Journal: Japan Focus*; daughters, Lili and Yumi, both translators; son, Ken, orchestra conductor; and her brother, Iriye Akira, Harvard historian for many years.

I met Kyoko in early 1976 when Professor J. Thomas Rimer invited me to take part in a small conference on modern Japanese poetry at Washington University. For nearly forty years following that, she helped and enlightened me in classical Japanese literature with her easy erudition.

The special 2015 issue of Josai University's Review of Japanese Culture and Society *is dedicated to Kyoko's unpublished translations and her essay, "A Childhood Memoir of Wartime Japan."*

Burton Watson

May 27, 2017, *Japan Times*

Burton Watson, the foremost translator of classical Chinese prose and poetry into English and my co-translator of the anthology of Japanese poetry *From the Country of Eight Islands* (Anchor Books & University of Washington Press, 1981), died on the first of April, in a hospital in Chiba. He was ninety-one years old.

I knew Mr. Watson since the early 1970s, so for the rest, allow me to call him Burt.

I came to know Burt because the publisher of my book *Spring & Asura: Poems of Kenji Miyazawa* turned to him for an introduction. Andrea Miller, of the Asia Society of New York, had sent a batch of my translations of modern Japanese poetry to *Chicago Review*, and its student editor and poetry editor, Alexander Besher and Curt Matthews, decided to devote one issue to my translations. Then, they started a publishing house, calling it Chicago Review Press, with the idea of doing a series of Japanese poets in my translation. *Spring & Asura* was the first.

The evening Burt invited me to his apartment to go over my translations remains vivid. Before we started work on the list he'd made on a yellow pad, he offered beer. Thereafter, every time we finished our cans, he'd ask, with a twinkle in his eyes, "Another?" And each time I nodded, he would unfold his long legs to get up from the low table and fetch two cans of beer from a refrigerator at the other end of a spacious, bare room. In the few years after arriving in New York City, I had come to fancy myself to be a good enough imbiber not to get drunk on mere beer, but I found I was wrong that evening.

Besher and Matthews' plan for Japanese poets proved a bit too optimistic, though they managed to get out four volumes in the series and Burt wrote introductions to three of them. Aside from *Spring & Asura* (1973), these were *Poems of a Penisist* of Takahashi Mutsuo (1975) and *See You Soon* of Tomioka Taeko (1979). For each poet, he showed easy familiarity, though each was very different from the other.

If Miyazawa was a modernist in the 1920s, Takahashi had emerged as an openly gay poet around 1960, whereas Tomioka was a poet Burt characterized this way: "A native of Osaka, resident of Tokyo, and visitor to New York, she has the big city dweller's savvy and refusal to be awed by affectation or cant."

Of these, Tomioka, who had spent some time here, came again after my translation came out to attend the staging of her play at La Mama, and I remember her dismissing women's libbers as "triflers" when we met and chatted. So I was surprised several years later when I read her book with feminists Ogura Chikako and Ueno Chizuko excoriating Japanese male writers on the way they described women.

By the time Chicago Review Press gave up on the Japanese poets series, Burt was long back to Japan, living in Osaka, but when I proposed a large anthology of Japanese poetry, he readily agreed to work on it with me. When the work was done, it was Burt who came up with the poetic title incorporating one of the ancient names of Japan, Yashimakuni, "Country of Eight Islands."

He wrote me regularly, typing up each aerogram fully. He wrote about the places he visited. He said he liked to check out the places mentioned in the writings he was translating. Likewise with food. Once he wrote how he loved to go to a *yatai* after a public bath. While drinking and eating, he'd ask the woman or man cooking and serving food what this or that was made of.

Later, when he sent me *Stories of Osaka Life* by Oda Sakunosuke (1990), as he did many others of his books, I realized that, when he was making queries at *yatai*, he was translating *Meoto zenzai*, Oda's fond

1940 story that was later turned into a film (1955). It's about a love affair between Ryūkichi, a merchant's spoiled, married son, and Chōko, a geisha. Ryūkichi, a gourmand of sorts, takes Chōko to down-and-out eateries, explaining each establishment serves a dish that's the best of its kind. So Burt had to find out what those mysterious things were. In his translation of this story, *Hurray for Marriage, or Sweet Beans for Two*, all the unfamiliar food items come with brief explanations.

Once a peer reviewer of his translation of a Chinese classic pointed out that it was wordy. He took the criticism to heart and retranslated the whole thing, he wrote to me.

Burt dropped out of high school to enlist in the Navy in 1943, reached Japan aboard a Liberty ship, a month after the country had surrendered. When he returned to the United States, he went to Columbia College to study Chinese on the G.I. Bill. In 1951 when he was completing his master's, the theoretical physicist Yukawa Hideki, the first Japanese to win a Nobel Prize (1949) then teaching at Columbia, introduced him to Yoshikawa Kōjirō at the University of Kyoto. So he went to Kyoto to become the great sinologist's assistant. By the late fifties, he had embarked on translating a long string of Chinese classics, beginning with the big *Ssu-ma Ch'ien: Grand Historian of China* (1959).

As he tells us in *China at Last* (2013), for all his work on Chinese classics and poetry, Burt did not visit the country for the first time until 1983—thirty-seven years after he'd begun studying Chinese. For most of that time, and afterward, he lived in Japan. In our long association he never told me, and I never asked him, why, though sometimes I wondered.

That wonderment may be misplaced, of course, for the answer can be simple. Donald Richie, whose life was almost the same as Burt's except for the field of interest, once said to me: "You, a Japanese, prefer to live in New York; I, an American, prefer to live in Tokyo."

Rand Castile

June 17, 2017, *Japan Times*

Rand Castile, a curator of Asian arts who was compared with Sherman Lee, died on May 16. He was seventy-eight years old. I moved to New York, in 1968, because he and his wife, Sondra Myers, sponsored me.

I met Rand a year earlier in Kyoto because of James Byars. Later an internationally renowned conceptual artist, of whom Rand once said, "If I were not convinced he is a genius, I would think he is a madman," Byars was, when I first met him, an eccentric American. He walked about in tuxedo, a Lincolnesque top hat, with a red rose in his lapel, occasionally handing out large, scarlet square envelopes he held under his arm. Opening one, you found a smaller envelope, say, blue. Open that one, you found an even smaller one, say, white. They were all made by a famous Japanese paper craftsman, says Sakagami Shinobu, who has just published a book, *James Lee Byars: Days in Japan* (Floating World Editions, 2017).

One day Byars invited me to his happening, "A White Carpet," telling me to do something white. It was there that I met an unusually handsome man of medium height, Rand Castile. After introducing himself and finding that I was an English major at Doshisha University, he asked if I could help him as an interpreter in the coming days. He was studying *chadō*, the Way of Tea, at Urasenke, and he wanted to visit some of the *chashitsu*, tea huts.

As it turned out, Rand, on a Fulbright scholarship, had lost the bulk of the notes on tea ceremony that he made in the preceding half a year and all its paraphernalia. He had parked his motorcycle by a bank to get some cash, when his briefcase containing the notes was stolen from its rack. The *Kyoto Shimbun* headlined the theft with Sen no Sōshitsu XV's appeal for the return of the notes, if not the briefcase, to no avail.

To spend time with Rand and visit places was eye-opening. Though a six-year resident of Kyoto by then, I had visited only a few of the many notable temples that dot the ancient city. I'd been to none of the tea huts or, for that matter, kilns making "tea bowls," either as a tourist or otherwise.

Rand had a quiet, persuasive intellect, which rendered everything to seem and sound fresh, fascinating, and of utmost importance. One morning, he played a record for me on a portable player and hummed along with it, explaining how it worked. Thus, Beethoven's Sonata for Cello and Piano No. 3 in A Major—probably by Mstislav Rostropovich and Sviatoslav Richter, in retrospect—became a discovery to me and, thereafter, a treasure. (Not that I had known anything about the sonata before then.)

Rand seemed to grasp the heart of anything effortlessly, quickly. Once we went to Ōyamazaki on the border of Kyoto and Osaka to see Tai'an, "Waiting Hut," the oldest, and the smallest, tea hut that survives. According to tradition, Sen no Rikyū built it, and moved it near Hideyoshi's camp during the climactic Battle of Yamazaki in 1582. A few minutes after we entered the two-tatami room and sat down, Rand started describing the distinctive features of the "grass hut"—the ceiling, the pillars, walls, *tokonoma*—as if he had already examined each, at length.

As I learned in time, Rand was perfect for studying *chadō* and destined to become a great curator. Like most Japanese, I'd thought of *chadō* as a means of learning traditional manners and refinement. In truth, it embodies "Japanese history, art, aesthetics, philosophy, and life," as Sen no Sōshitsu XV wrote in his foreword to Rand's book *The Way of Tea* (Weatherhill, 1971).

Rand said of the art of serving tea: "Tea ceremony, like Indian ragas and jazz, is ninety percent improvisation and ten percent technique when conducted by a master."

When his time in Japan was up, Rand said that he and his wife would sponsor me if I wanted to come to New York City. I jumped at the offer, without much thought. If I had given any thought to it, I might have hesitated. He was far from well-to-do, with two young daughters to raise, and he was just a few years older than I was.

When I arrived here, he was teaching at St. Thomas Choir School, while serving Japan Society as director of education, which he'd become upon return from Kyoto. In 1971, when the society's own building was completed near the United Nations Headquarters, he became the founder-director of Japan House Gallery. For the next fourteen years, he curated more than forty exhibitions of Japanese arts.

He featured several living artists, such as New York-based Ushio Shinohara, the Neo-Dadaist who famously constructed a motorcycle with jelly beans. But Rand's forte was in traditional arts. He brought a great many National Treasures and Important Cultural Properties from Japan to New York. The most impressive of them all may well have been the one he curated and mounted to mark the 75th anniversary of the Japan Society and 10th anniversary of his creation, Japan House Gallery: *Horyu-ji: Temple of the Exalted Law.*

No exhibition from Japan's oldest Buddhist temple, domestic or overseas, had ever been attempted. It was truly "unique and epoch-making," as the Japanese commissioner of cultural affairs noted.

In 1986, Rand moved to San Francisco to become director of the Asian Art Museum, expanding his scope and coverage beyond Japan. Ten years later, even as his plan to move the museum to a larger building was approved and under way, he abruptly announced his resignation, pleading fatigue.

If you take a look at the Hōryū-ji catalog, and you will understand why. To plan and execute an art exhibition like that, you must raise funds and manage an intricate, delicate web of negotiations with responsible parties, line up art historians and translators, while maintaining attention to a range of details to the very end. Rand had done this work for a quarter of a century.

John Ashbery

September 2018, *Words Without Borders*

Toward the end of 1973, I was about to move from my apartment on the Upper East Side to one in Chelsea when I received a card. To my surprise, it was from John Ashbery saying he liked my translation just out, *Spring & Asura: Poems of Kenji Miyazawa*. Not that I'd known him in person. It was my fifth year in New York, where I'd moved as soon as I finished my graduate studies in English and American literatures, in Kyoto, and I recognized the name Ashbery only because it was in one of the books I bought here, such as Donald Allen's *The New American Poetry*, as I started translating Japanese poetry, though it's possible that Michael O'Brien, the poet who had helped me translate Miyazawa, told me about him.

During the 1960s, Japanese college courses in English poetry stayed with safe greats: Sidney, Shakespeare, Herrick, Dryden, Keats, Shelley, Tennyson, Browning, Dickenson, Whitman. I'd read Pound because my poetry teacher, Lindley Williams Hubbell, taught "Hugh Selwyn Mauberley" with notes that he mimeographed for us. Thanks to Hubbell, too, I'd read some Eliot, including "The Waste Land." But even Hubbell, the 1927 recipient of the Yale Younger Poets prize for his *Dark Pavilion*, did not cover Beat poets, despite the fact that Ginsberg and others were all the rage in Japan around 1960—something I learned belatedly—only a few months ago, in fact—in writing about Shiraishi Kazuko's book of poems in Tsumura Yumiko's translation, *Sea, Land, Shadow*.

Ashbery had included his address, and it was, to my further surprise, on the street I was moving to. I wrote him at once to thank him. Was I also forward enough to tell him I'd be his neighbor soon and propose to meet him? Perhaps. Along with *Spring & Asura*, I had three other translations out that year: *Poems of Princess Shikishi* (a chapbook), *Ten Japanese Poets*, and a special issue of the *Chicago Review: Anthology of Modern Japanese Poets*. So, not long after settling down in the new apartment, I went to see him, only half a dozen buildings west of me.

That evening, when asked what I would like to drink, I said vodka—my drink since a few years earlier, when the two women who asked me to "teach" them haiku, Eleanor Wolff and Carmel Wilson, invited me to a restaurant called Napoleon. My college days in Japan just over, I wasn't used to American restaurants with a battalion of liquor bottles or, for that matter, American etiquette. Thus, when Miss Wolff, asked me, "What would you like to drink?" I was at a loss. Quickly discerning my plight, she, who had spent her youth in Paris, summoned a *garçon*—and the *garçon* recited a long list of liquors. Confused, I meekly said, The first one. That was vodka. Thus it had become my drink during the soirées before each haiku session at either of the two ladies' places.

Ashbery fetched me a drink. He didn't drink himself, saying he was on the wagon. I got drunk fast. And what did I prattle on about? The art of translation! I was full of myself, to be sure.

In the following days, and years, when I stepped out the front door of my building to go to work, I'd occasionally see him, and when he happened to see me, he'd smile. Most often, I'd see him walking away. In those days, in New York City, dogs could drop their feces anywhere on the street and their owners weren't required to collect them. Was he negotiating those hazards as he walked? I had read a story about Wallace Stevens: A woman who lived in a house on a street Stevens took every morning to his insurance company would sometimes see him stop and walk backward a couple of steps, as if rearranging the rhythm of the verse he was composing in his head.

I learned—probably from Robert Fagan, the poet who was helping me translate at the time and for a long time afterward—that Ashbery was the poetry editor of *Partisan Review*, and I sent him Ozaki Hōsai's haiku, a batch of 150, all translated in one line. Hōsai (1885–1926) was among the haiku writers who started ignoring the two basic requirements of the genre: the form of 5-7-5 syllables—defining the haiku as a verseform of three lines is a foreign invention—and the inclusion of a seasonal indicator, *kigo*. To my surprise again, Ashbery accepted the whole set, without comment, and published it in the January 1979 issue of his magazine. For a magazine to accept so many haiku at once may have been unheard of, before or ever since, in Japan, let alone the United States.

In the summer of 1982, Kanaseki Hisao, a scholar of modern American literature whom I knew arrived in New York under the aegis of the US Information Agency, to visit a dozen artists, Ashbery among them. Since Ashbery lived on the same block, Kanaseki came to visit me after interviewing him and said Ashbery told him that he learned about the genre *haibun*—a short essaylike prose piece written with a *haikai* spirit, usually accompanied by a haiku or two—from the anthology of Japanese poetry that I translated with Burton Watson, which had come out in the previous year under the title *From the Country of Eight Islands*. I was happy, then, to see Ashbery's book of 1984, *A Wave*, include "37 haiku," composed all in one line, *and* six *haibun*. A few years later, when a chance arose for me to write a book about English haiku, in Japanese, I included four of Ashbery's *haibun*.

When that book, *Eigo haiku*, with the English title *Haiku in English: A Poetic Form Expands*, came out in 1987, the Japan Society had an event for it, and its auditorium was packed—clearly because of the popularity of haiku, but also because of Ashbery's participation. And because of him, a *New Yorker* writer came and during the reception talked to me, with a small tape-recorder in one hand. But I evidently failed to say anything that would have tickled the suave readers of the weekly. Whatever she might have written didn't make it to "The Talk of the Town."

One day in 1989, Ashbery telephoned me to say he was in trouble: A Japanese professor who had invited him to Japan for a round of readings told him he couldn't come with his partner, though Ashbery told the professor he'd happily cover his expenses. So I called Kanaseki, and

Kanaseki called the professor, and the matter was settled. Kanaseki had much greater academic weight in Japan. In a recent letter, Ashbery's partner, David Kermani, told me that the professor was "not a nice person" in Japan, either, so the two visitors took to calling him "Mr. T"— a popular figure in the US entertainment business at that time. So it was Ashbery, and his book *A Wave*, that I chose when the Tokyo poetry publisher Shoshi Yamada agreed to do a book by an American poet in my translation. My translation, as you can imagine, endlessly flummoxed the publisher's editors, however much they were used to some of the more intractable modern Japanese poetry. Ashbery's poetry, in stark contrast to his art reviews in *New York* and other magazines, was infamously "opaque" or, as Larissa MacFarquhar put it in the *New Yorker* (September 5, 2017), of the kind that made readers wonder "why he had to go so far out of his way to contort his sentences, if 'sentences' was even the right word for whatever they were."

There also was my cultural and literary deficiency. For example, I didn't know that Sabrina in "Description of a Masque" originally came from Milton's masque *Comus* (though I had majored in English literature) until my poet friend Geoffrey O'Brien pointed it out to me. I had thought the name referred to the heroine of Billy Wilder's film of that title with Audrey Hepburn. So I provided my translation of Ashbery's "Masque" with half a dozen footnotes, though that was an exception.

Ashbery, who had lived in France about ten years, said that, when his poems were translated into French, he helped his translator. But I did not bother him with my translation. It wasn't just that he evidently didn't know Japanese, but I knew that once I started asking him questions, I would have drowned him.

I must add that I was particularly presumptuous in translating *A Wave*. At the time, I read somewhere an article about him—perhaps in the *New York Times Magazine*—that Ashbery worked for a set amount of time every morning, without fail. I decided to copycat him and tried work on translating *A Wave*, for a certain amount of time every day, regardless.

Nami hitotsu came out in 1991. It looked more impressive, I dare say, than the original, from Viking. With 300 pages, it was three times heftier than the ninety-page original. Shoshi Yamada is famous for turning out beautiful books, and my translation was stylishly produced, with the cover design incorporating the sculptor Noda Masaaki's painting "Inducement." The book came with a pamphlet, a selection of writings on Ashbery: an essay Geoffrey O'Brien wrote for the book as well as excerpts from commentaries by Harold Bloom, Helen Vendler, Alfred Corn, Richard Howard, Charles Berger, and Anita Sokolsky. In my translator's afterword, I contrasted Ashbery with Gary Snyder—who had written a blurb for *Spring & Asura*. To do so, I quoted the two poets' autobiographical statements included in Paris Leary and Robert Kelly's anthology, *A Controversy of Poets*, and ended with my translation of Snyder's poem "Civilization." In essence, I wanted to have Ashbery represent "culture," Snyder "nature."

When I received copies from Tokyo, I took a couple to Ashbery. During some chitchat, he asked how it came about that I translated a book of his. I told him that, back in 1973, he had sent me a card complimenting *Spring & Asura*. He said he didn't remember doing that at all.

A few weeks later, we had a party with him and several other poet friends of mine reading in Lenore Parker and Robert Fagan's loft. My photographer friend Kakizaki Seiji, who had taken some memorable shots at the party for my first books eighteen years earlier, was on hand to take some good photos.

Nami hitotsu was praised by a number of Japanese poets. Among them, Shiraishi Kazuko wrote a long review, concluding that through my translation she could see "one gleaming wave" in the offing of "mystery and maze." But *Nami hitotsu* didn't sell—in fact, of all the books Shoshi Yamada published, they lamented a few years later, it sold the least. It is still available from the publisher, if not from Amazon or any other bookseller.

I might have expected something like that. Knowing that it would cost a bundle if the publishers got involved, I talked to Ashbery. He agreed to skip his publisher, giving his personal permission for the translation and its publication free of charge.

Following *Nami hitotsu*, there appeared two Ashbery books in Japan, as far as I can tell. One is *Selected Poems of John Ashbery* in the Shichōsha series of modern American poetry in collaborative translation. The series is based on the idea that if a translator and a poet work together, the result will be best—that a poet should be able to transform a mere translation into "poetry." In the case of the Ashbery volume, which came out in 1993, the poet was Ōoka Makoto, a prolific literary critic who himself did a good deal of translation from French, and the translator the scholar of American literature Iino Tomoyuki.

(As I write this, I remember my vague puzzlement two decades ago. In 2000, when Ōoka spoke at the annual Sōshitsu Sen Lecture Series at Columbia University, Ashbery was in the audience and at the dinner that followed, and I wondered why. Now I know. Ōoka had worked on Ashbery's poems.)

In 2005, Iino Tomoyuki published a book of essays on Ashbery under a title that may be translated *John Ashbery: Poetry "in Praise of Possibilities,"* abundantly quoting Ashbery's poems in his own translations. The established house Kenkyūsha, famous for its English-Japanese and Japanese-English dictionaries, published the book.

Have these two books affected Japanese readers' understanding of John Ashbery? That is hard to guess. Some may have found inspiration in the way he wrote; but Japanese poets have been writing in quite unconventional ways for a long, long time.

Michi Kobi

"I Became Temporarily Blind, Deaf, and Paralyzed"

March 31, 2016, *Japan Times*

My actress friend Michi Kobi died on March 1 at age ninety-one. For most of her long life, her internment during the Second World War weighed on her. It was what *Fortune* magazine in its April 1944 issue plainly called "U.S. imprisonment of persons of Japanese descent."

I knew about that part of her life during my three-decade-long friendship with her. But inattentive as I am, it only recently occurred to me, for example, that the artist she had taken me to meet in the 1980s, in Upper Manhattan, must have been Miné Okubo. Famed for her drawings of her internment, *Citizen 13660*, Okubo, too, had been in the Topaz War Relocation Center as Michi had.

Yes, I knew Michi was an actress. But, again inattentive in the familiarity of friendship, I never asked her about her acting career in any significant way. One question I remember asking was a tease: What about your relationship to Isamu Noguchi? Yamaguchi Yoshiko (Li Xiang-lan) married the sculptor when she was appearing on Broadway as Shirley Yamaguchi but divorced him, it is said, because he had such a rigid notion of what a Japanese woman was or wasn't like. Michi's response was: "Oh, he was just a friend."

As you may find out on the Internet, her acting career reflected the way the U.S.-Japanese relations changed over the years.

Michi began to appear in a TV series in 1954, with *The New Adventures of China Smith*. I can't tell what role she played in it, but her last TV acting seems to have been in the "Gaijin" segment of *Law & Order*, in 2004. According to IMDb, that story had to do with "the murder of a prominent Japanese model visiting New York [that] may have been a Yakuza-related murder for hire." At the time a Yakuza killing or two in the U.S. were in the news.

Michi's first movie, *Tokyo After Dark*, in 1959, had to do with an overzealous American MP in Tokyo who shoots a Japanese teenager dead. In the late 1950s, I knew murders and other problems created by U.S. soldiers stationed in Japan were making headlines. But, in the film, Michi plays the MP's fiancé, a kimono-clad chanteuse at an establishment called Ginza Sukiyaki (!).

Her next film, *Hell to Eternity*, in 1960, dealt with the internment as a background story. Its protagonist is a Hispanic boy adopted by a Japanese American family who enlists in the Marines after his family is packed off to the Manzanar Relocation Camp, and becomes a hero in the Battle of Saipan—by saving 800 Japanese lives. In it Michi played what she called a "Honolulu fun girl," but the film may have led her to confide to a reporter for *The Victoria Advocate*, in October of the same year, that she'd begun to write a play about her experiences during World War II in relocation camps, though she added, "That isn't working out too well."

The old Texas newspaper called Michi "a beautiful girl, a talented actress, a person of charm and intelligence," but she was in her mid-thirties by then, and she was probably growing weary of the fun-girl routine. "They just don't write meaty parts for Oriental girls and nobody would think of casting me as anything but an Oriental girl," she said. She had toured for two years with *The Teahouse of the August Moon* as "the gentle and innocent maiden." The Broadway comedy, along with its film version with Marlon Brando, won the Pulitzer, Tony, and other prizes, but it was full of stereotypes and was later condemned as racist.

Michi was born in 1924, the year the U.S. enacted an immigration act based on eugenics, formalizing racial inequality as a foreign policy. In his testament shortly after Japan's defeat in 1945, the Showa Emperor sought the origins of the Pacific War in the U.S. not rejecting "yellow-white discrimination" as Japan asked after the Great War.

Michi's father, Okamoto Rikikazu, had arrived in the United States in 1902 when he was seventeen, and took a M.D. He went to Japan and married Kobinata Ito in 1923 and brought her to Sacramento. That was where Michi was born. But her father died of tuberculosis when she was three years old. Her mother took her to San Francisco, put her in a Methodist orphanage so she might learn her own trade. She took her daughter back when Michi was nine, but the value reversals at the Christian orphanage and in the hemmed-in Japanese immigrant community confounded Michi.

Then came Pearl Harbor and, with it, the "barefaced hostility from students and teachers at school," as Michi put it. To list some of the epithets that suddenly began to be hurtled at residents of Japanese descent from one of Miné Okubo's drawings, there were "Aliens-citizens, a Jap is a Jap," "Send them back to Tojo," "Sabotage," "Can't trust them," "Spy ring," "A Jap looks like this," "Stab in the back," and "Bank Freeze Jap."

In March 1942, the order came that they "voluntarily" leave the West Coast. Then, for those who failed to do so like Kobinata Ito, who couldn't give up her beauty shop quickly, came the forced "relocation"— first herded to the Tanforan Assembly Center, in fact a racetrack south of San Francisco, then transported by train carriages, with the shades down, for three, four days to Topaz in a Utah desert.

"I became temporarily blind, deaf, and partially paralyzed before entering Tanfaron for about 10 days," Michi wrote in 1988.

She recovered from these experiences and made a successful acting career. As she did so, her initial idea of writing a play expanded into a large novel covering the Japanese immigrants to the U.S. Around 2002 she asked me, "What might a young woman in the early 1900s have read?" She continued to struggle to turn various historical strands into a coherent story, but was apparently unable to finish it. Maggie Stein Nakamura, one of her friends who looked after her in her last days, reports that Michi had "nightmares" for fear that her writings might disperse with her death.

Part of the reason for her obsession and fear may have been the number of articles on the grave injustice seventy years ago that have recently increased. The most recent one I've read, on NBC News, is "Behind Barbed Wire: Remembering America's Largest Internment Camp," and it gives the recollections of five surviving inmates in Tule Lake of a maximum-security prison camp.

I once asked Michi about her surname, and she said it was her mother's surname shortened because no one in Hollywood at the time would bother to pronounce a name like "Kobinata." Too long. It might also have had something to do with the fact that her mother practically abandoned her in the relocation center in Topaz, remarrying.

In New York, Michi was active in redressing the damages done to Japanese-Americans during the Second World War.

Bong-san I
My Korean Friend Who Cherished Her Japanese Teachers

March 31, 2014, *Japan Times*

My Korean friend in Pennsylvania, Bong-san, has written she will be turning ninety at the end of this year. Whenever she mentions her age, I am surprised, as I was this time: She can't be that old!

Of course, I should know better. During the 1970s, when she worked for my employer, the New York office of a Japanese trade agency, she already had grown-up daughters. Yet, because she was the very image of the Buddhist goddess of happiness and prosperity, Kisshōten, I did not really imagine she would ever age.

Also, I was inattentive.

In the early part of that decade, I occasionally wrote a letter for her—a letter addressed to the U.S. Embassy in Seoul guaranteeing her responsibility for the conduct and expenses of the person she was inviting to this country.

It was only some years later that I realized she was reacting to the Immigration Act of 1965, which had famously removed nationality and ethnic quotas on immigration.

Korea was among the countries that saw a dramatic exodus of their people heading to the United States as a result. From the 1960s to the 1970s, Korean immigrants here jumped ninefold, from 27,000 to 240,000.

At any rate, while she was with us, I didn't really know much about her life. It was after she left and we started corresponding that I learned bits and pieces of her life during Japan's colonial rule and the several years after Japan's defeat—"the liberation" of Korea. Japan annexed Korea in 1910, and ruled it for the next thirty-five years.

In her recent letter, she calls the latest spats between Japan and Korea "ugly, infantile, and lamentable." She mentions some of the heinous things she has heard Japan did in her country in the past. One was Japan's attempt to force Korean people to adopt Japanese-sounding surnames. It ignored the tradition of a country that "puts special importance on ancestral histories," she wrote.

I say "the heinous things she has heard," because, if Bong-san suffered the brunt of Japan's colonial rule, she does not say. This is true of her perfect command of Japanese, the result of another of Japan's arrogant measures in Korea, the imposition of Japanese on Korean people. In writing, she retains the prewar style of kanji and kana. It is the style Mishima Yukio (1925–70), for one, never abandoned. He was born about the same time Bong-san was.

Rather, she remembers how wonderfully she got along with Japanese friends and teachers in Korea.

"Most of my teachers while I was in school were Japanese, but they all cared for us from their heart, loved us, and poured their heart and soul into making good human beings out of us. Each time I think of them, I want to see them again, and I become teary-eyed."

She has described some of her teachers for me.

In third and fourth grade, for example, her teacher was Nakasuna Sensei, a large woman. Childless, she had a special cushion made for her dog to sit on, but she was so partial to Bong-san she insisted she spend Sundays with her, driving Bong-san's mother up the wall.

Nakasuna Sensei's husband was, Bong-san heard, a security guard at an agricultural station, though he was formerly a high-ranking military officer. That story sounds highly plausible. In the years when Japan created and maintained a military force far too big for such a poor nation, many field-grade officers are known to have had to struggle in finding jobs in non-military life after they were decommissioned.

In fifth and sixth grade her teacher was Hirose Chieko, Bong-san remembers. Hirose Sensei was "petite, slim, and so stylish she looked like a Westerner, looking marvelous in her indigo suit." But she was known to have a terrible drunk for a husband, who created rows with her, "an intelligent, gentle-hearted soul."

Bong-*san* hated the man for it, even though she never had a chance to see him. She also hated him for producing a girl, Yuki-chan. Unlike her "beautiful" mother, the child wasn't nice-looking, though she was her good playmate.

Hirose Sensei openly wept at Bong-san's graduation, "trying to push back tears with a handkerchief as she repeatedly asked her to remain in touch," even as Bong-san was overjoyed she'd been accepted by a "first-rate school." She truly loved Korea, Bong-san reflects.

The school that accepted Bong-san, I found, was the Shukumei (Sookmyung) Women's School for Higher Education—a university since 1948.

Established by a member of the Korean Imperial family, the school was strongly supported by the Japanese, among them Fuchizawa Noe (1850–1936), the Christian who had studied in the United States on her own. Bong-san remembers her as an elegant educator always dressed in a blue kimono.

Among the other people at the school Bong-san continues to admire to this day are school principal Nomura Seinosuke and "the honorary principal" Oda Shōgo. Of the two, Oda was also a professor of Korean history at the Imperial University of Keijō (Gyeongseong, today's Seoul). Reading some references to his work reminds us how difficult it is to write a history of a country that was once a colony.

"Imperial universities" (*teikoku daigaku*) were the highest institutions of learning the Japanese government established, beginning with the one in Tokyo, in 1886. The Keijō University, in 1924, was the sixth (before Osaka, in 1931, and Nagoya, in 1939). Today, however, having been a professor at one such university makes Oda suspect, even though his position as a historian seems admirable.

Oda, lead author of the five-volume *History of Korean Peninsula* (1927), argued that "history must be a record of fact," and he rejected as "of little worth" and "opportunistic" anything that's written on the basis of "a ruler's policy or the author's prejudice." He was a "positivist" in that respect, and his stance was daring. Yet Oda's position may be dismissed as "fantasy" in the milieu in which he did his work—or so Katsurajima Nobuhiro, of Ritsumeikan University, suggests in his paper that's online, "History Compilation in Colonial Korea and Historiography."

Little wonder the joint effort some years ago to write a history satisfactory to both Korea and Japan went nowhere.

Bong-san II

A Korean Woman Recalls the Tragedy of Two Wars

August 30, 2015, *Japan Times*

"My Dear Abe-san, the moment you became prime minister, you totally messed up Japan's relations with Korea," Bong-san, my Korean friend in Pennsylvania, has recently written. "You seem to argue that the Japanese could not have possibly forced young Korean girls to become 'comfort women,' but to me, a 90-year old woman who lived in that period, the conclusion is that the Japanese *deceived* poor farm maidens. Which is more heinous, forcing someone or deceiving someone is self-evident."

Not that Bong-san thinks I have some private conduit to Abe Shinzō. She was mainly responding to my twenty-year-old article I'd sent her about how my family was repatriated from Taiwan following Japan's defeat in 1945.

Briefly, in the late 1920s my father emigrated from Fukuoka, Kyūshū, to Taiwan, which Japan had acquired in 1895 as a colony. Japan was in a chronic economic funk following the boom during the Great War, and he, a high-school graduate, tried a dozen jobs but none of them suited him.

The economy in Taiwan was not much better. But in the end he found a job as a cop, rose to become an officer of the Special Higher Police, and, after Japan started war with the United States, United Kingdom, and the Netherlands, was sent to Java, where he became a Dutch POW upon Japan's defeat.

My mother, a schoolteacher with four children, had to decamp for Japan. With most ships sunk during the war, it took the family five to six months from Guanshan (Kanzan), southeast of Taiwan, to Fukuoka, spending a month in a ship alone, from Keelung to Ōtake, in Hiroshima.

This story—the lengthy, arduous return to Japan part of it in particular—reminded Bong-san of her own life-or-death struggles that began with Japan's defeat. That's because Japan's defeat reversed Korea's political situation.

The Soviet Union declared war against Japan on August 9, the day the United States dropped an atomic bomb on Nagasaki, and in no time the once-vaunted Kwantung Army collapsed. In Manchukuo there were 1,550,000 Japanese, a large portion of them Korean Japanese. The U.S.S.R. would capture more than half a million of them, mostly soldiers, and send them to Siberia as POWs.

The rest became refugees and stragglers and tried to return to Japan, via China, the Soviet Union, and Korea. An estimated total of 176,000 died in the process, nearly half of them "pioneers" who had emigrated to Manchuria by "national policy" (Tsunoda Fusako, *80,000 Dead Without Grave Markers*, 1976).

At the same time, Soviet influences, which had deep roots in Koreans' demand for independence, quickly rose and spread throughout the Korean Peninsula.

For its part, the United States declared, on September 2, 1945, the day of Japan's formal surrender, that the U.S. and U.S.S.R would divide Korea into north and south along the 38th demarcation line for each to occupy one half. Then, just five days later, the United States put the south under military rule.

This upheaval threw Bong-san and her husband into great difficulty. She had been born fourteen years after Japan annexed Korea in what was now "south Korea" and married a man in "north Korea." Her husband had worked for a prefectural government. That meant he had worked for Japan's colonial government. So now he was branded "pro-Japanese." In addition, he was from "a local family with influence" and therefore "an exploiter of peasants and workers."

Thus with political and social standards upside down, the couple found the north grew untenable by the day, forced to live "as if stepping on thin ice." Finally, they managed to "escape to the south" in the confusions of the May Day of the following year, 1946, Bong-san holding her infant daughter in her arms.

It was in the north, and while escaping to the south, that Bong-san witnessed or heard about the miseries that the Japanese, now refugees and stragglers, suffered. "Russian soldiers looting and violence, the mass typhus in the concentration camps for the Japanese, the ghastly brutalities inflicted on the wave after wave of Japanese stragglers fleeing south on foot from Manchuria, and other things," Bong-san writes, "may have been deserving punishments the Japanese had brought upon themselves for starting the war. Still, I choke up when I reflect how sinful mankind can be."

More than 30,000 Japanese would perish in the north.

All that was "unbearable and painful to those like me who had been purely educated with the Japanese Nation's virtues," she adds. After the primary school where most of the teachers were Japanese, she was accepted by the Shukumei (Sookmyung) Women's School for Higher Education, founded by the Korean imperial family and Japanese educators.

"During the 35 years after making Korea into its own territory, Japan had done its best to raise it to its own level in every respect: governance, education, transportation, culture, agricultural reform," but all that proved "great pains but all in vain" upon Japan's defeat, except for the governing system, Bong-san writes.

But the travails for Korea had just begun.

With the fierce U.S.-U.S.S.R. conflicts worsening, there was first the 4.3 Incident in 1948, on Jeju Island. Touched off by the islanders' demand for Korean unification of the north and south as well as for independence, the small "revolt" would turn the island into a killing field. In the next seven years, 70,000 to 80,000 people were murdered.

In June 1950 the Korean War broke out. Truce talks started a year later. In that sense, the war was "relatively short," but it was "exceptionally bloody," a *History* website notes, adding that nearly five million Koreans died. The Korean government's official estimates of deaths are smaller. Either way, the war produced a large number of casualties.

"Almost all of south Korea turned into a wasteland (as did north Korea)," Bong-san writes. But "with the war ending in a draw," and the split between north and south "hasn't changed a bit to this day, when the 70th anniversary has arrived since Korea's independence" from Japan.

"Big countries trample upon small countries for their own national policies." Her lament is universal.

> *I always called her Bong-san, but the Chinese character for her surname 方 may be closer to "bang" in Korean pronunciation. Following the Korean custom, she kept her original family name in the United States, until, apparently for legal reasons, she switched it to her husband's, Joo 朱. Her full name at death was 朱允厚 or Joo Yun-He, as she romanized it.*
>
> *Bong-san died on March 5, 2020, at age ninety-six, her youngest daughter telephoned to inform me from ManorCare, Lansdale, Montgomeryville, PA.*

IV

Talking about Books and Such

An Unnaturally Smooth Naturalization?

April 24, 2006, *Japan Times*

I became an American citizen on March 31. The steps for citizenship were simple and easy, and the process took an unexpectedly short time. I experienced neither "the law's delay" nor "the insolence of office."

In early October last year, my young lawyer friend Donald Parker filed an application for naturalization for me. A month later, I received a receipt of the application from the U.S. Citizenship and Immigration Services. Though it said I should expect to hear about the date and place of my interview "within 540 days," a week later another notice came summoning me for fingerprinting. The date was December 1. The fingerprinting was followed by another notice—this one giving the date and place of the interview: March 16. The interview did not take more than ten minutes, or so it seemed, and the citizenship was granted on the spot. The ceremony took place two weeks later.

So the whole process took less than half a year. That length of time could exasperate some, I know, but I was in no hurry. After all, I arrived in this country nearly four decades ago. And the officials who dealt with me were kind and pleasant.

The first were the guards at the entrance to the building on Varick Street housing the INS office to which I was summoned for fingerprinting. Apparently Hispanics, they were apologetic and solicitous. I use crutches, the granite staircase right behind the revolving door was steep, and the correct entrance was elsewhere. The young, svelte, long-legged beauty of (maybe) Chinese extraction handling the fingerprinting

218

equipment was quiet and self-effacing. INS or the Immigration and Naturalization Service was the name of the Citizenship and Immigration
Services before it was absorbed into the conglomerate Homeland Security Department.

The officer who interviewed me in mid-March at the USCIS in the
Jacob Javits Federal Building, which is near the southern end of Manhattan, was also solicitous as she guided me to her office. I told her that
I used to visit the building to use the Commerce Department library.
During the interview she asked perhaps a dozen questions, in a more or
less perfunctory manner, as my lawyer friend had predicted. She gave
me no written tests. Then she said, "You've been approved. Congratula-
tions!" As I rose, I was briefly overwhelmed.

There were some personal moments during the interview, if I may
call them that. At one point, either because she had an accent or because
she did not look like someone from Western Europe, I asked where she
was from. Poland, she said. So I mentioned my "Polish niece," Aneta
Glinkowska, and the vodka she brought for me from her "old country."
She complimented me on my pronunciation of my niece's family name.
She also wondered how l liked Polish vodka.

My time with her, in any case, did not give me a chance to glimpse
the one thing I had associated with naturalization interviews: the different attitudes officers take to different applicants. Some years ago an English journalist who, being married to an American, decided to become
an American himself, wrote about the unpleasantness he overheard in
the next room. His own interviewer was polite, even deferential to him,
but the one in the next room, who was testing someone of color whose
English was far from fluent, was definitely not. She did not try to hide
her irritation and contempt.

I was reminded of this when I translated a poem by Cheon Mihye
not long before my own interview. Born to long-time Korean residents
of Japan, Cheon decided to become a Japanese citizen when she married
a Japanese. Her experience at the Japanese naturalization office was a
replica of the Englishman's in America. Again, her own interviewer was
kindly and considerate, but throughout the interview she heard beyond

a thin wall the insolent voice of an official interviewing an Asian woman whose Japanese was halting at best. But I did not glimpse anything comparable, perhaps largely because there were no interviews going on near my officer's room.

The naturalization ceremony two weeks later was held in the oak-paneled Ceremonial Courtroom of the brand-new building housing the U.S. District Court, Southern District of New York. The tall, barrel-chested court officer, when my turn came, at once guided me to one of the leather-upholstered chairs in the front row, rather than to any of the wooden pews. Soon guided to the seat next to me was a middle-aged Hispanic woman elegantly dressed in black, with a dark, round hat. During the last part of the ceremony the one who sat in her place was a young, stylishly dressed Englishman.

Receiving our documents and identifying each of us were six people: a young black woman coupled with a middle-aged male Japanese-American (perhaps), a young Hispanic woman coupled with a middle-aged Caucasian male, and a young Asian woman coupled with a Caucasian male of an indeterminate age. When the processing was over, the court officer asked us to give a hand to these six because, he said, they were paid so little.

Then, after some moments of hushed waiting, the bailiff announced the arrival of Chief Judge of the District Court Michael Mukasey. A smallish, white-haired man appeared and placed himself in the middle of a long, empty dais. The bailiff made us repeat the Oath of Allegiance after him. Then the judge gave a speech, recalling how his own ancestors came to this land eighty years ago. He then stepped down from his dais and shook hands with each of us as the bailiff called out our names, one by one, to hand each the certificate of naturalization. When I shook hands with the judge, I was once again briefly overwhelmed.

Out on the street in the unseasonably warm day that was March 31, did I wonder about the seeming disconnect between immigration policy debate and implementation in the United States? I do not recall, but I became an American citizen as huge, unprecedented waves of immigration-reform demonstrations were rising. It was a few years before I came here that the revolutionary Immigration Act of 1965 abolished the quota system by nationality and ethnicity. It has since altered the demographic face of the United States. Today this country admits about a million immigrants every year and allows more than half that number to naturalize.

The ABC's of Life

March 25, 1985, *Mainichi Daily News*

When a McGill University professor recently asked me to talk about Japanese poetry at his seminar in international business, I thought of Amaya Naohiro and his poetry collection. Amaya, a career bureaucrat at the Japanese Ministry of International Trade and Industry (MITI), published a book of poems upon his retirement, in 1981.

MITI is the parent agency of the office where I've worked since the end of the 1960s, and Amaya held high positions throughout the last decade of his service at MITI. Yet it was only several years ago that he became a presence in my mind. That was when I heard about his exchange with Japanese journalists upon his return to Tokyo from the United States, where he had had a particularly trying round of negotiations on Japanese exports.

When some reporters pointedly asked why he, a man representing the government trade agency of a proud economic power, had acted like a sycophant, making so many "unwarranted" concessions, his reply was: If you were a military power, you might be able to behave like a bully to your client. But if you are a merchant, which is what Japan is, you can only try to please your client, and if you fail to, for whatever reason, you can only step back and bow.

More recently, I read in a newspaper profile an account of Amaya's session with Japanese automakers. The session took place when the United States government was demanding that Japan put "voluntary quotas" on its automobile exports, while the Japanese auto manufacturers were in no submissive mood, asking indignantly, why should they curtail their exports when the American consumer evidently liked what they had to sell? At one of those sumptuous restaurants in Akasaka or some such place, where Japanese businessmen and politicians are said to get together and concoct nefarious schemes, Amaya, apparently a teetotaler, forced himself to drink and practically groveled before the chieftains of the auto industry, begging them to accept the quotas as proposed by the United States.

The automakers, though they agreed to a compromise in the end, were furious and are said to have called Amaya "a prostitute catering only to foreigners" and other names. The outcome of the quotas for the Japanese auto makers has been ironic. By holding down the number of cars, they've been able to sell more expensive models, thereby making far more money than they'd expected to.

Not long after this encounter—if there was such an encounter—Amaya Naohiro, then vice minister for international affairs, retired from MITI. A few months later he privately printed a collection of thirty-one-syllable tanka, called *A Clerk's Idle Mumblings in a Nation of Townspeople (Chōnin-koku tedai no kurigoto)*. As he explains it, the title derives from his view that if Japan is to be compared to a business establishment, the Japanese people will be the master of the shop, the prime minister and his cabinet officers the managers, and the bureaucrats the clerks.

If the title is only mildly ironic, his view of Japanese business in the international market is sardonic, even despairing. He likens the international market to a casino guarded by men armed with swords, and says Japan is like a fellow who wants to barge in there without carrying a big sword, gamble without paying proper stakes, make a clean sweep of the joint, and get away with it. In some of the poems, he asks rhetorically:

To watch the buyer's expression in selling stuff—
    isn't that the vendor's A, B, C's?

To surround a castle on three sides, leaving one side open—
    isn't that the A, B, C's of laying siege?

To lie low in a blizzard and wait for fine weather—
    isn't that the mountain-climber's A, B, C's?

At one point Amaya likens Japan to a burglar and asks:

To hold one's breath and slip in, pussyfooting—
    isn't that the burglar's A, B, C's?

And recalling the Battle of Imphal, one of the more disastrous defeats Japan suffered during the Second World War, he says:

Because a general at Imphal didn't know how to retreat
    100,000 soldiers turned into white bones

Such epigrammatic pieces appear mostly in the section bearing the title of the book. There are four other sections to this tanka collection, among them one consisting of poems on flowers, such as:

A camellia drops, a carp swims near it in a spring pond;
    the water undulates and grows still again

Some people will no doubt hold verses like this dearer. To me, though, *A Clerk's Idle Mumblings* is attractive mainly because its author, while a bureaucrat, managed to find the time to record his political musings in the centuries-old tanka form. And I find many of his arguments contain a grain of truth, even though it may be a bit cruel to say Japan is an international burglar.

Amaya Naohiro's father, Naojirō (1888–1966), was a lieutenant general in the Japanese army.

Drinking in Mr. Cavett

June 16, 1986, *Mainichi Daily News*

One problem I have in trying to tell a story or give an answer is that I usually become distracted by what I'm saying and get bogged down before reaching the end of what I might have started out to say. I was reminded of this once again the other night when I spent several hours with Dick Cavett—yes, of the Dick Cavett Show. How did I end up finding myself in the company of the famous TV host?

One day I had a call in my office where I get quite a few telephone inquiries. One such inquiry several years ago was from a Tennessean or Kentuckian who was convinced that his farmland had a wealth of oil hidden under it and wanted a Japanese oil company to drill it for him. Another call, from Michigan, led the caller, a sanguine gentleman by the name of Gordon Peterson, to invite me, along with my wife, to vacation in his town, and we spent some glorious days on Lake Superior.

One unforgettable incident occurred when Mr. Peterson's boat arrived in one of the few ports on Isle Royale, the only place in the United States where wolves have been allowed to remain in the wild. Mr. Peterson started to maneuver his boat to fill the tank, when it stopped moving. He found out the propeller was missing, and in no time spotted it on the bottom of the lake, clearly visible through the water whose transparency is known worldwide.

Somehow the pin holding it to the tail end of the axis had fallen off; it was all right as long as the propeller was pushing the boat forward, but the moment its rotation was reversed, it fell off, too. Just like that. A pole with a hook attached at the end and a similarly equipped rope was tried, but neither worked. Finally, a wiry middle-aged man at the gas station who had been busily helping us from the outset took off his clothes, dove into the cold water, and salvaged the gear.

Another unforgettable thing about Isle Royale is the quiet inlet where we parked the boat to spend the night. For the few hours before sunset, the quietude around us filled with fairly large insects, which waddled, rather than flew, through the air and would flop on the water from time to time. I had the feeling that it was the same insect President Carter described in his piece about trout fishing, which I had read in a magazine a few years earlier. Soon gulls congregated about us and began catching some of the fat, juicy aerial waddlers either in the air or as they landed on the water.

Anyway, as I picked up the phone the caller identified himself so simply, unpretentiously—no doubt as simply and unpretentiously as he later said Groucho Marx had responded when one day he found himself standing next to the great comedian and started to talk to him—that I at once caught and missed his name.

It was only midway through our conversation, when he said he was calling from Montauk and I said we used to vacation there in the summer until a few years ago and he asked where and I said at Sepp's Cottages and he recognized the place, that it began to dawn on me who the caller was. For the eastern tip of Long Island was where I began spending two weeks of the summer as I began to live with a woman who became my wife not many years afterwards. And as we cruised the prettier section of the resort town, my wife—or was she, at the time, still in the "anti-social cohabitation" stage with me, as her mother put it—said that one of the houses was inhabited by a TV host we often watched.

We stopped vacationing there because its popularity grew, and what was a half-deserted, forlorn place when we began our annual trip turned into a typically congested resort place. One restaurant we thought we liked for its rustic air, for example, was renovated and expanded, and nattily dressed folks began to visit it in big expensive cars apparently from miles away.

Also, about the time we began to lag in our eagerness in making reservations at Sepp's Cottages, a friend of ours in North Carolina told us about a small island off the coast of South Carolina and said we might like it there. So, although I was a bit ashamed to behave like a bastard who turns fickle about a resort place as his purchasing ability increases, and although the water there in the semi-tropical region of South Carolina struck us as too warm the first time, we've been returning to the island since then—except when my Michigan caller graciously offered his place for us and an opportunity to drink directly from Lake Superior.

Speaking of drinking Lake Superior water, you'd be amazed by the innumerable gnats that instantly gather all about you when you stop the boat to fish even if you are a couple of miles away from the land. And drink Mr. Cavett did not. Not as much as I did, anyway. That may be why (although I really doubt that's really the why of it), whereas I often can't finish a story, every story he told us through the evening we spent together was a perfect anecdote.

I said "us," because Daniel Furuya, an aikido teacher from Los Angeles, was with us. Indeed, the telephone call and the evening together came about because Mr. Furuya, a friend of Mr. Cavett's, wanted to see me because of my book, *The Sword & the Mind*. And Mr. Furuya was right in saying some of the card tricks Mr. Cavett showed us were "spooky," as I found out at The Players, a musty, exclusive club. But I may be losing track of myself again. . . .

Kissing Encounters

July 11 and July 25, 1988, *Mainichi Daily News*

In his book *A Lateral View* (Japan Times, 1987), Donald Richie has an essay on "Japan's odd relation to the kiss." He begins it by noting that as early as 1883 Edmond Goncourt jotted down in his journal an observation made during dinner by "someone who had lived in Japan for many years" that "the kiss did not exist in Japanese love-making." Things have changed since then, and now every Japanese seems to be doing it. Still, the Japanese acceptance of this particular use of the lips is limited, Richie concludes, to just one thing: "an exotic adjunct to the act of making love."

When I read this essay I remembered an account Saitō Mokichi (1882–1953) has left of witnessing kissing in Europe. Though now in the main known as a tanka poet, Saitō was a physician who ran a hospital for the mentally ill and it was as a psychiatric student that the Ministry of Education sent him overseas. From January 1922 to the middle of 1924 he studied at the Neurological Institute of Vienna University, then at the Kaiser Wilhelm Institute, in Munich. Amy Heinrich, who has written a full literary biography of this poet-psychiatrist in English, *Fragments of Rainbows* (Columbia University Press, 1983), judges that the 5-7-5-7-7-syllable tanka he wrote while diligently pursuing his research in Austria and Germany are unremarkable but some of his prose pieces describing "the scenery and culture of Europe have an immediacy and drawing power that is lacking in the poems." One such prose composition may be an account entitled "*Seppun*," "Kisses."

In this piece Mokichi first tells us about two couples he saw kissing "for nearly an hour" in Vienna, the sculptural depictions of Amenophis IV kissing his child and another king kissing a god which he saw in the Cairo Museum, and two murals of Giotto he saw in Padua, one of them depicting Judas kissing Christ. He ends his report with a speculation on the origin of the word *seppun*.

What makes "Kisses" so memorable is what might be called pristine frankness mixed with clinical wonderment. Mokichi saw the first hour-long osculation—to use a word I learned from Richie—while taking a walk in the afterglow one summer evening in 1922. He describes the kissing couple he came upon in a street thus:

> The man was ganglingly tall, skinny, and had wild hair. He had very terrible clothes on. Somewhat stooping, he was holding the woman with his right arm over her left shoulder and his left arm firmly around her hips. His mustache a little overgrown, what little I could see of his face was pale. The woman was stretching up and, with her arms around his neck, kissing him. She had an ancient hat on. Therefore, it was difficult even to imagine her facial features.
>
> As I saw this spectacle in the evening dark, I thought I encountered something eerie. So, after passing by them, I looked back at them. The man and the woman remained erect, immobile. I walked ahead somewhat and looked back at them again. They remained as was. Though I began to feel a little uneasy, I told myself to calm down, backed up somewhat, and up close to an oak tree, watched the kissing. The kissing lasted forever. About an hour later, I detached myself from the tree and hurriedly left the place.
>
> 'That's long. Very long indeed,' I said to myself.

After witnessing this spectacle, Mokichi goes to a pub, downs a large mug of beer in a few gulps, ponders the matter, has another mug, and goes back to the same street, but he sees the kissing couple no more. As he snuggles into his bed that night, he feels exultant and mutters to himself, "I saw something nice today, something very nice."

His second encounter is precisely dated: January 1, 1923. To seek a sign of good fortune for the New Year, he climbed a hill rising behind Vienna. When he had climbed quite high, he looked back down and spotted two people coming up the same path he had taken:

> They were a man and a woman. They were so far away that they were indistinct, and it was pleasant to watch them grow large little by little. Suddenly, in the midst of the path they casually held each other and began kissing. The kissing couple did not separate for quite a while.
>
> Embossed like a dot in the mountains and water, the human beings the size of miniature dolls spent almost an hour kissing. Finally they disentangled themselves and came closer and closer to where I was. Then they walked past in front of me.
>
> As they did so, I stared at them with a feeling resembling contempt. The man was skinny, his features sharp. Dressed for mountain-climbing, he was carrying a rucksack. The woman was on the plump side, her features ugly. Wearing a white jacket, she was also carrying a rucksack. It appeared that they planned to go over the mountain and seek lodgings somewhere in the forest. Before long they became invisible behind the valley.

Despite the talk of contemptuous staring, Mokichi again felt exultant. He climbed down the mountain in a great hurry, had dinner at a restaurant, saw a cinema, went home, wiped his body, and went to bed, muttering to himself again—yes, "I saw something nice today."

Now, as Richie points out in "The Japanese Kiss," though there is "a perfectly good Japanese word for 'kiss,'" most of those who do the kissing in Japan today—i.e., young people—use the bastardized English word for the act, *kissu*. Obviously, kissing remains a largely Western custom. Indeed, the "perfect word," *seppun*, itself isn't that old.

When did the word *seppun* come into being? This is the question Saitō Mokichi tried to puzzle out toward the end of his essay, "Kisses." As a reputable psychiatrist who had studied and received a Ph.D. in the West, he apparently felt he just couldn't describe the kissing scenes he had witnessed and let the matter go. So he ended his account with some scholarly musings on the origin of the word, *seppun.*

Mokichi starts out by saying that the word, which consists of two Chinese characters meaning "touch" and "lips," had become part of daily usage in Japan by his time, but that it doesn't appear in a giant dictionary of Chinese compiled in China in 1711. If it wasn't part of the Qing-dynasty Chinese, what did translators do when they worked on the Bible? Earlier in his essay Mokichi has referred to Giotto's mural depicting Judas kissing Christ, which he'd seen in Padua, and quoted Matthew 26: 40-45 in Japanese translation where the word, of course, occurs. Because the Bible had been translated into Chinese before it was into Japanese, he checks a Chinese translation of the Bible and finds that the word invented to fill the Biblical need is entirely different—something like "intimate billing."

He then points out that in the Japanese translation he has quoted, the word, though written in a combination of Chinese characters whose Sinified pronunciation is *seppun,* is given a different reading: *kuchizuke.* Difficult or non-standard Chinese characters used in the Japanese language are given Japanese readings. The practice was much more extensive in the earlier days when compulsory education was less so.

As Mokichi goes on to note, in the earlier usage, *kuchizuke,* "mouth-touch, mouth-attached," meant not kissing but "habitual remark," rather like "being attached to mouthing something." He sees, however, that some of the more recent dictionaries or the supplements to older ones list the word as meaning "kiss."

Does this mean, he asks, the Japanese language had no equivalent of "kiss" in the old days? Well, it did, in the word of *kuchi-sui,* "mouth-suck," whose recorded usage may go back to the early thirteenth century. Mokichi, professing to find the word *kuchi-zuke,* "mouth-touch," not quite right, wonders if it's possible to revive *kuchi-sui,* "mouth-suck." He rejects the possibility on the ground that you can't really say you "mouth-suck" Christ's forehead or a lady's hand.

Mokichi wrote his essay sixty long years ago, and I'm sure that by now lexicographers and scholars of Japanese literature have uncovered the first use of the word *seppun* or even pinpointed who coined it. The redoubtable Donald Keene, for example, has said in his tome *Dawn to the West* (Holt, Rinehart and Winston, 1984) that a word for 'kiss' was listed in English-Japanese dictionaries compiled some years before the Meiji period (1868–1912) began—though he has done so without saying what that word is.

Such etymological inquiries aside, it seems that even after the coinage of *seppun* and despite the centuries-old existence of *kuchi-sui,* kissing was something the Japanese men and women didn't feel quite comfortable doing.

Shunga: The Art of Love in Japan, by Tom and Mary Anne Evans (Paddington Press, 1975), the largest collection of erotic ukiyo-e prints I own, does have some pictures of kissing men and women. But in stark contrast to the graphic exuberance in the depictions of coital acts, most of the depictions of kissing suggest men and women so tentative and half-hearted that one can't help concluding, as Richie does, that they regarded kissing as no more than "an occasional practice, a further perversion." The paucity of references to the act in classical literature is as attested to by our poet-scholar Saitō Mokichi.

Not that I think it necessarily desirable for the Japanese to start kissing everywhere, for every purpose—to have the act convey "affection or reverence or sorrow or consolation or any of the other things," in Richie's words. A resident of the United States for the past twenty years, I still very much doubt if I'd ever get used to the sight of a Japanese grandpa kissing his daughter goodbye at a station in Tokyo or a pious Japanese dame kissing the hand of a bonze in Nara, should such things ever begin to happen.

Meanwhile, I, for one, would like to continue to live under the illusion that when some young beauty kisses me, even if it's no more than a peck on the cheek, she means to convey something more than a passing affection.

Panties Talk

1990, *Coffee Break*

"What's the color of your panties today?" I ask Mary Jo. Mary Jo is a schoolteacher whose overflowing sensuality seems to mesmerize toddlers, adolescents, and men of considerable judgment alike. For this evening's tutoring she's wearing a red blouse, red skirt, red stockings, red shoes.

She turns around, beams: "Red, of course!"

"Did you buy those panties for yourself or for your hubbie, Jim?" I ask Brenda. Brenda is a farm girl who happens to work in a Manhattan office. She wears nothing under her one-piece dress today, she says, but was out during lunchtime to buy some undies.

She giggles, her eyes bright: "For Jim!"

Why so much interest in panties? asks Ueno Chizuko in her book *The Theater Under the Skirt* (*Sukāto no shita no gekijō*, Kawade Shobō Shinsha, 1989), with the subtitle: "Why are people obsessed with panties?" Ueno is a Japanese university professor in Kyoto, who proposes to establish "a new brand of Marxist feminism through a critical re-examination of structuralist sociology, cultural anthropology, and semiotics." She also writes haiku. In *The Theater Under the Skirt* she contemplates modern-day panties—or, as she puts it, "a piece of cloth that eats into the crotch and attaches itself closely to the sex organ." The book became a bestseller.

Why do human beings, both male and female, cover their genitalia? The question, though seemingly simple, has little universal applicability.

For example, the current issue of *Natural History* (August 1990) has a story about the Matis, a small tribal people in Brazil who apparently find the idea of covering genitalia either novel, alien, or ritualistic: as far as the accompanying photographs show, women and children go about in the buff, while men engaged in a tribal ritual wear briefs—but of the kind obviously made in the outside world. Many such peoples are known to exist in the world. For that matter, until only several decades ago most Japanese women didn't think of using pieces of cloth specifically designed to cover their genitals, except during menstruation. Ueno Chizuko herself cites her own grandmother, who, born in 1886, refused to wear anything like panties throughout her life.

The question has to be: Why do human beings cover their sex organs when they do? The immediate answer: Because the genitals are something to hide. But why hide? For one thing, Christianity, Buddhism, and probably many other religions have regarded the sex organs, especially the female part of the duo, as the most tangible instrument that hampers the promoted mode of living: asceticism.

But let's not get deep into religion. *The Theater Under the Skirt* glides over the question of religion, and my knowledge of this human activity is nil. Let's just note, as Ueno does, that when Adam and Eve were given fig leaves to hide their private parts, those parts became terribly conspicuous. And let's posit, with Ueno, that one purpose of covering the genitalia has to be to "reveal" their existence by "hiding" them. Then we may see her analogy between the "penis cases" worn by the men of a highland tribe in New Guinea and modern-day panties.

The penis cases, made of gourd shells, are practically the only thing those men, known for their misogynistic culture, wear. With their awkwardness and all, the sole function of the cases must be, observers have judged, to exaggerate the existence of the phallus.

Modern-day panties, some would suggest, are more utilitarian; some friends of mine aver they will *not* wear them unless for hygienic reasons. However, in the minds of both manufacturers and users, today's panties, like swimsuits for women, have lost much of their utilitarian value. The sharply decreased (and still decreasing) sizes, the ever-flimsier materials used, and the fancier designs of panties point to the increasing importance of their aesthetic role of accentuating that which they cover and hide: the sex organ. John Keats said, "Heard melodies are sweet, but those unheard / Are sweeter." Or, as Ueno puts it, "What's created by the imagination is always richer than the reality."

(Besides, it may be that as the Korean woman writer Lee Yeong-hui has recently said in commenting on a poem in the *Man'yōshū,* "Only a man utterly in love can attain such a poignant expression as 'Your vagina looks so lovely.'")

So modern-day panties are meant to titillate men's imaginings, to stoke up their lust. Or are they? Not quite. An informal panel discussion of young men suggests that in love-making men seldom pause to admire the panties of their partners. (Kim, a young friend of mine, says her experience confirms this.) Come to think of it, only decrepit old men like me may derive any pleasure from inspection of panties—especially those advertised in the likes of *Victoria's Secret.*

Why, then, are women so careful in selecting their panties? Because women are narcissistic, because panties have become an autoerotic device, says Ueno Chizuko. As she puts it, today's panties are "a small piece of cloth that attaches itself to the wearer's sex organ and whispers to it whenever she walks."

Either as an accentuating or autoerotic device, panties now work to "objectify" the woman and her sex organ, says Ueno. If continued, the process may lead to the extinction of the human race, she argues. To follow that argument, you must read *The Theater Under the Skirt.* For now, let me quote one of her haiku to end this piece:

Spring ferns and their kind fill up under my pink dress

Ueno Chizuko became a professor of sociology at the University of Tokyo in 1995 and served in that position there until 2011.

Lee Yeong-hui attracted attention for her books arguing that Japan's oldest extant poetry anthology Man'yōshū *was written in ancient Korean.*

Results of Carnal Prohibition Are No Surprise

April 25, 2010, *Japan Times*

When the Vatican "scandal" erupted, I happened to be reading Minakata Kumagusu's writings on homosexuals—to be exact, his writings as selected, with comments, by Inagaki Taruho (1900–1977). I was doing so because Inagaki won Japan's literary "grand prize" for his book *The Aesthetic of the Love of Boys (Shōnen'ai no bigaku)* the year it was set up, in 1969, and he did so at the urging of one of the judges, Mishima Yukio.

Minakata (1867–1941), who worked for the British Museum from his twenties and early thirties, was mainly a naturalist. But his encyclopedic knowledge extended to a number of other fields and subjects. Male same-sex love, which he discussed at length in his letters to Iwata Jun'ichi (1900–1945), was one of them, the voluminous correspondence apparently prompted by an innocuous question Iwata asked, in 1931. Iwata would later achieve his fame for his work on the subject as it relates to Japan.

So, in one letter, Minakata began a paragraph touching on the Roman Catholic Church and sodomy by referring to the Confucian thinker Ogyū Sorai (1666–1728): "Sorai, who grew up to be an adult among monks, in Kazusa, simply states that monks always think about sexual acts, because they have to try to pretend to do otherwise."

Sorai says that "in his political discourse for the eighth Tokugawa shogun," Minakata noted. At the time, Buddhism was the government-sanctioned religion, and "female violation," along with meat eating, was among the cardinal sins for the monks. They could be crucified for it.

But with the introduction of the freedom of religion at the start of the Meiji period, those bans were lifted and Buddhist monks could eat meat and have sex as they pleased. As a result, Minakata told Iwata, "in the Shingon School, it is no exaggeration to say that monks and such are all men of lascivious conduct." He knew what he was talking about. He lived not far from the holy Mt. Kōya, where Kūkai the Great Proselytizer (774–835) established his version of the Shingon School.

In contrast, "in the Ikkō School, there is little to talk about" in that regard, because its followers "are internally content, as Tachibana Haruakira says in *Idle Talk at the Window to the North*." The Ikkō School, practically suppressed during the Tokugawa Period, accepted marriage among its priests. Haruakira, better known as Nankei (1753–1805), was a physician who left accounts of travels through Japan.

"Something like 'meditating in the state of clear water' is, in truth, identical to masturbating in your mind." Here Minakata used the word *shisuikan*. "Stopping your mind to meditate" or *shikan* is the basic means of seeking enlightenment in Zen. He, in effect, dismissed any such thing as a sexual duplicity.

"In the West, too, Roman Catholicism bans female violation. Because of this, they engage in sodomy," he continued. "In addition, they concocted something called the Holy Mother on which there is not a single word in the Bible, and they have vied in making the most beautiful lady out of her, obsessed as they are less with praying to her in veneration than with the thought of doing it with her."

Minakata knew something very similar happened at Mt. Kōya. When young, he was surprised to visit the temples there, he told Iwata. He saw so many beautiful women—heavenly maidens and female Buddhas—painted on screens and such. Mt. Kōya's reputation as excluder of women still held then, but it was obvious that "the monks were totally obsessed with women."

Those who disliked women, on the other hand, "worshipped Mañjuśrī in adolescent form by taking the word *śrī (shiri)* to mean 'ass' or else had pretty young boys painted in the portraits of patriarchs where they had no part." Either way, "there was no one who did not want to do it."

The results of carnal prohibition have been well known from the outset, of course. As Minakata told Iwata, *Nihon ryōi ki*, Japan's oldest extant collection of homiletic tales, from the ninth century, includes a story about a monk who fell in love with a statue of Kisshō the Heavenly Maiden—that is, Mañjuśrī—and left buckets of semen. There has long existed a how-to volume on sex with acolytes attributed to none other than the Great Proselytizer.

Minakata concludes: "Not doing what you want to do—nay, trying hard to show you are not doing it, you waste your time only on such exterior things and never have time to listen to the religious principles." He then refers to the 240 B.C. Chinese compilation of philosophical thoughts, *Lulan*, to quote an observation: "If you have something you can't force people not to do, let them do it as much as they want to." Minakata adds: "If you do something too much, you get surfeited and stop doing it."

The ancient Chinese wisdom reminds me of America's "war on drugs," one of the most self-righteous, the most egregious, and the most destructive policies this country has ever devised for the world, other than outright wars. But let me not digress. Here my subject is sex.

Hendrik Hertzberg has pointed out, in *The New Yorker* (April 19, 2010), that practically all the Vatican "controversies" have had to do with sex: "abortion, stem-cell research, contraception, celibacy, marriage and divorce and affectional orientation." The latest, pedophilia, is a mere public rehash of what has been known for centuries.

In his article "Indulgence," Hertzberg also mentions Martin Luther, and that reminds me of the religious rebel's words I have liked ever since a friend gave me *Bartlett's Familiar Quotations* four decades ago: "There is no more lovely, friendly and charming relationship, communion or company than a good marriage." Or, as he is supposed to have put it in a verse: "He remains a fool his whole life long / Who loves not women, wine, and song."

Women can easily be men, and why not?

Genji: The Long and the Short of It
Reading Royall Tyler's New Translation

March 10, 2001, *Japan Times*

In the February 2002 issue of the monthly *Eureka*, Kawazoe Fusae gives a rundown of translations of *The Tale of Genji*—not only into foreign languages, but into modern Japanese as well. In doing so, the noted *Genji* scholar reminds us of the profound influence of Arthur Waley's translation, which appeared in six installments, from 1925 to 1933.

The French, Swedish, Dutch, German, Italian, and Hungarian translators made their versions from Waley's English. The process of secondhand translation is dubious at best, but the result was remarkable. European readers came to rank the eleventh-century Japanese author Murasaki Shikibu with Cervantes, Balzac, Jane Austen, Boccaccio, and Proust.

The Waley translation also provoked the one translator of *Genji* into modern Japanese who counted at the time: the poet Yosano Akiko (1878–1942). Yosano, who by then had made two translations (one partial and published in 1912; the other complete but lost in the Great Kanto Earthquake of 1923), apparently felt betrayed by the extravagant praise Japanese intellectuals gave Waley's work. Masamune Hakuchō, for one, announced that Waley "revived the original that appeared to be dead." For the modern Japanese reader, Murasaki's language is hard to decipher, said the foremost advocate of Naturalism of the day, whereas Waley's translation is easy to comprehend.

Yosano had read *Genji* since her early teens and didn't like this. "You do not read literature only for its meaning but for its unique language," she wrote. "*The Tale of Genji* does not exist separate from the beauty of Murasaki Shikibu's language." She was dangerously implying that *Genji* could properly be appreciated only in Japanese.

Yosano, in any case, set to work on a third translation and completed it while battling her deteriorating health. She wanted to demonstrate, Kawazoe suggests, that a translation into modern, colloquial Japanese would be superior to Waley's English translation.

Waley's work also provoked Tanizaki Jun'ichirō (1886–1964). "Mr. Waley's English translation of *Genji* is reputed to be the one great translation in recent years," the novelist wrote in his guide to prose, *Bunshō tokuhon* (1934). But the praise may be misguided because Waley has greatly "supplemented" (*oginau*) or amplified the original, he said. To make this point, Tanizaki cited a passage from Waley and translated it into Japanese to show that Waley used twice as many words as Murasaki's original.

You might say that if Yosano's nationalistic reaction was rather strange, so was Tanizaki's analysis. If you translate a translation back into the original language, you may well end up expending more words. Also, in his third (and for him, definitive) translation of *Genji*, he used one third more words in restating what Murasaki said. If modern Japanese requires more words than classical Japanese in saying the same thing, English can certainly require more words than Japanese in doing the same, can't it?

The aim of Tanizaki's analysis was even more questionable. He wanted to advance the claim that the Japanese people are laconic, Westerners loquacious. The only other example of Western verbosity he cited was Theodore Dreiser.

And yet, where Tanizaki saw Waley exemplifying the Western proclivity to say things that the Japanese would rather leave unsaid, Edward Seidensticker simply saw a translator's willfulness. In publishing his translation of *Genji*, in 1976, he said that Waley's "amplifying and embroidering," which is "continuous," impels one to conclude that "Murasaki Shikibu has the worst of it all the way." This criticism was notable because it came from a scholar who professed his indebtedness to Waley to be so deep that preparing a new translation "felt like sacrilege."

So, let us look at the passage Tanizaki quoted to make his case. It occurs at the start of "Suma" chapter. Prince Genji, the protagonist of the story, decides to exile himself to a remote coastal village because of the troubles he has created for himself in the Capital. Here's how Waley imagined Murasaki would have written in English:

> There was Suma. It might not be such a bad place to choose. There had indeed once been some houses there; but it was now a long way to the nearest village and the coast wore a very deserted aspect. Apart from a few fishermen's huts there was not anywhere a sign of life. This did not matter, for a thickly populated, noisy place was not at all what he wanted; but even Suma was a terribly long way from the Capital, and the prospect of being separated from all those whose society he liked best was not at all inviting. His life hitherto had been one long series of disasters. As for the future, it did not bear thinking of! Clearly the world held in store for him nothing but disappointment and vexation.

Elegant and smooth Waley certainly is. But he is also extravagant. How much so becomes immediately clear when you put this side by side with Seidensticker's rendition.

> He thought of the Suma coast. People of worth had once lived there, he was told, but now it was deserted save for the huts of fishermen, and even they were few. The alternative was worse, to go on living this public life, so to speak, with people streaming in and out of his house. Yet he would have to leave, and affairs at court would continue to be much on his mind if he did leave. This irresolution was making life difficult for his people. Unsettling thoughts of the past and the future chased one another through his mind.

As Tanizaki noted, Murasaki doesn't say anything like "It [Suma] might not be such a bad place to choose," and Seidensticker doesn't,

either. When it comes to something like "the prospect of being sepa-
rated from all those whose society he liked best was not at all inviting,"
the only thing the original says is *"furusato obotsukanakarubeki,"* "the
hometown would worry him." Even though Seidensticker's translation
of this sentence, "affairs at court would continue to be much on his mind
if he did leave," may not be too "economical of words" (his characterization of Murasaki's style), altogether he uses a quarter less words than
Waley in re-creating in English what Murasaki describes (100 versus 134
words).

Little wonder Tanizaki pointedly noted that Waley may add *seim-
itsu*, "precision," but in doing so he loses *anji*, "suggestiveness."

So, how does our third translator into English, Royall Tyler, handle
the same passage?

> There was Suma, yes, but while someone had lived there long ago, he
> gathered that the place was now extremely isolated and that there was
> hardly a fisherman's hut to be seen there—not that he can have wished to
> live among milling crowds. On the other hand, merely being away from
> the City would make him worry about home. His mind was in undigni-
> fied confusion. He reflected at length on what was past and what was yet
> to come, and the effort brought many sorrows to mind.

Here, I might note the changes in *Genji* scholarship over the past
century.

When Waley decided to translate *Genji*, the scholarship wasn't
extensive. I have tried to find out what annotated texts Waley may have
used, but learned only that whatever texts he may have had were unlikely
to have been fully annotated. This may not have mattered much to a linguistic genius who famously observed: "since the classical [Japanese]
language has an easy grammar and limited vocabulary, a few months
should suffice for the mastering of it." Still, the truth is, even dedicated
Japanese scholars of classical Japanese finds *Genji* opaque.

By the time Seidensticker started his work, a fully annotated text
with interlinear notes indicating who is saying what was out, and he

could use several other texts and consult translations, including those by Yosano and Tanizaki. Whether what he saw in Waley was the impetus or not isn't clear, but Tanizaki started translating *Genji* into modern Japanese in 1935 and in the end produced three different versions (published in 1941, 1954, 1960). And Seidensticker was a Tanizaki translator.

Genji scholarship has greatly expanded in Japan and elsewhere since Seidensticker's days, producing highly specialized studies such as the one by my friend Doris Bargen focusing on spirit possession in the tale, *A Woman's Weapon* (University of Hawaii, 1997). Among the theories advanced has been an argument—initially elaborated by Japanese scholars, then taken up by some of their American counterparts—that since *Genji* is mostly written in the present tense, an attempt should be made to re-create the effect in English (and other languages) as well.

It may be in reflection of these developments that Tyler acknowledges the existence of the Waley and Seidensticker translations but doesn't talk about either the way Seidensticker spoke of Waley's. On the other hand, he makes clear that he differs from Seidensticker in the assessment of the basic matter: Murasaki's prose. Where Seidensticker speaks of a language "brisker and more laconic" than Waley's English suggests, Tyler speaks of "the tale's many long sentences" and "its evenness of flow." And each, naturally, tries to re-create his view in translation.

So, in the opening part of the passage referred to earlier, Waley deploys five sentences, Seidensticker three, and Tyler just one, which is what Murasaki does, though this observation assumes that such comparative parsing in such different languages has any value. Despite his best effort, Tyler often fails in this particular endeavor. But his effort is commendable. As may be expected, Tyler uses even less embroidery than Seidensticker—in this passage, 88 words versus 100.

What is curious in this light is Tyler's decision to apply the 5-7-5-7-7-syllable pattern to his translation of tanka. *The Tale of Genji* is full of them—795, by Tyler's count. As he notes, however, Japanese is a polysyllabic language, so applying the syllabic count in English translation means embroidery. Indeed, Tyler's verse translations are often as extravagant as Waley's prose translation. Some prefer nettles, as Seidensticker put it in translating the title of one of Tanizaki's stories. Tyler's decision nonetheless strikes me as a strange error. The contrast between verse and prose is conspicuous.

Is Tyler's translation superior to those by Waley and Seidensticker? In the overall accuracy, yes. Will it supersede them? Probably, no. I say this because on the question of faithfulness to the original alone, a translator faces many choices.

Take the word *himegimi* that occurs a few sentences after the passage we've seen, in the original. It would normally be translated as "princess." Yosano, who usually makes explicit the person suggested or referred to but unspecified, translates it as *wakai fujin*, "(his) young wife." Waley names the person, Murasaki. Tanizaki, who attempts to be as rigorously faithful to the original as he can, uses the word as is and in the footnote tells the reader that Murasaki is meant. Seidensticker follows the example of Waley. Tyler translates the word as "his darling." Which is better? Which do you prefer?

Genji's Poetry of Spirit Possession

July 22, 1997, *Japan Times*

Among the best-known literary offshoots of *The Tale of Genji* is the nō play *Lady Aoi (Aoi no ue)*. Composed about 400 years after Murasaki Shikibu wrote the famous romance, it presents Lady Rokujō as a jealous, vengeful soul who kills Lady Aoi by means of spirit possession *(mono no ke)*.

Why is Rokujō jealous? Because she, a widow with a daughter, is no more than one partner of the polygynous Genji the Shining Prince, while Aoi is his (then) "principal wife." Why vengeful? Because during a festival Aoi's servants insulted her by perpetrating violence against her carriage.

What makes this play particularly unforgettable is the imaginative way it depicts the avenger-avenged relationship: it shows the target of Rokujō's fury, Aoi, only as a folded "short-sleeve" kimono *(kosode)* laid on the stage floor, which Rokujō crouches down to strike with her fan. As may be expected, in the second half of the play where the protagonist *(shite)* reveals her true self, the actor wears a white *han'nya* mask, a face horribly deformed with jealousy.

Thus *Aoi no ue* impresses upon us, cogently, concisely, the very antithesis of the "vanished world of elegance and refinement" that the mention of *The Tale of Genji* often evokes: a dark world of jealousy, hatred, and murderous intent, that comes with spirit possession, exorcism, and, at times, even death.

This is good; after all, love in a polygynous world can't be all song, dance, and poetry.

The trouble with *Aoi no ue,* argues Doris Bargen in her startlingly intense book *A Woman's Weapon: Spirit Possession in* The Tale of Genji (University of Hawaii Press, 1997), is that the play gets the true import of the Rokujō-Aoi episode wrong. This is a serious matter because *Aoi no ue* crystallizes a one-sided view of spirit possession that practically all readers of the *Genji,* Japanese and non-Japanese, have accepted and followed.

There are of course reasons for the general acceptance of the view.

During Murasaki's days, when someone suffered inexplicable emotional distress, the custom was to judge that the person was "possessed" and to look for a possessor. In that milieu, those suspected of being possessors, the circumstances warranting, would develop self-doubts. As Murasaki tells us, that is exactly what happens in the Rokujō-Aoi relationship.

Aoi falls ill, and her exorcists, unable to pinpoint the cause, begin a search for the culprit. Hearing the rumors that she is one of the suspects, Rokujō, a woman of uncommon self-awareness, begins to wonder: "I do worry about myself and lament my fate, but I have no wish to do other people harm. Still, a soul, while brooding, might indeed wander off (to someone else)." These self-doubts are followed by her repeated dreams in which she finds herself physically abusing Aoi in retaliation for what was done to her during "the carriage quarrel."

There is, in addition, the fact that when Aoi in her agony and delirium pleads that she be spared, for a while, the oppressive incantations for exorcism, it is Genji himself that identifies the voice coming from his wife as Rokujō's.

Does not all this prove that the interpretation starkly given in *Aoi no ue* is correct? No, says Bargen. By deploying modern anthropology and psychology to examine the triangle entailing Rokujō, Aoi, and Genji, she concludes that Rokujō may be culpable but to focus on her culpability alone is to miss Murasaki's point.

Rokujō's anxiety about her own culpability must be considered along with her "defensive rationalization," Bargen argues, "that her conscious purpose is not to harm Aoi but merely to use her rival as a way to get at her real tormentor, Genji." As Murasaki observes with acute sympathy, the person of whom Rokujō, in her psychological battle, tries not to think but ends up thinking *(omowaji to omou mo mono o omou)* is not Rokujō but the "heartless" Genji.

Rokujō's nightmares in which she "pulls Aoi around" *(hikimasaguri)* and "strikes her" *(uchi-kanaguru)* reveal, Bargen notes, that Rokujō's "plight is not unlike that of a prophet who foresees his fate but is helpless to alter it." Therein lies her tragedy.

As for Aoi, whose arranged marriage to Genji has never been satisfactory from the outset, the primary cause of her mental disorders is of course Genji's promiscuity. That much is understood. Yet when at the height of her suffering, just before childbirth, she summons Genji to her bedside, in privacy, and speaks, and when Genji decides that the speaker was Rokujō the spirit possessor, not Aoi the possessed, most readers take Genji's judgment as stated. The very possibility that Aoi may have spoken her own mind is not considered.

Is Genji trustworthy? No, says Bargen. As the pivotal figure in the sexual entanglements, he is "in no position to analyze coolly the drama he has been drawn into." A man of considerable sensitivity, he "is pulled toward" the truth of the situation, yes, but "instinctively shies away from" it. To face up to the fact that he is the one to blame confers no advantage upon him.

In presenting her case, Bargen is particularly original in her analysis of the poem (tanka) Aoi offers—poetry in spirit possession is rare, Bargen adds—in which the pleading is made to "tie down my disturbed soul and make it stay" *(midaruru waga tama o musubi-todome yo).*

As Bargen sees it, the spirit possession involving Rokujō and Aoi is "an esoteric spiritual rite in which the psychologically allied women vent their repressed anger at a third party—Genji—and at the polygynous society that allows men to neglect their women with near impunity." Hence her judgment that the nō drama *Aoi no ue* misrepresents the role of the possessed woman as a folded robe, deprived of all agency.

Not only does the Rokujō of the play, made to embody uncontrollable rage, appear as the only figure that matters in the drama, but the one-sidedness is further emphasized by presenting Aoi as a "disembodied" figure. The *kosode* silently placed on the stage may be "emotionally charged," but "[Aoi's] presence is an absence." She is "an involuntary participant" throughout.

In Bargen's erudite and insightful book, the Rokujō-Aoi-Genji complexity is just one of five instances of spirit possession analyzed. She addresses with equal care the cases of Yūgao (whose sudden death is one of the first harrowing moments in *The Tale of Genji*), Murasaki (not the person who wrote the story, but another of Genji's wives; the description of her shifting psychological struggle is one of the many features that make the *Genji* enduring), the Third Princess (another wife, who, on account of Genji's neglect, ends up committing adultery), and Ukifune (whose struggle with two suitors, long after Genji's death, concludes the story).

A Woman's Weapon is a book of eye-opening feminist polemics and will prove indispensable to any reader of *The Tale of Genji*. It is illustrated with twenty-four carefully assembled paintings, fourteen of them in color.

Shining a Light on Turkish-Japanese Ties

June 27, 2005, *Japan Times*

Selçuk Esenbel was in town. For many years now a professor of history at Bogaziçi University, Istanbul, Selçuk was, when I met her more than thirty years ago, studying Japanese history at Columbia University. The fruit of that study is her 1998 tome, which she gave me during her previous visit to New York five years ago: *Even the Gods Rebel: The Peasants of Takaino and the 1871 Nakano Uprising in Japan* (Association of Asian Studies, 1998).

If the subject of this book, a peasant rebellion, *hyakushō ikki,* in the fourth year of Meiji period (1868–1912), confuses most Japanese, as it did me, that's because "peasant uprisings" are indelibly associated with the feudal Edo Period (1603–1868), but not with the "enlightened" Meiji. If it does, the subject of her article Selçuk gave me this time will dumbfound them. It deals with what she calls "a forgotten political legacy": Japan's extensive efforts to cultivate and maintain relations with Muslims until the country was defeated in the Second World War. The article, "Japan's Global Claim to Asia and the World of Islam: Transnational Nationalism and World Power, 1900–1945," was published in *The American Historical Review* (October 2004).

Selçuk's giving me her latest work as soon as we met was fortuitous. When we picked a restaurant for dinner, I knew one question I'd ask would be the correct roman spelling of a Turkish name which, from a Japanese transliteration, comes out as "Abdul Hannan Safa." I had just read

Yuasa Atsuko's *Roy to Kyōko* (Chūō Kōron Sha, 1984), which describes the author's life with Roy—Roy James—whose real name, Yuasa tells us, was that. As soon as I brought up the spelling question, Selçuk pointed to the last footnote of her article she'd just given me. It read:

> Roy James, who was a popular media figure in 1960s Japan, most likely would not have received such acclaim if it were known that his given name was Ramadan, the holiest of months in the Islamic calendar. James (who spoke stilted English but had the physical appearance of a Westerner) was the son of a religious cleric serving the Tokyo mosque who was a member of the émigré community from Russia.

James is a figure I had remembered from the decade before I left Japan, and I may have thought he was Turkish, but Yuasa certainly tells a story I hadn't imagined.

Abdul Hannan Safa's father was a lieutenant of the Turkish Army that fought the Soviets in Siberia and was defeated—perhaps in what Selçuk refers to as "the Basmaci uprising of the Turkic populations in Central Asia in 1922." He had come to Japan via Korea, and along the way married a compatriot. Their son was born in Keiō University Hospital, in 1929. Called "Hannan Boy," he grew up as the darling of the neighborhood mothers in Shitamachi, an enclave for the poor, as opposed to Yamanote, an enclave for the upper class, where Yuasa, who married him, in 1957, had grown up. Every day the Japanese women took him to a public bathhouse—to the women's section, of course, and that's why he liked women, Abdul Hannan would tell Yuasa. One day, while his custodians weren't watching, the boy almost drowned. His real mother was upset and wouldn't allow him to go to a bathhouse again.

Toward the end of the Second World War, as Turkey severed its relations with Germany and declared war against it, Abdul Hannan, like all other Turks living in Japan, became an enemy alien, was rounded up for hard labor, and almost died. In the confusion of the last phase of the war, not many Japanese knew, as Yuasa in her wealthy, pampered life certainly did not, that Turkey had become an enemy country.

Turkey, of course, became one of the victorious nations when Germany and Japan were defeated. But its changed status did not vastly improve Abdul Hannan's life, even though in the postwar chaos his—to the Japanese—unmistakably "Western" appearance of blond hair and blue eyes helped. With the stage name of "Roy James," and with cabarets and such becoming all the rage after the war, he started getting occasional jobs as a performer, in time becoming a highly successful MC, ranked as the most popular TV MC for sixteen consecutive years. His wit and vast and exact memory also made him popular among those holding corporate meetings. Unhappily, in his prime he was struck down with one of the rarest diseases in which the jaw bone grows uncontrollably. After several years of struggle he died, in 1982.

So, why had Abdul Hannan's father headed for Japan, of all places? As Selçuk explains, the impetus was Japan's defeat of the Russian Empire, in 1905. Muslim newspapers celebrated it as "the victory of the downtrodden Eastern peoples over the invincible West." Not just Muslims. I sometimes come across a taxi driver from Africa who thinks Japan is special because of the victory. Just the other day I was reading an account of Kishi Nobusuke as prime minister (1957–60), which noted that during his first extended Asian trip in that capacity, Prime Minister Jawaharlal Nehru, of India, reminded him of that victory.

Selçuk adds: "a Turkish nationalist feminist, Halide Edip, like many other women, named her son Togo." Admiral Tōgō Heihachirō annihilated Russia's Baltic Fleet in the Battle of Tsushima. Selçuk's own grandfather, then a young naval officer, saluted the admiral when he made a port call in Turkey. Or so I remember her telling me in the days we were romping about town more than three decades ago. (She recently corrected this, saying her maternal grandfather met another hero of the Russo–Japanese War, Gen. Nogi Maresuke, during his European tour, in 1911.)

Japan was quick to seize the idea of incorporating what Selçuk describes as "global enthusiasm" into its geopolitical strategy as a world power. Many Japanese earnestly studied Islam, some converted to Islam. Among the converts, Hadji Muhammad Saleh Suzuki Tsuyoshi organized the Hezbollah in Indonesia. Selçuk's account solved one puzzle I'd nursed since reading one of Laurens van der Post's stories based on his own experience: Muslim waiters, bellboys, servants, and such in Malaysia suddenly shedding their subservience to Europeans as they sensed their imminent retreat—even before Japan's assault in the region, in 1941.

You may wonder where "Kyōko" in Yuasa's *Roy to Kyōko* comes from. In Mishima Yukio's novel *Kyōko's House (Kyōko no ie)*, Kyōko, to whose "salon" the four main characters are drawn, was modeled on Yuasa Atsuko. Mishima was a member of her salon, and Yuasa arranged his marriage to Sugiyama Yōko, in 1958. Roy James was the MC at the wedding.

From the Outside Looking In
The Donald Richie Reader

August 5, 2001, *Japan Times*

Full disclosure: I've known Donald Richie for more than twenty years and, like many people who have known him for a long time, I count him among my good friends. Once, he helped me write a full-length book on the history of Japanese poetry out of a slim collection I had made of English translations of the one Bashō' haiku—yes, the one about an old pond and a frog. Another time, I committed an affront that would have prompted a different person to drop me. He simply waved it off with a smile. Richie is generous, considerate, and tolerant.

The first book I read of Richie's many volumes was *The Inland Sea* (1971). I read it because the agency where I work had a copy in its small library. It was among the books our Tokyo office had bought for its New York branch, assuming, obviously, that it was a tourist guide or else one of those books written to "introduce Japan to the West."

The Tokyo office wasn't completely off the mark: *The Inland Sea* does introduce Japan to the West. But it does so in a way whoever was in charge in Tokyo would have hastily decided not to send it to New York had he read the book.

Visiting Onomichi, for example, Richie goes to a shabby striptease theater; it advertises an "all-nude" show. Watching it, he recalls another one in a different place, one held "on the bare tatami of someone's living room ... cramped between the wife's sewing machine and the children's toy-box."

That show consisted of three acts: she-she, she-he, and she-solo,

Richie recollects. In the third act, the principal "she," a "pleasant young country girl . . . promptly produced a number of objects: a banana, a full beer bottle, a length of string. With no more preamble than a small smile, she peeled the banana with her fingers, inserted it, and bit off great chunks. When it was consumed, she deftly removed it and put the mess daintily on a square of tissues. . . ."

Richie doesn't let it go at that. If he did, Richie wouldn't be Richie, *The Inland Sea* wouldn't be what it is: a series of reflections on Japanese culture and society given in the guise of a journey of personal exploration. So, he goes on to describe the manner of the young stripteaser's departure to make a seemingly obvious point on routine Japanese behavior.

Her act over, "she made a low and formal bow . . . smiled a most charming smile and . . . said: '*Dōmo shitsurei itashimashita*,' a common polite phrase that might be translated as 'I have been very rude.' All of this was accomplished without the least suspicion of irony, and none was necessary. This is what you say when you must leave, when you have stayed perhaps a bit too long, when you wish to reassure and at the same time show an attractive degree of gentility."

Now, I read *The Inland Sea* in the 70s and I don't recall whether I wondered why the book captivated me (except for the sex part). But rereading these passages, and reading a number of pieces I hadn't seen before, in *The Donald Richie Reader,* edited and compiled by Arturo Silva (Stone Bridge Press, 2001), I did wonder: What makes Richie so good as a cultural observer and commentator? Now I think I know the answer. He has no cultural condescension, and he writes with enviable felicity.

These days, talk of cultural condescension may seem out of place. But it is still common. To give just two recent American examples, a woman journalist wrote a long article questioning if a feminist movement is possible in Japan, and an editorialist of a major daily openly cast into doubt the validity of Japan's judicial system when a U.S. soldier suspected of rape in Okinawa was handed over to the Japanese police. The "We beat Japan, didn't we?" or "Japan is a backward Oriental country, isn't it?" attitude persists.

To any member of Donald Richie's generation, condescension could have come naturally. Born in Lima, Ohio, in 1924, Richie arrived in Japan not long after the Occupation started, on New Year's Eve, in 1946. It was during the time when, to cite his own example, an "Occupier" watching a Japanese carpenter with a saw could say, with a smile, with no irony, "These people got a long way to go." Why? Because Japanese use strength when they pull the saw, while Americans do so when they push the saw. A "topsy-turvy world"!

It apparently didn't occur to this particular Occupier that from the Japanese perspective "the world" could have been so described.

Why didn't Richie have a condescending attitude? He was, after all, a young citizen of a freshly, overwhelmingly, victorious nation. The correct answer may be that it is a matter of temperament and character. Still, I think it is telling that his early literary (and perhaps philosophical) mentor was Lindley Williams Hubbell. In 1943, while his ship was docked in New York, Richie went to the Map Room of the New York Public Library, where the poet happened to work. Characteristically, Hubbell, then forty-two years old, established an easy rapport with the nineteen-year-old merchant marine. Hubbell went to Japan in 1953, became a Japanese citizen, and died in Kyoto.

Richie was also among the first to be drawn to Helen Mears' 1948 book, *Mirror for Americans: Japan*. Unlike Richie, a member of the Occupation, Mears was so bluntly critical of the premises on which the Occupation policy was based that General MacArthur, Supreme Commander for the Allied Powers, personally stepped in to prohibit the publication of the Japanese translation of her book. Richie heard about it, acquired a copy, and reviewed it, favorably, for *The Pacific Stars and Stripes*.

It is also telling that Richie counts among the "best books on Japan" Kurt Singer's *Mirror, Sword and Jewel*. Though not published until the early seventies, it is a collection of reflections on Japan during the decade of the thirties when the German-Jewish philosopher taught, first, at the Imperial University of Tokyo and, then, at the Second Higher School, in Sendai. To quote one of the more perceptive passages from Singer:

> Let [the foreigner], experimentally but unreservedly, behave according
> to Japanese custom, and he will instantly feel what a cell endowed with
> rudiments of human sensibility must be supposed to feel in a well-coor-
> dinated body. There is a bewildering number of conventions and taboos,
> in various degrees of unintelligibility; if these are mastered and observed,
> life becomes singularly easy and entrancing.

Drop everything and read Richie's funny piece on being a sole foreigner on the jury for the Competition for Cultural Films on Japan! It's
an excerpt from his journals, dated October 27.

Arturo Silva, who compiled and edited *The Donald Richie Reader*
ably, with dedication, says of Richie: "The man is charming, open, witty,
a cosmopolitan *flâneur*. The style, the prose, is as well. He is comfortable to read, smooth, steady, melodious. The art is disguised, remarks
flow naturally." I agree. I may only add, perhaps unnecessarily, that
Richie is blessed with a fiction writer's ease in deploying various styles
as occasion requires. Compare, for example, the brief, cogent profile of
Mifune Toshirō, the encomium to the epitome of culinary simplicity,
morokyū, the Chekhovian short story *Commuting*, and the obviously
well-informed, serio-comic discourse, "The Sex Market: The Commer-
cialization of a Commodity."

Silva, an eighteen-year resident of Japan, occasionally objects
to Richie as a long-standing friend might. One example concerns a
Watanabe Hanako. A vignette that appears in *Different People* (1987),
it describes the reaction of Richie's acquaintance, "the tofu man's wife,"
when she misses a train.

"Mrs. Watanabe stopped short in front of the closed doors now
sliding past and smiled. At a moment when we of the West would have
turned our mouths down, she turned hers up. It was not an ironic
grimace, common enough, nor was it mock despair for the benefit of
those looking on. The smile was innocent and natural enough to seem
instinctive."

This, as you may expect, prompts Richie to philosophical musings, to which Silva makes a simple response: "there are any number of

Japanese who miss their train—and curse." I agree with Silva, though from a reverse perspective. I take the subway every morning in New York City. Half of those facing the train doors sliding shut before them smile, not grimace.

Richie once wrote to me: "I, an American, prefer to live in Tokyo; you, a Japanese, prefer to live in New York." If he followed this with a wise cultural observation, as he must have, I don't remember it. But, if he had, it may have been a condensed version of what he says in "Intimacy and Distance: On Being a Foreigner in Japan" (from *Partial Views*, 1993):

> *Foreigners, says Alastair Reid, are curable romantics. They retain an illusion from childhood that there might be someplace into which they can finally sink to rest: some magic land, some golden age, some significantly other self. Yet his own oddness keeps the foreigner separate from every encounter. Unless he regards this as something fruitful, he cannot be considered cured.*

COUNTERCLOCKWISE FROM TOP LEFT: Party for translation of Ashbery's *The Wave*, Robert Fagan left, 1991; the Japan-U.S. Friendship Commission's 1999 prize for translation of *Breeze Through Bamboo: Kanshi of Ema Saikō*, with Nancy, Hiro, and Amy Heinrich, 2001; with Burton Watson— the prize above was given after Burt delivered a Soshitsu Sen XV Distinguished Lecture—with Hiro, Hamaji Michio, and Burt, 2001; with Ronald Homer Bayes, early 1990s; the day I became an American citizen, 2006; I served as Japanese judge of the UNIS Haiku Contest, 2006–2018.

Bedfellows of Those "Lax," "Insular" Japanese

May 30, 2011, *Japan Times*

Are some of those who write for the *New York Times* utterly unaware of the rest of the world—including, yes, the United States?

Take the article last month, "Culture of Complicity Tied to Stricken Nuclear Plant" (April 21, 2011).

"Given the fierce insularity of Japan's nuclear industry," the article by Norimitsu Onishi and Ken Belson triumphantly began, "it was perhaps fitting that an outsider exposed the most serious safety cover-up in the history of Japanese nuclear power."

Onishi and Belson went on to detail how the regulators "colluded" with the regulated not to reveal the possible flaw pointed out by "an outsider," a Japanese American inspector working for General Electric—without mentioning that GE was the designer of the troubled nuclear reactors. For that matter, they did not refer to the March 15 ABC News article "Fukushima: Mark 1 Nuclear Reactor Design Caused GE Scientist To Quit In Protest." The protest and resignation happened thirty-five years ago.

The rest of the Onishi-Belson story was predictable. The disaster was a result of the regulatory laxity created by "politicians, bureaucrats and industry executives"—and scientists, too—who are "single-mindedly focused on expanding nuclear power." These people form "the nuclear power village" where they work in a network of backslappers and backscratchers, rewarding one another with "lucrative positions" and such while ostracizing those who do not agree with them.

"Just as in any Japanese village," the reporting duo did not forget to add, as if the inhabitants of a village of any other country would act any different. Actually, there's no need to bring in the urban-rural split prevalent in every part of the world. The "village" could be a town, a gated community, a co-op building. But Onishi and Belson had to show off their awareness of anthropological peculiarities long ascribed to Japan.

Is complicity, along with collusion, one distinguishing trait of Japanese "culture"? It definitely is not. Remember the torrents of news articles on the "Deepwater Horizon Oil Spill" last year?

On April 20, 2010, BP's giant oil rig in the Gulf of Mexico exploded, killing eleven people. BP estimated the resultant oil leak occurring 1.5 km below on the sea floor at a rate far below what would later become an accepted figure. Outside scientists protested at once, but no matter. The U.S. government went along with the BP estimate. They said they had no independent means of measuring it. The rest, as they say, is history.

Onishi and Belson, let alone their *Times* editors, surely knew all this when the news came out that the earthquake and tsunami damaged the Fukushima nuclear reactors. Just glancing at the Internet for headlines, you at once come up with the following:

"U.S. exempted BP's Gulf of Mexico drilling from environmental impact study" (*The Washington Post*, May 5, 2010);

"Gulf oil spill: Is MMS so corrupt it must be abolished?" (*The Christian Science Monitor*, May 7, 2010);

"The Spill, The Scandal and the President" (*Rolling Stone*, June 8, 2010);

"Barton BP Apology Spurs Rebuke From Other Republicans" (*Businessweek*, June 17, 2010).

Complicity? Collusion? Backscratching? Single-minded focus on energy development? It was all there.

"MMS" in the *Christian Science Monitor* headline is Minerals Management Service, the government agency responsible for oil drilling and other resources development. The *Rolling Stone* article said of it: "According to reports by Interior's inspector general, MMS staffers were both literally and figuratively in bed with the oil industry. When agency staffers weren't joining industry employees for coke parties or trips to corporate ski chalets, they were having sex with oil-company officials."

I don't know if coke or sex was involved in "the nuclear power village."

"Interior" is the Interior Department, the overseer of the MMS, just as Japan's Ministry of Economy, Trade and Industry, the promoter of nuclear energy, is of the Nuclear and Industrial Safety Agency.

The U.S. government's report that came out in January, "Deep Water: The Gulf Oil Disaster and the Future of Offshore Drilling," characterized MMS's mission as "conflicted" by "oversight—and oversights." This outcome was inevitable or "mandated." The agency was tasked, the report said, to "awkwardly" combine "the two priorities, as a series of Congresses, Presidents, and Secretaries of the Interior—responding to competing constituencies in explicitly political ways—sought to reconcile the sometimes conflicting goals of environmental protection, energy independence, and revenue generation."

"Barton BP Apology" in the *Businessweek* headline referred to the infamous incident after President Obama worked out a financial deal with the British oil company to pay for the damages of the oil spill. During a subsequent hearing by the House Energy and Commerce Committee, Texas Republican Joe Barton accused Obama of perpetrating a "shakedown" on the company and "apologized" to its CEO, Tony Hayward. This was too much for even the Republican stalwarts, and they forced Barton to "apologize."

Did Barton's act change anything? No, sir. The House lawmaker went on to easily win his thirteenth term in the 2010 midterm election. Not only that, the House Republicans were able to "shellac" Obama.

Less than three weeks ago, on May 10, another pair of *Times* reporters gave an interesting twist to the matter with the headline: "Lag in Closing a Japanese Nuclear Plant Reflects Erosion of a Culture of Consensus." But that's another story.

To go back to Onishi and Belson, "insularity" is one of the half-dozen words with which foreigners have long delighted in saying the Japanese are a race apart—since Ruth Benedict's *The Chrysanthemum and the Sword*. And many Japanese, lest they disappoint them, have aped them. "Insularity," in fact, was among the reasons Edward Seidensticker gave in declaring he was leaving Japan for good, back in the 1980s. The famed scholar of Japanese literature announced his decision to divorce Japan, as it were, in his foreword to Jared Taylor's *Shadows of the Rising Sun*.

Seidensticker, however, went back to Japan, and died there. Taylor, who grew up in Japan and stated in his book that his Japanese is so good most Japanese took him to be a native Japanese over the phone, went on to gain prominence as a white supremacist.

"Gaijin" Putting Down Roots in Japan

May 25, 1999, *Japan Times*

"The future. Tentatively, she considers it. . . . What will it be like for her when she's old and, as seems likely, alone? . . . In a little place like this one? . . . A very small place then, a six-mat room, with a cat—no, that will never be allowed, and anyhow Japanese cats are different, nervous and suspicious. . . . Still, that's the idea. She'll be a nice old lady, still rather British, waylaying cats, worrying about dogs. Perhaps she'll write long, crotchety letters to the *Japan Times*."

This is Gwyneth Plummer, one of the several foreign residents of Tokyo whom Dianne Highbridge imagines and describes in her second novel, *In the Empire of Dreams* (Soho Press, 1999). (One of them is Teruko, a Japanese who's "returned native" after years in the United States; another, Lew, seems to be a non-resident, who's just visiting Tokyo on business.) These characters are loosely linked in a novel of ten more-or-less-independent chapters, each focusing on a single person.

Gwyneth has taught English to Yamamoto Tomokazu, who, because of his ability to speak English, is obliged to "attend" foreigners who come to his company for business deals, and Lew—the most fascinatingly fleeting of the main characters—is one such foreigner.

Tomokazu (Tommy), in turn, once asks Gwyneth to be a facilitator of sorts for his love for Liz, and that's how Gwyneth meets the Australian, a "sullen-looking girl, with droopy light-brown hair and some inadequately concealed spots."

And Liz, who some years back came to Tokyo from London on

scholarship to study a certain era of Japanese history (and thus may come closest to being the author's alter ego), counts, among her friends, Cathy, her compatriot who's "in love with pots and things," and Elaine, an American student who goes on staying in Japan in her struggle to complete her dissertation on a particularly obscure aspect of Japanese Buddhism.

Cathy is acquainted with Claudine because she teaches English at the company where Claudine's husband, Michael, works. And Claudine "knows" Elaine, in a way. At a train station a man commits suicide by throwing himself in front of an incoming car, and "the voice of an American woman" she hears, "Oh, God, it's a suicide!," turns out to be Elaine's, though this remains unrevealed to both.

Not that such linkages are deployed in this novel to present some sort of foreign residents' collective reaction to the country they've chosen to live in or visit. Rather, they are used to create a group portrait—a picture scroll, really—to depict a variety of people reacting, each in a different way, to an environment that originally isn't their own or, for a while, ceased to be. And in Highbridge's deft hand and observant eye, no one is made into a type.

Claudine, for example, could easily be cast as one: all sensitivity but little sense. Married to a well-paid businessman who she suspects is running an affair with a young, pretty Japanese "office lady" in his company, she has no real stake in acquiring knowledge about Japanese society, in the sense that Liz, Cathy, and Elaine do. But she isn't presented as an intolerant cultural shrew.

Claudine lives near the Yamanote Line and takes it almost every day. So encounters with gropers *(chikan)*—the bane of Caucasian women, as all accounts tell us—are inevitable. But here's the way one such encounter is described:

Once a man—an ordinary middle-aged man with a perspiring nose—rubbed himself against her, trapping her against the door. He got off at her station—it really was his station, too—and, beside her in the crowd pushing towards the stairs, muttered urgently in her ear, 'I rub you!' Claudine broke away and stood at the bottom of the stairs and laughed till he was out of sight.

Note the nice touch, "it really was his station, too." It continues:

"[There are] the mornings when sometimes, nobody's fault, she is crushed against someone much more attractive, smelling faintly of aftershave, whose face, near her own (because he's usually not very tall) maintains a polite neutrality to the last, but who is clearly finding the whole thing as interesting as she does. She likes Japanese men on the whole, their thick hair and neat bodies, their cool."

This is not to say, incidentally, that the man with whom she ends up having extramarital sex is Japanese, but Gary, another English teacher at her school. (The title of this fiction comes from the name of the love hotel where they go to do it.)

Living in a very different culture can be stressful, of course. Janet, another English teacher, is a large woman who in a rush-hour train "sometimes imagines herself a volcanic island risen out of a dark sea." Once she throws a Christmas party for her Japanese students and non-Japanese friends. In the course of the evening, she suddenly fills with emotion:

"She feels an affection for all gaijin, even Nigel [with his stinking feet]. Well, not necessarily all, not IBM executives or diplomats or people like that, they don't need it, or the young with their backpacks, on the way to somewhere else. The real gaijin, she thinks. The ones who can't go home, not just yet. The ones still here, still fumbling for the right words in a language made for not explaining, still searching for lovers whose embraces bring to mind no pain. . . ."

Then, Highbridge adds: "Janet is drunk."

After all her guests are gone, Janet hears the cry of a sweet potato man: "She scrabbles for money in her purse, finds her clogs in the shoe box, and dashes down the side passage, leaving the door swinging. There he is, at the end of the road, going slowly away from her. She can see through the snow the fire in the brazier glowing red on the back of the truck, and clumsily, slipping and sliding on the icy road, she runs after it, just managing to keep it in view."

One day in the early 1990s I received a letter for requesting permission to quote a passage from my translation, Chieko and Other Poems of Takamura

Kōtarō *(University of Hawaii Press, 1980). She'd like to cite some lines for her novel to be called* Reflections at the Water's Edge, *she wrote. Her name was Dianne Highbridge. In time I learned she was originally from Australia and, while studying at the University of London, won a scholarship to go to the University of Tokyo to research Hirazuka Raichō and other early women who pushed for women's liberation. Takamura (née Naganuma) Chieko, a painter, was one of them and did the cover design for the first issue of the group's magazine* Seitō (Bluestockings).

When Dianne's first novel, A Much Younger Man *(Soho, 1998), was published, she came to New York and I invited her for lunch at A Dish of Salt, whose proprietress Mary Ann Lum I knew. It was not long after a school-teacher near Seattle having sex with a student had become a scandal, and Dianne said that part of her book tour on the West Coast was canceled as a result. She had come to New York because the same publisher, Soho Press, had accepted her second novel,* In the Empire of Dreams.

It was because of this second novel that a decade later I interviewed her "on being a gaijin" for Inside/Outside Japan, *the desktop-published monthly I edited for my employer.*

In early 2019 I wrote her the usual "how are you?" Sometime later I heard from her designer husband Takahashi Masahiro that she had died, alas, of cancer. She had never told me about her ailment, even as she talked about the horses with whom she had grown up in Sydney.

Years earlier Dianne had told me that the novel for which she had intended to quote some lines from one of Takamura Kōtarō's poems had gone nowhere. If I remember correctly, the poem was "Two Under the Tree." It begins:

> *That's Mount Atatara,*
> *that glistening is Abukuma river.*
> *Sitting like this, with few words,*
> *I feel through my head lulled to sleep*
> *only the pine wind of distant times blowing light green.*
> *In this large landscape in early winter*
> *I burn quietly, holding your hand—let me not hide my joy*
> *from that white clouds looking down. . . .*

Remains of the Occupation Mentality

November 29, 2004, *Japan Times*

Sometimes a perception formed during an era, however unthinking, never seems to leave you. When I read, in a detailed chronology of Mishima Yukio's life, that Meredith Weatherby visited him in his hotel in New York and had an all-day discussion with him of his translation of *Confessions of a Mask (Kamen no kokuhaku)*, its timing threw me. Then I knew I still harbored "the Occupation mentality." The reverse side of it, that is.

The Weatherby-Mishima meeting in New York took place in January 1952, at the start of Mishima's first trip overseas. At the time Japan was still under the U.S. Occupation. As my late friend Herbert Passin, reminded the reader in his introduction to Theodore Cohen's *Remaking Japan* (Free Press, 1987), the Occupation lasted for nearly seven years or, to be exact, "six years, seven months, and twenty-eight days."

The Occupation meant, among other things, that a Japanese needed a permit to go overseas, and the permit required the signature of the Supreme Commander for the Allied Powers (SCAP). Naturally, only a few permits were issued. Mishima managed to get one because a top editor at the *Asahi Shimbun* was a classmate of his father, a former bureaucrat, and he was able to designate the young author as his paper's "special overseas correspondent."

What caught me off guard was this background superimposed on the image of an American visiting a young visitor to New York from the occupied land and talking about *his* translation of the young man's work. Yes, I had long known some of the illustrious students of Japanese literature and society since the war, Herbert Passin among them, studied the language in the special military language schools set up in preparation for an impending war with Japan. But I had somehow felt that Meredith Weatherby, who established the publishing house John Weatherhill, was of a different breed. Yes, I knew he had translated *Confessions of a Mask*. But I did not know he had done that so early.

The Weatherby-Mishima meeting confounded me also because Mishima had confirmed, less than two months after Japan's defeat, the famous Japanese about-face as the conquered to the conqueror.

"The Occupation force popularity, shall we call it, it's simply a bizarre popularity," Mishima wrote to a friend, in early October 1945, after visiting his haunt, the Ginza. "Shabby dirty Japanese in khaki and *mompe* attire mill around. . . . Enchanted by shopping Occupation soldiers and women reporters, there are, I tell you, crowds upon crowds of people, mouths agape, listening gratefully to (though can't hope to understand) the responses in English."

Where was the diehard enmity of yesterday?

Not that I was old enough to experience it. The month Mishima visited New York I was still a fourth grader on a small island, in Nagasaki. I doubt I knew Japan had waged a war a few years earlier. If someone had told me that an atomic bomb had destroyed a city nearby, it would have made no impression on me. A few months afterward, my family, till then split into two, reunited in a big city, Fukuoka. In April the San Francisco Peace Treaty was ratified in and the Occupation ended. Utterly beyond my ken.

In fact, it was after the Occupation came to an end that I was exposed to America for the first time and began to form a view of the country as powerful, glamorous, and, above all, superior. In Fukuoka, U.S. jet-fighters roared back and forth low above us, shaking our ramshackle, rented house, which was close to an American airbase. The Korean War was still being fought. My oldest sister, Nobuko, worked at a brand-new movie theater in the center of Hakata and occasionally allowed me to slip in to see American films. In *Tarzan*, the handsome man born to flaunt his body made a special impression on me. Outside the theater, I gawked at American soldiers: tall, good-looking, in uniform, with fancily dressed Japanese women on their arms.

Then I began to learn English. That was glamorous enough, but one day the teacher who taught English brought a gramophone to class and played a record in which Americans said exactly what the textbook said: "I am a boy. My name is Jack. I am a girl. My name is Betty. . . ." How exotic and unreal it all was! In time I formed the amorphous thought: the Japanese may study English but no Americans will study Japanese.

My sense of the Occupier-Occupied relationship was lopsided, of course. As I soon learned as regards Mishima's trip abroad, once the permit was given, the Occupation, via a Mrs. Williams—the name Mishima cites in his letter to his mentor, the novelist Kawabata Yasunari—asked the Department of State to arrange appointments for him, not just in the U.S. but in other countries as well.

Indeed, it may well have been Herbert Passin who played a decisive role in securing an overseas travel permit for Mishima. Chief of the Public Opinion and Sociological Research Division under SCAP at the time, he introduced the proper way of conducting opinion polls to Japan and he most likely knew the *Asahi* editor. I regret I was unable to ascertain this with him. Only after his death did I spot his name in Mishima's report on his trip, *Apollo's Cup*, as someone who asked a New York organization—the American Committee for Cultural Freedom—to look after him in this city. Furthermore, because of the death of his baby, Passin happened to be back in New York while Mishima was here and interpreted for him.

So I asked Donald Richie about Meredith Weatherby. It was at his recommendation that Weatherby/Weatherhill published a book for me. Donald responded promptly. Weatherby studied Japanese before the war and was working at a consulate when the war broke out, he wrote. While interred in Kobe, he translated a nō play and other things. When Mishima came to New York, he was at Harvard.

When Donald told me these things, his journals spanning nearly sixty years were being readied for publication. Now they are out: *The Japan Journals: 1947–2004* (Stone Bridge Press, 2004). To learn what Weatherby did after discussing *Confessions* with Mishima, you must read the book.

The Answer, My Friend, Is Blowing in the Wind

April 30, 2012, *Japan Times*

Until the *New York Times* pointed it out earlier this month, I had failed to notice, alas, that Tokyo had given cherry trees to this city as it had to Washington, D.C., 100 years ago ("Gifts From Japan, Less Celebrated in Manhattan," April 12).

I had known about the cherry trees in the nation's capital for some years, but it's only recently that I began to see, online, the *Washington Post* write about their imminent blossoming—yes, just as the Japanese do about the "sakura front": providing day-to-day forecasts as spring warmth creeps up north.

This shows, I marveled, how times have changed. If I can trust my memory to any extent, not long after arriving here four decades ago, I read some American horticulturalists regarded cherry trees as arboreal "weeds" that suck up all the nutrients from the soil and enfeeble all the others. No wonder, I thought, the cherry trees in Central Park looked somewhat ill-kempt.

Now I see the real reason was different. As the *Times* reported, even as the more than 3,000 cherry trees for Washington were planted *en mass*, the 2,500 trees for New York City were dispersed across Upper Manhattan—nearly a third of them, or 764 trees, near Grant's Tomb alone, according to the 1912 annual report of the City's Department of Parks.

Also, whereas the trees along the Potomac River were well tended over the years, those in Manhattan were not. Most of the trees west of Grant's Tomb, for example, were removed in the 1930s for renovation despite the fact that the area, Claremont Park, had been renamed Sakura Park and Grove.

The question is: Why such extravagant gifts to foreign cities? After all, when the U.S. decided on a return gift three years later, it gave Tokyo just forty dogwood trees—a fair international botanical gift, one would think, in normal circumstances.

The answer, partly, is that they were a gesture of gratitude.

The idea of bringing cherry trees to this country first came from people who simply admired cherry blossoms. Among them was Eliza Ruhamah Scidmore, a great world traveler who became the first female member of the National Geographic Society.

But when Ozaki Yukio, the mayor of Tokyo—a city at the time— learned of this, and that the First Lady, Helen Taft, was now involved, he pulled out all the stops. He had been searching for some way of conveying Japan's gratitude to the U.S.: President Theodore Roosevelt, serving as arbiter of the Russo-Japanese War, had made Japan the victor.

Ozaki's first attempt failed. The shipment of 2,000 trees to Washington, in 1909, had to be burned on arrival; they were found infested with insects. The shipment to New York in the same year was lost at sea: The ship carrying it sank.

Ozaki did not give up. He instructed scientists to develop insect-free cherry saplings. Thousands of farmers helped. It worked.

All "the many rare varieties having beautiful blossoms" were "very hardy," New York City's annual report stated, "as proved by their condition on arrival, after a journey of nearly three months, closely packed in the cases which were stored in the steamship hold in transit."

But, by the spring of 1912 when the planting ceremonies were held in Washington and New York, politics, domestic and international, had largely overtaken Japan's gratitude to the United States.

As early as March 1907, Roosevelt, who had conferred "victory" on Japan just a year and a half earlier, banned Japanese laborers' entry to this country. The resentment toward Japanese fishermen and immigrants on the West Coast had gotten out of control.

Japan's "victory" itself had fanned the fear of the Yellow Peril. Books imagining Japanese invasion of the U.S., such as *Banzai!* by Ferdinand Heinrich Grautoff and *The Valor of Ignorance* by Homer Lea, had appeared by the end of the decade.

That's why, during the planting ceremony near Grant's Tomb, on April 28, 1912, Japanese Consul General Numano Yasutarō warned of warmongers. "The occasional voice of an alarmist is heard proclaiming the danger of the war between the two countries," he said, reported the *New York Times*.

The war, as we all know, came, three decades later. And in it, the cherry blossoms played a fateful role as the symbol of a brief but beautiful life, youth illuminating its worth before scattering away.

Years before that, in fact, the idea that cherry blossoms were singularly Japanese had obtained. Yukika, Ozaki Yukio's third daughter, recalled, for example, how her elementary schoolteacher pointedly said in class, "The cherry blossoms are the soul of Japan, but there's a fellow who sold them to a foreign country." Yukika was born in the year the cherry trees were planted in Washington and New York.

Her father, a popular, distinguished politician later called "the deity of constitutional governance," had not "sold" the trees to the United States, but in the teacher's eyes, he had betrayed his country by giving them to aliens.

The great scholar of Japan's classical literature Yamada Yoshio was alarmed by the overt manifestations of these sentiments in the 1930s. He had written a history of Japanese love of cherry blossoms, meticulously citing poems and other paeans from the start of Japanese literature to modern times. His chronicle included the destruction of many fine cherry groves in the early part of the Meiji regime when the day's zeal was westernization. Everything extolled in Japanese tradition had to be condemned.

In any case, the Japanese had seldom, if ever, admired cherry blossoms for their transient beauty, Yamada argued. They were enchanted by their hallucinatory abundance. That—the classicist did not say this— was probably why Mayor Ozaki, when he decided to give cherry trees to Washington and New York, gave thousands of them, all at once.

Yamada may have been particularly aggravated by the song the French professor turned songwriter Saijō Yaso published in 1938. In it, air corps classmates vow to each other:

We're cherry blossoms having bloomed,
we're determined to scatter.
We'll scatter spectacularly
for our country's sake.

But Yamada's scholarly protests were to no avail. By then it was too late. Saijō's ditty, with the music Ōmura Nōshō composed for it the following year, went on to become an exceedingly popular military song. How many young lives were wasted as a result, we do not know.

This article requires some emendation in the description of Saijō Yaso's lyrics. When I wrote this article in 2012, I consulted Shigure Otowa's collection of popular songs, including military songs, Nihon kayō shū, expanded (Shakai Shisōsha, 1963), which treated the song "Cherry Blossoms of the Same Class" ("Dōki no sakura") as Saijō's, in association with military pilots. Recently I learned, however, that Saijō wrote the original version imagining the Japanese Marines that landed in Shanghai in July 1937 for, of all things, a girls' magazine, Shōjo Club, and titled it "Two Cherry Blossoms" ("Nirin no sakura"). It was set to music the next year but it didn't catch on. In 1944, toward the close of the war, Lieutenant Jōsa Hiroshi at the Naval Academy largely rewrote Saijō's lyrics, though keeping the line saying, "having bloomed, we're determined to scatter." The military song became immensely popular as special force (suicidal) missions grew prevalent.

In 1943, Saijō wrote lyrics for "Young Eagles' Song" ("Wakawashi no uta"), which suggested the cherry blossom as the symbol of bravery and willingness to give up life in an attack. Set to music by Koseki Yūji and turned into the theme song of a movie, "The Big Sky for a Decisive Battle" ("Kessen no ōzora e") became very popular. It was also called "The Song of the Naval Aviation Preparatory School" ("Yokaren no uta").

The scholar Yamada Yoshio's book History of Cherry Blossoms (Ōshi) *was published in 1941. It was a collection of poems and other descriptions of cherry blossoms since the oldest eras that he had begun to serialize in 1919 in the annual magazine of the Cherry Society, writing the last installment 1931. Its main argument was not that the Japanese loved cherry blossoms because they bloom and scatter "gallantly," but because they bloom in abundance.*

In 1938, he penned a separate essay to deplore the modern-day equation of the samurai to the cherry blossoms on the assumption that both readily give up their lives "gallantly." In the past the Japanese had taken up their brushes to write prose and poetry on cherry blossoms in praise of their abundance and splendor, Yamada argued.

Zen and the Art of Beatnik Haiku

March 28, 2004, *Japan Times*

Jack Kerouac (1922–69), the King of the Beats, started writing haiku with the belief that this short poetic form was an avatar of Zen, and pursued haiku and Zen to his drunken end. I do not know if this is common knowledge among those who continue to be enthralled by *On the Road*—published more than forty-five years ago!—but it is what comes through in the generous collection of more than 700 of his haiku Regina Heinreich has assembled in *Jack Kerouac: Book of Haikus* (Penguin, 2003). (Yes, as Weinreich notes, Kerouac added "s" to the word "haiku" to indicate plural, which is seldom done today.)

Among the earliest Japanese advocates of the notion that haiku embodies Zen was Bashō's contemporary Onitsura (1661–1738), and among the most famous in recent years is Nagata Kōi (1900–1997). Onitsura regarded *Teizen ni shiroku saitaru tsubaki kana*, "In the garden blooming white are camellias" as his signature piece. It was a response to a Zen master's query: "What's your haikai eye like?" Among Kōi's haiku is *Dai-banshun doron doro doro doro doron*: "Great late spring muddy mud mud mud muddy." I don't know whether this was a response to anything.

Yet Onitsura and Kōi are exceptions. The development of the haiku form has had such a tenuous linkage with Zen that most Japanese haiku practitioners today would probably be surprised to learn that in the United States the association of haiku with Zen has been pervasive. Here is, for example, how the Haiku Society of America defines the form: "An

277

unrhymed Japanese poem recording the essence of a moment keenly perceived in which nature is linked to human nature."

How has this come about?

The answer is simple: the influence of the Zen proselytizer D. T. Suzuki and the Zen devotee R. H. Blyth. Suzuki's many books arguing that Japanese culture is based on Zen started appearing as early as 1927, and Blyth's books simply asserting that "haiku is Zen" began to appear in 1949. Kerouac was so devoted to their books that he was aggrieved, Weinreich tells us, when one of Blyth's four-volume *Haiku* went missing.

As important, Kerouac's friend and guide in Zen was Gary Snyder, who practiced Zen and translated poems of the Chinese Zen mystic Han Shan, *Cold Mountain*. Kerouac gives an account of how Snyder told him how to express himself in haiku.

"A real haiku's gotta be as simple as porridge and yet make you see the real thing, like the greatest haiku of them all probably is the one that goes 'The sparrow hops along the veranda, with wet feet.' By Shiki. You see the wet footprints like a vision in your mind and yet in those few words you also see the rain that's been falling that day and almost smell the wet pine needles."

The haiku in question reads, in the original, *Nure ashi de suzume no aruku rōka kana*. One of the more than 20,000 pieces Masaoka Shiki wrote in his relatively short life, it is not often anthologized, probably because Takahama Kyoshi (1874–1959), the dictatorial inheritor of the conservative wing of the Shiki circle, did not include it when he made a selection of 2,300 of his teacher's haiku. But Snyder was right in praising the haiku. It has the on-the-bull's eye kind of immediacy associated with Zen.

In no time, Kerouac decided to call his haiku "pops," saying: "POP— American (non-Japanese) Haikus, short 3-line poems or 'pomes' rhyming or non-rhyming delineating 'little Samadhis' if possible, usually of a Buddhist connotation, aiming towards enlightenment." A tall order, whatever "enlightenment" may mean.

Still, he kept reading Buddhist sutras. One of his early pieces is endearing because Snyder described Kerouac in one of his poems.

My pipe unlit
    beside the Diamond
Sutra—What to think?

In his poem, "Migration of Birds," Snyder wrote:

Jack Kerouac outside, behind my back
Reads the *Diamond Sutra* in the sun.

Early on Kerouac also wrote:

Juju beads on
    Zen manual—
My knees are cold

Here, "juju," also called "juzu" and "zuzu," are the Buddhist prayer-beads. Among Kerouac's last pieces is:

Sleeping on my desk
    head on the sutras
my cat

Kerouac naturally wrote haiku-esque haiku which readily recall their Japanese counterparts, such as—

Frozen
    in the birdbath,
A leaf

In my medicine cabinet
    the winter fly
Has died of old age

"Frozen" brings to mind, for example, Buson's *Furuike ni zōri shizumite mizore kana,* "A straw sandal sunk in the old pond and the sleet." As for the image of a dead fly, Murakami Kijō (1865-1938) wrote *Fuyubachi no shinidokoro naku arukikeri,* "A winter wasp, with no place to die, is walking."

I first came across Kerouac's haiku in the second of the three different editions of *The Haiku Anthology* that Cor van den Heuvel has compiled. The selection of five Kerouac pieces in that Simon & Schuster book (1986) ends with one that may be called Kerouakian:

Missing a kick
    at the icebox door
It closed anyway

In a somewhat different way, the following two may be equally Kerouakian.

What is Buddhism?
    —A crazy little
Bird blub

Haiku, shmaiku, I cant
    understand the intention
Of reality

And, yes, porridge. He wrote one referring to it, which also reminds us of his life with his mother:

Christ on the Cross crying
    —his mother missed
Her October porridge

A devoted son, Kerouac lived many of his last years with his mother, Gabrielle.

The Complexities of "They" versus "Xe / Xim / Xir"

May 4, 2016, *Japan Times*

"The Economist's style guide," Amanda Hess pointed out in "Multiple Choice: Who's 'They'?" (*The New York Times*, April 3, 2016), "still calls the honorific Ms. an 'ugly' word."

That reminded me: When the word began to gain currency in the 1970s, my informal teacher of English, Eleanor Wolff, observed it sounded like a Southern mispronunciation of "Miss." Not that she looked down upon the Southern use of the language. For example, she urged me to read Eudora Welty, in particular her novel, *Losing Battles* (1970). Having never married, she herself stuck to "Miss." I admired her decision.

My teacher's and my own reservations notwithstanding, I did submit my translations of Japanese women poets to *Ms.* magazine, which Gloria Steinem and Dorothy Pitman Hughes had started in 1971. I even remember having been invited to their editorial office. And their magazine took a poem or two of Tomioka Taeko.

As the Wikipedia entry on the honorific tells you, "Ms." was not a neologism created by Steinem and Co., but the 1971 edition of the OED didn't list it. And, in the U.S., its adoption raged throughout the 1970s.

For example, the *Harpers Dictionary of Contemporary Usage* (1975), edited by William and Mary Morris, with an impressive "panel of consultants on usage," showed that a full seven out of ten of the panelists expressed a preference for "the established forms of address for women," even as fifty-six percent said they used "Ms." in correspondence.

These were in response to what Jean Stafford had written in a *New York Times* article. In it the writer had said that if she received an envelope addressed to her as "Ms." she would mark it, "Not acceptable to addressee. Return to sender"—after first checking to see if there was a check inside. Otherwise, she should be addressed as "Miss Stafford," she had written, or as "Mrs. Liebling," if inquiries had to do with her late husband.

Stafford had been married three times, first famously to the poet Robert Lowell, then to the *Time* staffer Oliver Jensen, and, finally, to the *New Yorker* writer A. J. Liebling.

Debrett's Etiquette and Modern Manners (1981), edited by Elsie Burch Donald, noted that "the contraction 'Ms' (pronounced miz)" was "not yet fully established."

But by the early 1990s, at least one man of erudition and great writer from Australia had become a convert. In *Culture of Complaints* (1993), which had started with a series of lectures under the sponsorship of Oxford University Press and the New York Public Library in 1992, Robert Hughes asked a rhetorical question: "What letter-writer, grateful for the coinage 'Ms,' which lets one formally address women without referring to their marital status, would willingly go back to choosing between 'Mrs.' and 'Miss'?"

It is all the more interesting, then, that Hillary Clinton, of all people, appears to insist on being addressed "Mrs. Clinton." If she wins the election this year, will she demand to be addressed "Mrs. President"?

No, I didn't mean to trace the usage history of "Ms." as I've seen it in the United States. Amanda Hess' subject in "Who's 'They'?" was the "gender binary" question raised in HBO's *Girls*, that is, by the show's creator Lena Dunham's sister who plays "a young queer writer and performer who identifies as a 'trans person with a vagina.'" She had proclaimed, "I hate, fear and am allergic to binaries."

It is bewildering and not the least confusing how sex has grabbed the headlines in this country for some years now. Most recently, "gay marriage" was treated as a life-or-death question. Then rape seemed to replace it. The hottest subject for the moment seems to be the toilet for transsexuals.

The "gender binary" argument originated in the 1970s, though the question back then wasn't called that. Besides, at that incipient stage, the argument was opposite—for differentiation between the two sexes, not for annihilation of it.

As it happens, my employer was in the McGraw-Hill Building. One day, McGraw-Hill, the biggest publisher at the time, issued a notice on English usage guidelines, announcing it would be giving copies of the guidelines to anyone interested. I got one at once.

The focus of the guidelines was, as I recall, on the avoidance of the pronoun "he" as representative of both sexes. As *Harpers Dictionary* put it, "rising protests" were "against the continuation of the traditional use of '*him*' and '*his*' when the person referred to is unidentified as to sex, as in 'Anyone who crosses that road on foot takes *his* life into *his* hands.'"

"Aside from recasting the sentence to avoid the problem, the only solution to date has been to use '*his* or *her*' or '*he* or *she*,'" the editors added. "Even feminists themselves have failed to come up with a single word which could mean either sex."

As I recall, John Kenneth Galbraith toward the end succumbed to the "he or she" construction, whereas Barbara Tuchman continued to call it barbaric to the end.

It did not take long before the term "political correctness" or PC gained currency even while the move to "overthrow gender-specific terms" wherever possible got underway. Thus, *chairman* became *chairperson* or simply *chair*, Hughes noted, "as though the luckless holder of the office had four cabriole legs and a pierced splat."

The *Australian* characterized this righteous intolerance as "a peculiarly American habit." The chaos that would ensue should this push for unisex be applied to Roman languages "hardly bears thinking about," he wrote, for there "every noun has a gender while, to make things worse, the word for the male genital organ is often feminine and the one for its female counterpart not uncommonly masculine."

Japanese should have few such problems, where no nouns are gender-specific and pronouns that are may be dropped altogether as they are modern-day inventions anyway. But who knows? The Japanese love to follow the American ways.

To go back to Amanda Hess, the singular "they" or "xe / xim / xir" or something else may replace "he" and "she" soon, although "they" has been used for some time where the person's gender is "unknown or irrelevant."

Japan's First Embassy to Washington

November 24 and December 9, 1986, *Mainichi Daily News*

Open House, Closed House

In this rapidly changing world, the one Japanese trait that American people, traveling or resident in Japan, continue to find unchanged and inscrutable, annoying, or plain dishonorable, besides, seems to be the Japanese people's reluctance to invite them to their own homes. "One does not often get invited home in Tokyo"—so reads the latest lament I've seen. It comes from Clyde Haberman, Tokyo bureau chief of the *New York Times,* who voiced it in a most enviably knowledgeable guide to Tokyo he wrote for those American travelers who might have to penny-pinch as a result of the recent rise of the yen.

The lack of this particular sociability on the part of the Japanese has been traditionally attributed to the pitiable size of their living quarters, of which the Japanese themselves had been acutely aware long before a representative of the European Community scandalized them by describing their abodes as "rabbit hutches." And in a vague, unthinking sort of way I had agreed to the view. I don't know anything about the houses for ordinary mortals in Europe, but those in the United States certainly are commodious.

In the decades following the Second World War "the Americans developed a housing style," observed Calvin Beale in a recent interview, "that I'm sure looks extravagant to people from other parts of the world." Mr. Beale is head of the population section, of the U.S. Department of Agriculture, and a distinguished demographer, so he's in a position to know.

To add a personal note, I had also suspected that the privy might have something to do with the parsimony of my compatriots in this aspect of social intercourse. My late father was gregarious and would bring home, on the slightest excuse, several people from his office and let those who couldn't make it to the last bus because of his merry-making stay overnight. I liked all that, but was rather uneasy about those young women—for men somehow found their way home, however late—using our miserable john.

At such a time I dared doubt my tyrant father's sagacity. Unlike the novelist Tanizaki Jun'ichirō, who found the traditional Japanese place for excretion "peaceful," "poetic," and "elegant" as he compared it with its Western counterpart, in *In Praise of Shadows (In'ō raisan)*, the Japanese privy was the one place I wanted to stay away from to the best of my ability.

It recently occurred to me, though, that the cramped living quarters and the unsavory privy might not be the primary reasons for the Japanese secretiveness. During our vacation this past summer I read a diary by Tamamushi Sadayū (1823–69), entitled *Daily Account of Crossing Over to the United States (Kōbei nichiroku)*. Tamamushi was one of the seventy-seven government officials and their aides who came to the United States in 1860 to exchange the ratifications of a commercial treaty.

Why such a large mission to ratify a treaty? Because Townsend Harris, the first U.S. consul in Japan, who negotiated the treaty, wanted the Japanese to see with their own eyes what his country was like, and the Japanese, who hadn't had many chances to go overseas because of their semi-isolationist policy, were more than willing. The mission, indeed, was the first of its kind that Japan had dispatched in centuries.

A Confucian scholar who got on the mission as a low-ranking aide, Tamamushi appears to have been among the most inquisitive and observant of the lot. He jotted down everything he saw, heard, and read. And one thing he did not tire of recording was the openness of the people he encountered, especially their readiness to invite him and his companions to their houses.

So, in Hawaii, the first place of landing, when he and his friends passed by an English house, "four women, young and old, though not a single man," came out of it, "joyfully" invited them inside, and guided them around. They brought out a variety of fascinating things, beautifully arranged them on a table, and politely showed each of them. One of the women played for the visitors an instrument that looked like a zither, then fed them home-made bread. Tamamushi and his companions were treated in like fashion at two other houses on the same day.

In San Francisco, to Tamamushi's chagrin, the members of the mission weren't allowed to saunter in the city freely. Still, during the brief free time given, he and his companions were invited inside "at each door" and entertained generously. The Japanese ambassador's restrictions became even tighter in Washington and other cities the mission visited, but Tamamushi continued to note the American people's eagerness to display their houses. At one point he contrasted this openness with the way his compatriots back home would hastily shut their doors at the sight of an alien. Though the Japanese are no longer that xenophobic, Tamamushi's reaction suggests that inviting a stranger to one's home wasn't part of Japanese tradition.

Tamamushi's experiences remind me of the first time I came to this country. That was in 1966, and the place was Redondo Beach, California, where I stayed with a family consisting of, by ticklish coincidence, four women but not a man: grandmother, mother, and two granddaughters. Many things about American life impressed me deeply then, but what at first surprised me to the point of apprehension was the family's utter openness concerning their living quarters. They left open even the door of the bathroom!

An Earlier Egalitarianism

Tamamushi's account, *Daily Account of Crossing Over to the United States,* also reminds us how things do and don't change. This is especially the case with the American egalitarianism Tamamushi witnessed and recorded. He first saw it aboard the *Powhatan,* the warship the U.S. government sent to transport the mission across the Pacific.

One day he observed a crew inspection ceremony. Describing it in his diary, he characterized the procedure as "strict." "Nevertheless," he wrote,

> even to the captain a crewman would merely take his headgear off but not give obeisance. On regular days the captain and his officers mix with their men, making no distinction between ranks, and even the non-military sailors give no indication of deferring to the captain unnecessarily.
>
> The captain and his officers, on their part, do not flaunt their authority, treating men as if they were their equals. As a result, their mutual feelings are close indeed and, if anything unusual occurs, they try to protect one another, each to the best of his ability; if something unfortunate happens to one of them, they shed tears and grieve. All this is just the opposite of what happens in my country.

By then, Tamamushi had witnessed the way the captain and his officers worked alongside their men during the violent storm they had encountered in the Pacific.

"In my country," Tamamushi added, "manners and protocol are so tight that one can seldom see one's lord, like a demon or god. In the same vein, any man of any rank flaunts his authority extravagantly and holds his subordinates in contempt. So, the mutual feelings are rare, and even when an unfortunate thing happens, expression of grief is not seen." Though he had to add "this does not mean I am upholding the customs of a foreign country," he could not help expressing the worry that in Japan, where hierarchy dominated everything, no one would exert himself in an emergency.

This democracy in America, so to speak, that Tamamushi observed aboard an American warship, is remarkable when you remember that extreme discipline prevailed in the U.S. Navy in those days. Commodore Matthew Perry, who had used gunboats in 1853 and 1854—the *Powhatan* was one of them—to force Japan to open itself to international commerce and diplomacy, was known as "Old Bruin" for his tough discipline. A little earlier, in 1850, Herman Melville had published *White-Jacket; or, The World in a Man-of-War,* whose descriptions of flogging and other forms of corporal punishment given to any violation, large or small, are said to have eventually led to the revision of naval regulations.

Even so, the general absence of hierarchical differences remains true of American society today, although our understanding of it may have become subtler.

Tamamushi's admiration for American egalitarianism was reinforced when the mission reached Washington and met some of the ranking officials, including the President, James Buchanan. For the formal meeting with the President, the Japanese side sallied forth in full regalia, though, as Tamamushi noted, the ambassador and his top aides were unable to bring along the correct formal attires specified for such an occasion by the Japanese protocol. President Buchanan, however, came out to meet them, simply dressed—"in dark wool, with no special decorations on." Moreover, like the captain of the *Powhatan*, the President did not flaunt his authority.

"When he entered or left the room," Tamamushi wrote,

> no one called out for those nearby to snap to attention. He was just like an ordinary man. To his left and right sat not only those in charge of various affairs but also women and children, fully dressed. There was no difference between men and women.... Even from where we were seated, we could see all the proceedings by craning our necks a little. Ordinary people stood outside the door to have a look, but no one tried to warn them off. It was like someone seeing his relatives or an official meeting people in the capacity of an ordinary citizen.

A few days before the mission left Washington, President Buchanan dropped by the hotel they were staying. "He was only with his coachman and three women. He was not accompanied by any servant, like an ordinary man. People who saw this didn't think it odd, and no one paid obeisance to him. He seated himself among us [to see a slide show]. It was impossible to tell who the President was."

This—American egalitarianism at the highest level—has changed. I don't know much about James Buchanan, but Abraham Lincoln, who was nominated as the Republican candidate for President while Tamamushi and his mission were still in Washington, is said to have set aside, as President, a few hours every morning to meet citizens who wanted to see him for one reason or another. Now an ordinary mortal meets the President either accidentally during his election campaign or in an elaborate setting devised to enhance his political fortune.

Masao Miyoshi's book As We Saw Them: The First Japanese Embassy to the United States (1979) *fully describes the embassy of 1860, including the death by seppuku of Tamamushi Sadayū, "the most lucid-minded of all the 1860 diarists." A samurai of the Sendai fiefdom, he worked for an alliance of northern fiefdoms after the Boshin War started in 1868. As a result, he was arrested, imprisoned, and ordered to kill himself, on the ninth of Fourth Month 1869. He was forty-six years old.*

Japan's Close Encounter with the West
The Iwakura Embassy

July 9, 2002, *Japan Times*

By reading, hearing, and by observation in foreign lands, our people have acquired a general knowledge of constitutions, habits, and manners, as they exist in most foreign countries.... Japan cannot claim originality as yet, but it will aim to exercise practical wisdom by adopting the advantages, and avoiding the errors, taught her by the history of those enlightened nations whose experience is her teacher.

So spoke Itō Hirobumi in San Francisco, on January 23, 1872. It was at the banquet the city gave the Iwakura Embassy, which had arrived at "the throat of the entire state of California" eight days earlier. Charles Lanman, American secretary of the Japanese Legation in Washington, who may have had a hand in the speech, reported that Itō delivered it "in a clear voice, so as to be distinctly understood by all present."

"With more than three hundred guests in attendance, it was a splendid occasion," wrote Kume Kunitake, who later prepared the remarkable document *Beiō kairan jikki*, now translated into English in its entirety as *The Iwakura Embassy: 1871-1873* (Japan Documents, 2002).

Wreaths made with green leaves interspersed with flowers decorated windows and walls. The crossed flags of the Rising Sun of Japan and the Stars and Stripes of the thirty-seven United States were hung in several places. The whole Embassy, Mayor Alvord of San Francisco, Governor Booth of California, officers of the army and navy—all sat at a raised table at the head of the room. A band played during the banquet. The food was elegantly presented and very delicious.

San Francisco's welcome befit the embassy's ambitions. The mission was planned to tour the United States and Europe with the kind of daring that characterized the Japan of the day.

There was, first, the size and composition of the embassy. Made up of nearly fifty officials, it included about half the leaders of the new regime. Iwakura Tomomi, the ambassador, was Minister of the Right and the third-ranking officer in the administration. Among his four vice-ambassadors were Councilor of State Kido Takayoshi and Minister of Finance Ōkubo Toshimichi. The speech-maker Itō Hirobumi, another vice-ambassador, was Senior Councilor of Public Works.

Equally weighty was the timing. The Meiji government, created just three years earlier, had brought forth a transformation "unprecedented in Japanese history," as Kume put it in the preface to his five-volume report. There were three factors that made it so: "1. Arresting shogunal power and restoring direct rule by the emperor; 2. Amalgamating the scattered authority of the feudal domains and thus making a unified polity; 3. Reversing the isolationist 'closed country' policy."

Any one of these would be hard to pull off at any time, Kume pointed out, but pulling off all three at a time of rapid change, as his government had, was "almost heaven's act, not man's." Indeed, even as he labored over his report, the samurai who were deprived of privileges were rebelling, and the peasants who felt overtaxed continued to revolt. In addition, the tour, as initially planned, was to last for ten months.

Imagine: In the United States, half the cabinet and sub-cabinet officers, plus the Speaker of the House, vacating the country for most of a stressful political year—say, right after the Civil War—in order to see what the rest of the world looked like! As the late Marius Jansen, of Princeton University, observes in his foreword to the five-volume translation, "A historian would be hard-put to find another [such] instance" in the world. Furthermore, the mission actually took twenty-two months to complete its tour.

Little wonder the departing party felt compelled to extract from the men staying home a written pledge not to introduce any significant policy changes while the embassy was away. The pledge was signed, only to be ignored.

The Iwakura Embassy wasn't meant, of course, just to observe the "constitutions, habits, and manners" of "those enlightened nations." In his speech in San Francisco, Ito referred to "the Treaty Powers." After opening the country, in 1854, Japan had quickly been saddled with a series of treaties granting extraterritoriality but securing no tariff autonomy. Nearly twenty years later, the time for their renegotiation was coming up. One goal of the embassy was to assess, from a weakling's perspective, the state of affairs in those Treaty Powers.

In the event, that goal took an ironic turn. The grand, indulgent receptions Americans gave the embassy everywhere they went—in San Francisco, Chicago, and Washington—generated the hope that the United States had a soft spot for Japan. The reality of international power politics couldn't be more different. When they finally sat down to talk, they learned, in short order, that Secretary of State Hamilton Fish and his deputies had no intention of yielding an inch. It would take three more decades, in fact, for Japan to be able to persuade the Treaty Powers to give up extraterritoriality and allow Japan tariff autonomy.

Still, the palpable sense of realpolitik gained from that experience led what some historians call a coup d'état after the embassy's return. While the mission was away, a plan to send an expeditionary force to Korea to appease the discontented samurai had been hatched. Ōkubo Toshimichi and Kido Takayoshi, knowing such an oversea venture could be fatal to Japan, scotched it, driving its planners out of power.

That and other diplomatic and political affairs were, however, outside the purview of Kume's "true account." As he explained, on such matters there already existed reports other members of the embassy had filed. What Kume dealt with instead were the results of the embassy's principal aim of observation and learning, and he fulfilled his task brilliantly.

Kume Kunitake was blessed with two traits that mark a good reporter: the ability to observe and compare and the ability to write well. In view of the astonishing differences he confronted between his own country and those he visited, I must add a third: the ability to maintain an intellectual poise. The vastness of the lands, the opulence, and the awesome industrial superiorities that he witnessed could have intimidated him, as indeed such things cowed his compatriots in later generations. But he did not lose his equanimity.

That he was a scholar trained in Chinese classics certainly helped. He was also well informed of current affairs of the world. His fiefdom, Hizen, today's Saga, was relatively small, but it was responsible for the port of Nagasaki, Japan's only window to the globe while the country was closed.

Kume could readily cite ancient sources. In Washington, D.C., for example, in describing the horrors of slavery that the Unite States had abolished a mere seven years earlier, he observes: "In the *Chou li*, the section dealing with the responsibilities of governors and officials forbids the selling of human beings as if they were oxen or horses." As Martin Collcutt, of Princeton University, who translated the volume covering the United States (Vol. I), explains, *Chou li*, or *The Rites of Chou*, is "a collection of traditions and administrative precepts attributed to the Chou dynasty," compiled in the fourth and third century B.C.

Here, because Kume's description of the slave trade is so vivid and detailed, I must also note the assumption that he (and his colleagues) had superior informants. When he writes, for example, "Households which bought slaves considered them part of their property," and indicates the word "property" in English, one recalls John Quincy Adams' argument before the Supreme Court, in 1839, that Spain could reclaim the ship Amistad but not the slaves because, whereas a ship could legitimately be claimed as property, human beings could not.

To give another example of Kume's familiarity with Chinese classics, at one point he refers to the *Kuan-tzu*, a collection of writings attributed to Kuan Chung, who died in 645 B.C. The reference occurs in one of the many passages where Kume reflects on the embassy's most important finding: the crucial role of international trade in a nation's prosperity.

The occasion was the embassy's visit to the Mint House (then so called), in Philadelphia. Shown "displays of foreign coins, including Ancient Greek and Roman coins, and old and new coins from various countries in Europe and from China and Japan," Kume realizes that the West has kept the values of coins precise, treating them, correctly, as "a medium for trade and commerce." The East, on the other hand, has been careless about them, at times even minting extravagant gold coins to be used as gifts. This partly explains why, despite the advice given in the *Kuan-tzu* and other ancient texts, "The peoples of Japan and China, from ancient times until now, *have put commerce outside their field of interest*" (italics in the original). Consequently, the West has prospered, but the East has not.

Kume's Chinese sources can be far more recent. In Paris, he posits that the French are, in temperament, "akin to the Japanese, invariably excelling in their ingenuity, but quite the opposite of the British and Germans in their weakness for reckless daring and their lack of diligence and perseverance."

Citing this passage, I can't help but imagine Pierre Loti cringing to learn that a Japanese visiting his country a few decades before he went to Japan thought his compatriots resembled the Japanese. Kume, in any event, had a source: *Ying-huan chih-lueh.* Andrew Cobbing, of Kyūshū University, who translated the volume that covers France, Belgium, Holland, and Prussia (Vol. III), explains that it is "a ten-volume gazetteer by the Chinese scholar Hsu Chi-yu," published in 1850.

The members of the embassy were guided to a wide variety of places: girls' school, botanical garden, ironworks, shipyard, glass factory, chocolate factory, racetrack, palace, prison, millionaires' residence, the school for the deaf, and the school of anatomy (these two in Russia), to name only a few. And in each place they were provided with detailed explanations and demonstrations.

Some of the accounts of such places are marvels of condensed information displaying the reporter's knowledge and his ability to absorb details. One outstanding example is Kume's description of the porcelain factory at Sevres on the outskirts of Paris. Kume was from a domain famed for its porcelain industry, but even so!

Gemlike vignettes enliven many accounts. For example, there is the embassy's visit to the Woolwich Arsenal in London, the largest in the world at the time. When someone expressed admiration for the stupendous

technological prowess on display, General Sir David Wood, comman-
dant of the arsenal, responded (and Kume was careful to note it): "The
sole purpose of all these things is in the last analysis the spilling of human
blood. How can they be for the good of a civilised world? I am utterly
ashamed of them." This appears in the volume covering Great Britain
(Vol. II), which Graham Healey, of the University of Sheffield, translated.

It was crucial for the embassy to have an accurate grasp of where
nations stood in political development. Japan was going through
wrenching changes, but so were some of the more important countries
in Western Europe. In summarizing the history of France, Kume tells us
what has been happening in the neighboring countries as well:

> Following the defeat of Napoleon in 1815, France reverted to a monar-
> chy, which lasted for the next thirty-three years until, in 1848, there were
> more uprisings, clamouring for popular rights and sending waves of
> unrest across neighbouring lands. Consequently, the Italian states, too,
> were finally unified in 1860, and Austria, where the vision of feudalism
> still persisted, made sweeping reforms in 1867 to introduce an entirely
> constitutional system.

Of the five most powerful empires in Europe, Germany had been
unified only a few years earlier, in 1870–71, while Russia was "the most
backward." Despite the "prodigious efforts" made since Peter the Great
onward to develop itself, it was a country which "the great European
powers" looked down upon as "an upstart youth."

In fact, Russia was a revelation for the embassy. Japan had a "delu-
sion" that Russia was "the largest and most powerful country . . . perpet-
ually stalking the land in a rapacious mood and nursing ambitions of
conquering the world." In reality, it was a vast land where progress was
stymied because "wealth (was) concentrated in the hands of the powerful" and the great majority of its people, still no better than serfs though
recently liberated, had no incentive to work to improve themselves.

And it is in recounting the embassy's travels to Eastern Europe
and Russia, which were "mostly cold and barren," that Kume makes
one arresting observation: "For all the talk about civilisation and

development, when the whole world is taken into consideration these notions amount to no more than the light of a star on the ground in one corner of the world"—as P. F. Kornicki puts it in restating Kume's words in English. Kornicki, of the University of Cambridge, translated the volume covering Russia, Denmark, Sweden, Italy, and Austria (Vol. IV).

Political development was not only in flux, but its variety offered plenty of food for thought. If "the governance of Russia" was at one extreme, characterized as it was by "imperial absolutism," the United States was at another extreme and was proud of it.

"Of course, no man-made constitution" (or law) "will be perfect," Kume becomes philosophical in reflecting on democracy in America. "If you give power to the people, the power of government will be reduced. The more you promote liberty, the more lax the laws will become. It is a natural principle that if you gain something in one direction, you lose something in another."

"However, the American people . . . see no fault in their democratic system, only perfection," Kume goes on to add ruefully. "Because they think their system is the best in the world, they encourage everyone to adopt a similar one." With due respect to Martin Collcutt, I would translate part of this passage: "They love the beauty of it so much that they try to make the whole world adopt their national policy." But no matter; Kume's point is clear and it is a sentiment that remains alive today.

So, after all this, what was Kume's conclusion? It was at once a statement of fact and a declaration of intent.

"European countries at the present day stand at the pinnacle of civilisation," Kume said. "They are immensely rich and powerful, their trade is on a huge scale, they excel in arts and manufactures, and their peoples live pleasant lives and are extremely happy. It is natural to assume . . . that it is peculiar to this continent."

"However, the truth is otherwise," he concluded. "*It is since 1800 that Europe has attained its present wealth; and it is only in the last forty years that it has achieved the truly remarkable level of prosperity we now see*" (original emphasis).

In other words, given forty years, Japan could and should attain the European level of industrial progress.

Tanaka Akira, of Hokkaidō University, who edited Kume's 1878 report for Iwanami Shoten and has written the introduction to *The Iwakura Embassy*, says in the original editor's note that Kume Kunitake uses "extremely many" kanji, Chinese characters. Having translated several passages from his edition for a newsletter, I certainly remember coming across many a kanji I could not puzzle out. But Kume's ability to use Chinese at will is precisely what makes his writing at once daunting and dazzling. I understand that the primary aim of the publisher of the English translation was to see to it that Kume's rhetorical mastery was conveyed.

Here are two passages from the volume covering the last leg of the embassy's tour (Vol. V), which Eugene Soviak, of Washington University, Tsuzuki Chūshichi, of Hitotsubashi University, and Graham Healey translated.

On July 10, 1873, the Swiss government invites the embassy to go on a cruise on Lake Geneva. The previous day a telegram from the Japanese government had told them to return to Japan immediately.

From the stern of the boat, the musicians' charming melodies floated away on the breeze to drift across the lake, so light and airy as to put one in mind of [Taoist] immortals taking wing to rise up to Heaven. The snow and ice of Mount Blanc glittered, and by the town of Nyon mist shrouded the waters of the lake and the summer mountains were a hazy green. . . .

We sailed below the walls of an ancient castle [the Chateau de Chillon] near Vevey and finally arrived at Chambon, at the head of the lake. Just to the south of this point, the river Rhone debouches into Lac Leman. On its way to the lake, it flows along a narrow plain with mountains on either side. The river is a torrent which scours this alluvial plain before emptying with a roar into an arm of the lake, foaming tumultuously and muddying the waters. The mountains which flank the river are precipitous, towering overhead like wild waves about to break. . . .

On August 9, 1873, the party reached the port of Point de Galle, in Ceylon.

A promontory like an elephant's trunk curves round the south-west side of the bay, and a lighthouse fifty feet high stands at its tip. On the seaward side of the lighthouse lie submerged reefs, dangerously jagged rocks and a scattering of islands, both large and small. The waves rush towards the shore like a never-ending procession of white horses; after galloping some dozens of yards, they break over the rocks. Here and there spray leaps upwards, like snow-flakes flying through the air. It is as though a thousand whales were doing battle.

Kume Kunitake became a distinguished historian and lived until the ripe old age of ninety-two, dying in 1931. But, first, he became a victim of the emperor worship instituted by the Meiji government. In 1892 he was forced to resign from the Imperial University for writing that Shinto was nothing but "an ancient folkloric custom." He then saw Japan slide into militarism—a disappointment for a man who ardently hoped for a harmonious development among nations.

Itō Hirobumi, whose speech I quoted at the outset, visited Europe again, in the early 1880s, this time for the specific purpose of preparing a constitution for Japan. The result of that one-and-a-half-year stay was the Meiji Constitution, promulgated in 1889. He went on to serve the Meiji government with distinction, becoming prime minister twice. In 1909 he was assassinated by An Jung-geun, leader of the movement to oppose Japan's dominance of his country, Korea. Japan annexed it the following year.

Itō, in fact, became the only one among the top leaders of the embassy to survive long enough to influence the entire course of Meiji Japan. Kido, who was all for Westernization, died in 1877. Ōkubo, who, with Kido, pulled off the coup d'état I mentioned, was assassinated the next year. Iwakura died in 1883. So, other than the coup d'état and the administrative and judicial reforms Ito pursued, tangible effects of the Iwakura Embassy are hard to assess.

But the embassy's mission was to observe and learn. And Kume showed how well that goal was met. His report, sumptuously illustrated, sold well. There is little doubt that many Japanese learned a great deal about the rest of the world from *The Iwakura Embassy*.

Undergoing the Third Degree
in Prewar Japan

February 2, 2016, *Japan Times*

In the 1930s a translator of Japanese literature from New Zealand was jailed and tortured by the Japanese police. His name was Max Bickerton or, more fully, William Maxwell Bickerton.

I had wondered about this translator for a long time—for an esoteric reason. I translate haiku in one line, and Bickerton is one of the very few people who have done the same, as I found in *The Classical Tradition of Haiku: An Anthology* (Dover, 1996). Faubion Bowers, who compiled it, gave a copy to me.

The book lists some well-known and not so well-known haiku in translation by a variety of hands. In it Bickerton's source is given as *Issa's Life and Poetry* (Asiatic Society of Japan, 1932). Issa is Kobayashi Issa (1763–1824), who described daily life in haiku in a readily understandable way. An example:

Once more in vain the stepchild bird opens its beak.

When I first wanted to learn more about Bickerton some years ago, I didn't find much on the Internet. But when I did the search recently, I found a wealth of information about him, including an obituary, by Sir Herbert Vere Redman, in the February 1967 bulletin of The Japan Society of London.

Equally important, there was an article by Bickerton himself, titled "Third Degree in Japan." It originally appeared in the *Manchester*

Guardian, then was reprinted in the September 1934 issue of *The Living Age*, a magazine published in Boston.

William Maxwell Bickerton was born in Christchurch, New Zealand, in 1901. After graduating from Victoria College (now University), he taught at high school for one year in Maori territories and, at age twenty-four, went straight to Japan. There he "plunged almost completely into Japanese life" and "started serious study of the Japanese language on arrival." To make a living, he taught English at the Tokyo University of Commerce at Hitotsubashi (now Hitotsubashi University), where Vere Redman was his colleague, for four years. Bickerton followed this with six years at the First Higher School.

He had an innate linguistic talent. In short order, he translated Issa and the brilliant but short-lived woman writer Higuchi Ichiyō (1872–96). What put him in trouble with the police was his translation of "some of the proletarian writers of the late twenties," as Vere Redman put it in his obituary, though he didn't mention the ordeals he had to go through as a result.

"The inhuman treatment in the police cells," Bickerton began his account, "is calculated to break the spirit of any prisoner." He was "confined in a cell measuring 12 feet by 5.5, in which there were never less than nine, and sometimes as many as fourteen, other prisoners." He was made to stay there for twenty-four days, "never allowed to have a bath."

"The brutality of the jailers is beyond imagination," the New Zealander added. The "almost daily sight of other prisoners being stripped and beaten with sticks till their backs were a row of weals or kicked till they could not stand up—and all for very minor infringements of discipline—was hard to bear."

Bickerton wasn't beaten by jailers like them, probably because he was a British subject. Instead, he was beaten, more insidiously, by "two plain-clothes police officers named Ogasawara and Suga" in police headquarters. At the outset Ogasawara said to him: You have probably heard "tales of torture from your Left-wing friends" but they are "untrue." Then the two officers proceeded to make him taste "the third degree" Japanese style.

They stomped on his toes, kicked him on the leg, smacked his face, punched him on the ear, banged his head against a cupboard. They made him sit up straight on the chair and gave him "a crack across both legs above the knee" with a baseball bat, each time he refused to answer a question. They switched the baseball bat with "a bamboo fencing stick (*shinai*)" and whacked him with it across both legs above the knees, endless times.

They raised the *shinai* above his head and struck it with force, in the same place, each time they did it.

What were the police after? They demanded to know exactly how Bickerton spent his monthly salary from school. They pressed him on who had given him a copy of the banned Communist Party's periodical *Sekki* (now *Akahata*) from which he had translated "the confession of an agent-provocateur." They wanted to know if he knew a woman named Ōtsu Toshi, who said she knew him.

But all these beatings stopped two weeks before he was handed over to the British Consul. By then all "the bruises had gone."

That was in the spring of 1934. Just before Bickerton met his ordeals, the Marxist economist Noro Eitarō, sickly but often jailed and tortured, had died after he was carried to hospital from Shinagawa Police Station. A year earlier, the writer Kobayashi Takiji had been killed by torture. He had published a novel describing harsh labor conditions on a crab cannery ship and other stories. Bickerton had translated and published them, though anonymously, in England.

No, Max Bickerton wasn't tortured for translating haiku, let alone doing so in one line. But only six years later, in 1940, a total of fifteen haiku poets were arrested, jailed, interrogated, and, at times, subjected to the third degree. What was their crime?

These poets had moved away from the traditional haiku, rejecting, among others, the requirement of the inclusion of seasonal words (*kigo*). Conservatives charged that the disregard of *kigo* was "liberal" and even led to the denial of the Emperor System. The army (war) minister stated in the Diet, "Liberalism is the hotbed of Communism."

Were the Japanese police particularly bad? In reprinting Bickerton's account from the *Manchester Guardian*, the editor of *The Living Age* prefaced it with this note: "A young New Zealander, imprisoned by the Japanese for radical activities, tells of his adventures in a jail that sounds worthy of these United States."

Looking Back at Seventy Years
Before the War's End

October 1, 2015, *Japan Times*

This is the seventieth anniversary of Japan's defeat in the Second World War. What happened seventy years before that? This is a game I sometimes play when a notable year comes around.

Go back by seventy years from 1945, you get to 1875. That was the eighth year of the newly constituted regime of Meiji, and the country was still unstable.

The tax system had been "reformed" two years earlier, from rice to land, but the burden did not change. Peasant rebellions continued to erupt in many parts of Japan. The samurai class, their stipends and status deprived, revolted here and there, with the Satsuma Rebellion, the biggest one of its kind, to take place two years ahead.

That year Japan took two international steps that continue to reverberate today.

In May, it signed a treaty with Russia for Japan to take the Kuril Islands and for Russia Sakhalin. Japan's claim since the Second World War that the four islands of the Kuril archipelago closer to Hokkaidō are part of its territory is based on this agreement.

War, of course, is merciless. The Cairo Declaration (November 1943) simply asserted that Japan had "stolen" all its territories, while the Potsdam Declaration (July 1945) infamously threatened Japan with "prompt and utter destruction." Also, the San Francisco Peace Treaty (1951) and the U.S. Senate ratification of it weren't precise on territorial definitions.

Some say that the problem was with the 1875 treaty itself. Written in French, a foreign language for both Russia and Japan, it wasn't really "official" and was prone to interpretative manipulations. It was also the days of territorial free-wheeling. Russia had sold Alaska to the U.S. in 1867.

In September, two Japanese warships landed on Ganghwa-do, the island west of Seoul, provoked the Korean defense force there, and "won." This unprovoked act of belligerence was rooted in Japan's so-called "Conquest of Korea Argument" that had come forward in the first year of Meiji. The idea had then receded for domestic political entanglements. But by 1875 the situation had changed.

For one thing, in 1871 the U.S. had tried gun-boat diplomacy against Korea to open it, a country that adamantly stuck to its isolationist, "expel-the-barbarian" policy, but failed; two decades earlier the same tactic had worked against similarly isolationist Japan. Still, within Korea, the isolationist force was weakening.

At the same time, other Western powers, led by Great Britain, "the biggest Asian invader" at the time, encouraged Japan to "open" Korea. Britain's minister to China and Sinologist, Sir Thomas Francis Wade—yes, the one who left his name in the Wade-Giles system of romanization of Chinese—supported the idea, with force if necessary.

Thus, in early 1876, Japan forced upon Korea an unequal "amity treaty," even as the country was struggling with similar treaties Western powers had imposed on it. Japan was just beginning to learn the international legal deceptions, so it turned to its government's French legal counsel, Gustave Émile Boissonade, to write the document.

The Japanese-Korean treaty that included the stipulation that Korea be a sovereign, rather than China's tributary state, would lead to the Sino-Japanese War in 1894, which, despite its name, was over the same question, Korea's sovereignty. Japan annexed Korea fifteen years later. The annexation ended with Japan's defeat in 1945, but Japan's thirty-five-year subjugation still rankles in Korea.

To step out of East Asia to take a look at the United States for a minute, in the year of 1875 the country ratified a "reciprocity treaty" with

Hawaii that, among others, specified that no third power might acquire the island kingdom. Then, in 1898, it annexed it and, in 1959, incorporated it as a state.

Now, one of the more important books that appeared in Japan in 1875 was Fukuzawa Yukichi's *Outline of the Theory of Civilization* (*Bunmei-ron no gairyaku*). Fukuzawa, who had visited the United States in 1860 on an embassy to ratify the treaties of 1854 and 1858 and toured European countries in 1862 on a mission to renegotiate the opening of four ports that it had agreed to four years earlier, was inspired to write this *Outline* by books such as the French historian François Guizot's *Histoire de la civilisation en Europe* (1828; English 1846) and the British historian Henry Thomas Buckle's unfinished *History of Civilization in England*.

In his book, Fukuzawa pointed out that "civilization is of utmost importance," defining it as "the way human society gradually moves toward improvement," adding that this was "common knowledge of the world," which said that countries were divided in three categories: "the very best among the civilized," "semi-civilized," and "barbaric." In the first category were "various countries in Europe and America"; in the second, "Turkey, China, Japan, and other Asian countries"; and in the third, "Africa, Australia, and others."

We may assume Fukuzawa included Australia in the barbaric category because Britain had only recently stopped treating the continent as what its own social reformer Jeremy Bentham had condemned as the "thief-colony."

Fukuzawa stressed that civilization was needed, be it for "institutions, learning, commerce, war, or politics," and that for it to work, a dualistic system is necessary. This was because, he explained, at least two entities were required to allow "rationality" (*dōri*) to occur between them, whereas a monistic system does not allow that. He picked Japan and China, both in the semi-civilized category in his scheme, to demonstrate his point.

Japan was "extremely fortunate" in that two entities—that which was spiritually "revered" (emperor system) and that which was militarily "powerful" (state)—coexisted for seven hundred years till then. In contrast, China did not have much luck in that respect, for there, that which was militarily powerful was also that which was spiritually revered for much of its long history. That is, it enjoyed little separation of church and state.

If Fukuzawa's view of civilization and his analysis of the histories of Japan and China have held any validity for the last 140 years, you might say that Japan almost annihilated itself by gradually eliminating dualism in the first seventy years. It permitted the military to exalt the emperor to such a degree as to achieve a divine status for its own advantage.

In the meanwhile, China has held onto monism, Communism, for the second seventy years. The latest news is that Chinese President Xi Jinping has revived Confucianism, which, Fukuzawa judged, does not prevent monism.

Returning from Taiwan after Japan's Defeat

August 26, 2017, *Japan Times*

August is the month to remember the atomic bombings of Hiroshima and Nagasaki and Japan's surrender that followed. As it happens, my mother and her four children, including me, who were refugees from Taiwan following Japan's defeat, landed in Hiroshima in April 1946, and, in less than two years, moved to Nagasaki.

Not that my family was affected by atomic radiation effects in any direct way as we know it. Ōtake Port, Hiroshima, where we landed, is a little north of the U.S. Marine Corps Air Station Iwakuni and twenty-seven kilometers southwest of Hiroshima ground zero. Tobishima, a tiny island in northern Nagasaki, where we moved from my father's hometown in southern Fukuoka where we traveled after Hiroshima, is seventy kilometers north of Nagasaki ground zero.

But I thought of Hiroshima, Nagasaki, and Japan's defeat because Sumiko, my niece in Kitakyūshū, sent me my mother's old *rirekisho*, "resume," and the resume, simply giving the date and place of birth, a list of jobs, and repatriation from Taiwan, shows how entwined my family was with Japan's history after it plunged into the imperialistic contest in the late nineteenth century.

For one thing, I had long thought that my mother, Michiko, moved to Taiwan as an adult and became a schoolteacher, just as my father, Masao, a policeman, did. Instead, I learned that she was born there and studied to become a teacher.

Japan took Taiwan after the Sino-Japanese War in 1894–95. A

Taiwanese friend of mine who wrote a short history of China-Taiwan relations noted that China's Li Hongzhang, who negotiated the surrender terms with Japan's Itō Hirobumi, was happy to cede Taiwan to Japan. China, which had begun seriously to administer the island as a province only a decade earlier, regarded it as "barbaric."

It may have been around 1906 when Japan completed the first round of the modernization of the colony, emphasizing hygiene, sanitation, industrialization, and education, that Michiko's father (perhaps with his spouse) migrated there from Kagoshima. It was in December 1910 that she was born in Anping, Tainan City, her resume says. She went to the Tainan First Girl's Higher School. Called the National Tainan Girl's Senior High School today, it does not reject its origins; its website shows the original Japanese school song, alongside its current one in Chinese.

In 1929, Michiko graduated from the First Normal School in Taipei, today's National Taipei University of Education, and became a public-school teacher. Here "public school," *kōgakkō*, was the elementary school for Taiwanese children, for the school for Japanese children was called *shōgakkō*, though the distinction was later erased, to be called "people school," *kokumin gakkō*, in imitation of *Volksschule*. The Governor-General's Office promoted education earnestly. By the early 1940s, the school attendance rate in Taiwan was over seventy percent—about the same as the United States at the time.

In 1937, Michiko married Masao. Masao was born in 1908 in a village in southern Fukuoka. Unable to find any suitable job after higher school, he got a one-way ticket to Taiwan from his father. Japan was going through prolonged economic doldrums for some years before the stock market crash struck the United States in 1929. Taiwan was in no better economic condition, but he finally landed a job on the police force. Advancing quickly, he was sent to the Police Academy in Tokyo and became an officer on the Special Higher Police.

From 1937 to 1942 Michiko stayed out of teaching evidently to give birth to children. She resumed teaching just ten days after I was born, her resume shows. In the meantime, Michiko and Masao had moved to Guanshan, Taitung, probably because Masao was assigned there.

Soon after their marriage, the China Incident occurred, later called the Second Sino-Japanese War. One of Masao's younger brothers would be drafted, seriously wounded, and die of the wounds a month before I was born. A few months after my birth, Masao was sent to Java, becoming a colonial administrator with twelve servants in a newly acquired land.

Japan surrendered on August 15, 1945. In Taiwan, it was on October 25 that year that Governor-General of Taiwan Andō Rikichi signed the instrument of surrender with Cheng Yi of Chiang Kai-shek's Republic of China. Later Gen. Andō committed suicide, indignant that he was suspected of war crimes; Gen. Yi was executed for proposing to surrender to Mao Zedong's People's Republic of China.

On March 2, 1946, Michiko and her children evacuated Guanshan to be repatriated to Japan—though mother and children were all born there so "repatriate" might not be the right word. On March 26, the family's ship left Keelung, Taipei. It took nine days to reach Ōtake Port. There were 6,500 departures from Taiwan's biggest port that day, records show. Altogether, there were 510,000 refugees from Taiwan. With those from other areas—Manchuria, Korea, China, and elsewhere—added, a total of five to six million Japanese, soldiers and civilians, are estimated to have repatriated to Japan.

Masao was retained in Java for possible war crimes by the Dutch who returned to their former colonies for revanche. He was cleared and returned to Japan by the summer of 1946. By then Gen. Douglas MacArthur's Occupation had abolished the Special Higher Police.

Having a teaching certificate helped Michiko. After living on the second floor of a cattle barn a farmer rented my family for a year and a half, she found a teaching post in Tobishima, Nagasaki, in November 1947. It was there, too, that Masao found a job, with a coal company on an island that originally had only a small fishing village. The two were more fortunate than many others.

In a few years Masao found a job in a big city, Hakata, and moved out with some older children. Michiko followed with the rest as soon as the school term was over, leaving the island where she was my first elementary schoolteacher.

Going with the Flow in a Japanese Trade Office

June 24, 2013, *Japan Times*

Leaving the New York office of the Japan External Trade Organization (JETRO) after forty-four years of employment is an occasion to look back.

I arrived here in the fateful year of 1968. It started with Martin Luther King Jr. shot dead, and ended with three American astronauts flying around the moon and returning to earth. In between, Robert F. Kennedy, running for president, was shot dead, and Chicago police's violence during the Democratic Party Convention was televised.

Next spring I was hired by JETRO—though its New York office was called Japan Trade Center at the time. A young American couple had sponsored me, and I'd come here on a tourist visa. But the rules on such things were not as uptight as they are today. The immigration act that abolished racial and ethnic preferences and has since transformed America's demographic contour had become law just four years earlier.

The raging Vietnam War created an oppressive air. But the Americans I knew were laid back and kind, even as the civil rights movement and sexual revolution were cresting.

When it comes to the matters my employer tracked, U.S. sales of small cars "made in Japan" had just started to skyrocket, easily overtaking the top import car till then, the Volkswagen Beetle, in a few years. One thing I remember in that regard is what my sponsor's mother said. "Hiro, the name Toyota is unfortunate," she told me. "It reminds us of Japanese Christmas toys. A few days after you open the boxes, they break down and have to be thrown away."

U.S. trade deficit with Japan quickly came to the fore. Congress held hearings in 1970. Looking back, the funny thing is the size of the deficit at the time: $1 billion a year. Today, it's $60, $70 billion a year. Even taking into account the inflation, the amount around 1970 was small.

And think of all the reasons thought up to explain the trade imbalance: cheap labor, cheap capital, dumping, predatory trade practices, Japanese refusal to buy foreign products, Japanese inability to understand consumerism.

Another funny thing: The Japanese product at the center of contention at the time was textiles, not autos. It produced one of the more famous episodes in the annals of translation/interpretation. When Prime Minister Satō Eisaku came to Washington and met President Richard Nixon to discuss various matters, Nixon pressed him on textiles: Control your (expletive deleted) textiles.

In response, Satō may have said what a Japanese politician under similar duress would: *Zensho shimasu.* A year or so later Nixon expressed his (expletive deleted) displeasure. He told U.S. textile manufacturers that Satō had lied. The Japanese had promised him, "I'll take care of it," Nixon insisted. Exactly how Satō's interpreter rendered the prime minister's response remains unknown. He kept his mouth shut until his death. The guess is "I'll do my best."

Two decades on, Japanese imports of U.S. textile products exceeded Japanese exports to the United States in the same category. The top item was used jeans.

In August 1971, Nixon removed the fixed exchange rates, the main part of the 1944 Bretton Woods Accord, and embargoed shipments of soybeans en route to Japan, throwing my office into turmoil: Japan as a trading nation was finished!

I learned later that Nixon's embargo forced Japan to seek other sources for soybeans, among them Brazil. The Latin American country was eager to help. One result: further destruction of Amazon rainforests—later, and to this day, U.S. environmentalists' big concern.

It is remarkable to reflect how the U.S. pressure on Japanese trade did not let up until some years after the summer of 1995 when President

Bill Clinton reached an auto agreement with Japan with great fanfare. In between Nixon and Clinton, there was Ronald Reagan, who clamped down on Japanese auto imports as soon as he became president, in 1981. During his campaign against Jimmy Carter, he had put himself forward as an ardent free trader. His numerical limits on Japanese cars would lead Japanese automakers to switch from small, cheap cars to big, expensive ones.

Four years later, there was Reagan's Treasury Secretary Jim Baker. He worked out the Plaza Accord, in 1985. He meant to rein in Japanese exports by forcing a sharp appreciation of the yen against the dollar. That purpose failed. Instead, the measure directly led to the Japanese Bubble—or so some have argued.

Regardless, for more than a dozen years now, most of U.S. attention has been on China. Many may no longer remember the Japanese plaint in the 1990s: Japan "bashing" had turned into Japan "passing."

The United States now runs a trade deficit with China of $300 billion.

Of course, if you take a larger historical perspective, you may say that most of U.S. attention has been on China since Richard Nixon, following Henry Kissinger's Machiavellian machinations, flew to Beijing and met Mao Zedong, in the summer of 1972. Or since 1949. The Communist takeover of China that year spawned the harmful "Who Lost China?" recriminations in this country. Or since long before then. The Pacific War started because of the U.S. insistence that Japan move out of China.

The year of President Clinton's auto accord, 1995, was the fiftieth anniversary of Japan's defeat in the Asia-Pacific War. To mark the occasion, I invited a couple of people to speak to the monthly lunch meetings I ran in my office at the time. One was Faubion Bowers, Supreme Commander for the Allied Powers Douglas MacArthur's aide-de-camp and personal interpreter.

A year before the war started, Bowers, a fresh Julliard-trained pianist, had accidentally seen kabuki while in Japan and fell in love with it. After returning to this country, he studied Japanese at the Military

Intelligence Service Language School. His mastery of Japanese was such that he received two citations during the war. That's how, I imagine, he became MacArthur's personal interpreter.

He was later called "the Savior of Kabuki" because he liberated kabuki from Occupation censorship. The Japanese government decorated him for it years later.

At the lunch meeting, Bowers discussed, among others, how he had agreed to Japan's prewar slogan "the Greater Far East Asia Co-Prosperity Sphere," how he could not stomach furious racial misconceptions of all the combatants involved, and how little the war that had killed three percent of the Japanese population had accomplished.

He ended his talk by citing a haiku of his Japanese friend, the playwright, stage director, novelist Kubota Mantarō. The haiku described how Kubota felt when the war was over.

Nani mo kamo akkerakan to nishibi-naka

All gone, nothing left to say, in the westerly sun

BOOKS BY HIROAKI SATO

Poems
That First Time: Renga on Love & Other Poems. St. Andrews Press, 1988.

History and Criticism
One Hundred Frogs: From Renga to Haiku to English. Weatherhill, 1983.
One Hundred Frogs: From Matsuo Basho to Allen Ginsberg, originally a chapter of above, illustrated. Weatherhill, 1995.
Snow in a Silver Bowl: A Quest for the World of Yūgen. Red Moon Press, 2013.
On Haiku. New Directions, 2018.
Forty-Seven Samurai: A Tale of Vengeance and Death in Haiku and Letters. Stone Bridge Press, 2019.

Compilation
Erotic Haiku. IBC Publishing, 2004.

Biography
Persona: A Biography of Yukio Mishima by Inose Naoki (adapted and expanded). Stone Bridge Press, 2012.

Translations, Poetry: Anthologies
From the Country of Eight Islands: An Anthology of Japanese, with Burton Watson. Doubleday & Company [paper] and Seattle: University of Washington Press [hardcover], 1981. *PEN recipient.* Paperback edition reissued by Columbia University Press, 1986.

Japanese Women Poets: An Anthology. M.E. Sharpe, 2007.

So Happy to See Cherry Blossoms: Haiku from the Year of the Earthquake and Tsunami by Mayuzumi Madoka (adapted), with Nancy Sato. Red Moon Press, 2014. *Kyoko Selden translation prize recipient.*

Translations, Poetry: Individual Poets

Poems of Princess Shikishi. Granite Publications, 1973.

Ten Japanese Poets. Granite Publications, 1973.

Anthology of Modern Japanese Poets. Special issue of Chicago Press, 1973.

Spring & Asura: Poems of Kenji Miyazawa. Chicago Review Press, 1973.

Mutsuo Takahashi: Poems of a Penisist. Chicago Review Press, 1975. Reissued by University of Minnesota Press, 2012.

Lilac Garden: Poems of Minoru Yoshioka. Chicago Review Press, 1976.

Howling at the Moon: Poems of Hagiwara Sakutarō. University of Tokyo Press, 1978.

See You Soon: Poems of Taeko Tomioka. Chicago Review Press, 1979.

Chieko and Other Poems of Takamura Kōtarō. University Press of Hawaii, 1980.

A Bunch of Keys: Selected Poems by Mutsuo Takahashi. The Crossing Press, 1984.

A Future of Ice: Poems and Stories of a Japanese Buddhist, Miyazawa Kenji. North Point Press, 1989.

Osiris, The God of Stone: Poems of Gōzō Yoshimasu. St. Andrews Press, 1989.

Mutsuo Takahashi: Sleeping Sinning Falling. City Lights Books, 1992.

A Brief History of Imbecility: Poetry and Prose of Takamura Kōtarō. University of Hawaii Press, 1992.

Right Under the Big Sky, I Don't Wear a Hat: The Haiku and Prose of Hōsai Ozaki. Stone Bridge Press, 1993.

String of Beads: Complete Poems of Princess Shikishi. University of Hawaii Press, 1993.

Basho's Narrow Road: Spring & Autumn Passage. Stone Bridge Press, 1996.

Breeze Through Bamboo: Kanshi of Ema Saikō. Columbia University
Press, 1997. *Japanese-US Friendship translation prize recipient.*
Reiko Koyanagi: Rabbit of the Nether World. Red Moon Press, 1999.
Not a Metaphor: Poems of Kazue Shinkawa. P.S., A Press, 1999.
The Girl Who Turned Into Tea: Poems of Minako Nagashima. P.S., A
Press, 2000.
The Village Beyond: Poems of Nobuko Kimura. P.S., A Press, 2002.
Santoka: Grass and Tree Cairn. Red Moon Press, 2002.
Howling at the Moon: Poems and Prose of Hagiwara Sakutarō
(Expanded). Green Integer, 2002.
Running in the Margins: Poems of Akira Tatehata. P.S., A Press, 2003.
Toward Meaning: Poems of Kikuo Takano. P.S., A Press, 2004.
Miyazawa Kenji: Selections. University of California Press, 2007.
The Modern Fable: Poems of Nishiwaki Junzaburō. Green Integer, 2007.
The Iceland: Sakutarō Hagiwara. New Directions, 20014.
Hagiwara Sakutarō: Cat Town. New York Review of Books, 2014.
    (Reconstituted edition of the 2002 *Howling at the Moon*).
Inuhiko Yomota: My Purgatory. Red Moon Press, 2015.

Translation, Prose

The Sword and the Mind. The Overlook Press, 1985.
Legends of the Samurai. The Overlook Press, 1995.
Mishima Yukio: Silk and Insight: A Novel. M. E. Sharpe, 1998.
My Friend Hitler and Other Plays of Yukio Mishima. Columbia Univer-
sity Press, 2002.
The Silver Spoon: Memoirs of a Boyhood in Japan. Stone Bridge Press,
2015. *Japanese-US. Friendship translation prize recipient.*

Books in Japanese

Eigo Haiku: Aru Shikei no Hirogari (英語俳句：ある詩形の広がり).
Tokyo: Simul Press, 1987. A survey of American and Canadian
haiku, discussing nine haiku writers, three *haibun* writers (including John Ashbery), a renga by Rod Wilmot, Sato, and Geoffrey
O'Brien, and haiku by American high school students.

Manhattan Bungaku Mampo (マンハッタン文学漫歩). Tokyo: JETRO, 1992. Essays on literature, with two sequences of tanka.

America Hon'yaku Musha Shugyō (アメリカ翻訳武者修行). Tokyo: Maruzen, 1993. Essays on translation.

Yakusenai Mono: Hon'yaku ni Karemeta Bunka-ron (訳せないもの：翻訳にからめた文化論). Simul Press, 1996. Essays on translation and culture.

Translations into Japanese

Nami Hitotsu (波一つ). Tokyo: Shoshi Yamada, 1991. Translation of John Ashbery's book of poems, *A Wave*.

Hō wa Nichibei o Hedateru ka (法は日米を隔てるか), by Michael Young, Professor of Law at Columbia University. Tokyo: JETRO Press, 1989.

INDEX

319